WHAT THE CRITICS SAY:

A very worthwhile addition to any travel library. —**WCBS Newsradio**

Armed with these guides, you may never again stay in a conventional hotel.
—**Travelore Report**

Easily carried ... neatly organized ... wonderful. A helpful addition to my travel library. The authors wax as enthusiastically as I do about the almost too-quaint-to-believe Country Inns. —**San Francisco Chronicle**

One can only welcome such guide books and wish them long, happy, and healthy lives in print. —**Wichita Kansas Eagle**

This series of pocket-sized paperbacks will guide travelers to hundreds of little known and out of the way inns, lodges, and historic hotels.... a thorough menu.
—**(House Beautiful's) Colonial Homes**

Charming, extremely informative, clear and easy to read; excellent travelling companions. —**Books-Across-The-Sea** *(The English Speaking Union)*

...a fine selection of inviting places to stay... provide excellent guidance....
—**Blair & Ketchum's Country Journal**

Obviously designed for our kind of travel.... [the authors] have our kind of taste.
—**Daily Oklahoman**

The first guidebook was so successful that they have now taken on the whole nation.... Inns are chosen for charm, architectural style, location, furnishings and history. —**Portland Oregonian**

Many quaint and comfy country inns throughout the United States... The authors have a grasp of history and legend. —**Dallas (Tx.) News**

Very fine travel guides. —**Santa Ana (Calif.) Register**

A wonderful source for planning trips. —**Northampton (Mass.) Gazette**

...pocketsize books full of facts.... attractively made and illustrated.
—**New York Times Book Review**

Hundreds of lovely country inns reflecting the charm and hospitality of various areas throughout the U.S. —**Youngstown (Ohio) Vindicator**

Some genius must have measured the average American dashboard, because the Compleat Traveler's Companions fit right between the tissues and bananas on our last trip.... These are good-looking books with good-looking photographs.... very useful.

—**East Hampton (N.Y.) Star**

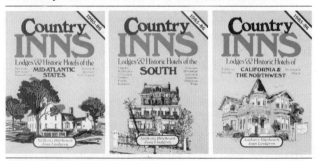

Country New England Inns

by
Anthony Hitchcock
and
Jean Lindgren

BURT FRANKLIN & CO.

Published by
BURT FRANKLIN & COMPANY
235 East Forty-fourth Street
New York, New York 10017

EIGHTH EDITION

Copyright © 1978, 1979, 1980, 1981, 1982, 1983,
1984, and 1985 by Burt Franklin & Co., Inc.

Library of Congress Cataloging in Publication Data

Hitchcock, Anthony
Country New England inns.

(The compleat traveler's companion)
Includes index.
1. Hotels, taverns, etc. — New England — Direct-
ories.   I. Lindgren, Jean, joint author.
II. Title.   III. Series: Compleat traveler's
companion.
TX907.H55   1985   647'.947401
ISBN 0-89102-309-7 (pbk.)

Cover illustration courtesy of
Woodchuck Hill Farm
Grafton, Vermont

Printed in the United States of America

Published simultaneously in Canada by
FITZHENRY & WHITESIDE
195 Allstate Parkway
Markham, Ontario L3R 4T8

1 3 5 4 2

Contents

INTRODUCTION   4

CONNECTICUT   5
  *Deep River • East Haddam • Essex • Glastonbury • Greenwich •
  Ivoryton • Litchfield • Madison • Mystic • New Preston • Norwalk • Old
  Lyme • Ridgefield • Riverton • Salisbury • South Woodbury • Tolland*

MAINE   26
  *Bar Harbor • Bath • Bethel • Blue Hill • Bridgton • Brooksville •
  Camden • Chebeague Island • Clark Island • Damariscotta • Deer Isle •
  Dennysville • East Waterford • Freeport • Georgetown Island • Hancock
  • Islesboro • Kennebunkport • Kingfield • Newcastle • North Waterford
  • Ogunquit • Searsport • South Bristol • The Forks • Weld • Westport
  Island • Winter Harbor • York Harbor*

MASSACHUSETTS   83
  *Barnstable • Brewster • Chatham • Concord • East Orleans • Eastham •
  Falmouth • Great Barrington • Harwich Port • Lenox • Martha's
  Vineyard • Nantucket Island • Newburyport • Northfield • Petersham •
  Princeton • Provincetown • Rockport • Salem • Sandwich • Sheffield •
  South Egremont • South Lee • Stockbridge • Sturbridge • Sudbury •
  Ware • Wellfleet • West Harwich • West Stockbridge • Whitinsville •
  Woods Hole • Yarmouth Port*

NEW HAMPSHIRE   168
  *Bradford • Bridgewater • Center Sandwich • Chocorua • Conway •
  Eaton Center • Francestown • Franconia • Glen • Haverhill • Henniker •
  Hillsborough • Intervale • Jackson • Jaffrey • Jefferson • Lancaster •
  Littleton • Lyme • Moultonboro • New London • North Conway • North
  Sutton • Plainfield • Portsmouth • Shelburne • Snowville • Sugar Hill •
  Tamworth • Temple*

RHODE ISLAND   215
  Block Island • Newport • Westerly

VERMONT   227
  *Arlington • Bennington • Bethel • Brookfield • Chelsea • Chester •
  Craftsbury • Craftsbury Common • Dorset • East Dover • Fair Haven •
  Goshen • Grafton • Greensboro • Jamaica • Killington • Landgrove •
  Londonderry • Lower Waterford • Ludlow • Manchester • Manchester
  Center • Marlboro • Mendon • Middlebury • Middletown Springs •
  Montgomery • Moretown • Newfane • North Hero • North Thetford •
  Peru • Pittsfield • Plymouth Union • Proctorsville • Quechee • Randolph
  • Ripton • Saxtons River • Shaftsbury • Shoreham • Stowe • Sunderland
  • Tyson • Waitsfield • Wallingford • Weathersfield • West Dover •
  Weston • West Townshend • Wilmington • Woodstock*

INDEX WITH ROOM-RATE AND   309
  CREDIT-CARD INFORMATION

Introduction

In this new edition, we have quoted the most recent room rates in a combined rate chart and index at the end of the book. Readers should note that the listed rates are *subject to change*. While the quoted rates are for double occupancy in most cases, single travelers as well as larger groups should inquire about special rates. We list daily room rates as based on the American Plan (AP, all three meals included), Modified American Plan (MAP, breakfast and dinner included), Bed and Breakfast (BB, either full or Continental breakfast included), or European Plan (EP, no meals). In many cases a tax and a service charge will be added. Be sure to ask. Children and pets present special problems for many inns. If either is *not* welcome at an inn it is noted in the description. These regulations also often change, and it is imperative that families traveling with either inquire in advance. Though many inns state they are open all year, we find that many close during slow periods. Call first to confirm your room reservations.

The inns described in this book were chosen for their inherent charm, based partially on their architectural style, location, furnishings, and history. We have made every effort to provide information as carefully and accurately as possible, but we remind readers that all listed rates and schedules are subject to change. Further, we have neither solicited nor accepted any fees or gratuities for being included in this book or any of the other books in this series. We have tried to be responsive to reader suggestions arising out of earlier editions of this book. Should readers wish to offer suggestions for future editions, we welcome their correspondence. Please write to us in care of our publishers: Burt Franklin and Company, 235 East Forty-fourth Street, New York, NY 10017.   JEAN LINDGREN
                                                       ANTHONY HITCHCOCK

Connecticut

Deep River, Connecticut

RIVERWIND

209 Main Street, Deep River, CT 06417. 203-526-2014. *Innkeeper:* Barbara Barlow. Open all year.

Riverwind, a whimsical country inn in an 1850s house, is filled with Barbara Barlow's collections of fanciful early-American and more recent mountain crafts—twig baskets, antique quilts, pierced tin, wooden folk art, and weathered advertising art—all displayed throughout fresh, painted rooms with polished pine floors topped with handwoven scatter rugs. Antique pine pieces house the collections: Barbara's grandmother's stoneware is displayed in an old pie safe in the dining room, where breakfasts are served at the antique harvest table. Barbara, who left teaching and her native Smithfield, Virginia, to open the inn and its antique shop housed in the summer kitchen, did the entire year-long restoration herself, with irresistible results. Sherry is set out in the parlor, where guests may chat or try their hand at one of the musical instruments. Each guest room has a special feature—a fishnet canopy bed, a large antique maple four-poster with a red-checkered patchwork quilt, or an old pine bed with hand-painted roses on the inset.

Accommodations: 4 rooms with private bath. *Pets and children:* Not permitted. *Driving Instructions:* The inn is in the center of town.

Photo courtesy Lorenzo Evans / New Haven Register.

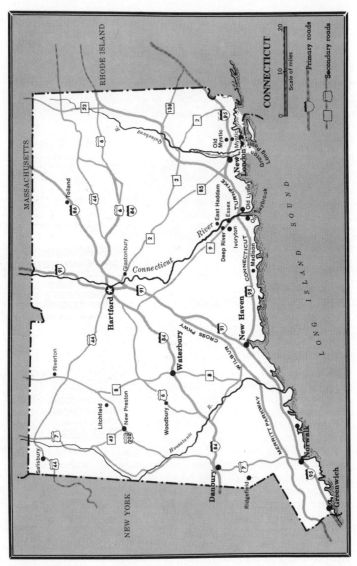

CONNECTICUT

Scale of miles
0   10   20

— Primary roads
---- Secondary roads

RHODE ISLAND

MASSACHUSETTS

NEW YORK

LONG ISLAND SOUND

Hartford

New Haven

Waterbury

Danbury

Norwalk

Greenwich

Mystic
New London
Old Mystic

Old Lyme
Essex
East Haddam
Deep River
Ivoryton
Madison
Old Saybrook

Glastonbury
Toland
Riverton
Litchfield
New Preston
Woodbury
Ridgefield
Salisbury

Connecticut River

Housatonic R.

Quinebaug R.

WILBUR CROSS PKWY

MERRITT PARKWAY

CONNECTICUT TURNPIKE

East Haddam, Connecticut

BISHOPSGATE INN

Goodspeed Landing, Route 149, East Haddam, CT 06423. 203-873-1677. *Innkeeper:* Julie Bishop. Open all year.

In 1818 this inn began as the Colonial home of a shipbuilder in a historic town on the Connecticut River. The beautifully restored house is decorated throughout with nineteenth-century antiques and Oriental rugs on wide-board floors.

This is the home and inn of Julie Bishop, whom most guests consider one of the nicest things about staying here. As an opera fan and past president of the Goodspeed Opera House Guild, Julie chose the inn for its proximity to the renowned playhouse. The walls of her kitchen, the true heart of the inn, are covered with autographed photos of performers. Breakfast is served here at the harvest table, and soft chairs are grouped around a wood-burning fireplace. It is almost impossible to choose a favorite guest room. Four have fireplaces, and all have antique furnishings. The Jenny Lind Room has a four-poster complete with fishnet-lace canopy.

Accommodations: 6 rooms with private bath. *Pets:* Not permitted. *Children:* Under six not permitted. *Driving Instructions:* From Route 9 take exit 7 to East Haddam. From the Goodspeed Opera House take Route 149 to the crest of the hill.

Essex, Connecticut

GRISWOLD INN

Essex, CT 06426. 203-767-0991. *Innkeeper:* William Winterer. Open all year.

The Griswold Inn has been in continuous operation since 1776 and has been carefully renovated over the years, with an overall effect which continues to be among the more pleasing in the state. The Griswold contains fine guest and dining facilities, and a fascinating collection of marine art is displayed on its walls. An extensive library houses a collection of reference material concerning the history of firearms.

Perhaps the most famous room in the inn is the Tap-Room, a paneled room with a pot-bellied stove that has a fire during the winter months. The room was built in 1738 as an early schoolhouse in Essex. It was rolled to the Griswold in the late eighteenth century on a bed of logs. Food is served in seven dining rooms, including the Covered Bridge Room, constructed from components of an abandoned New Hampshire covered bridge. The room's decorations include a collection of Currier and Ives steamboat prints and a number of temperance banners. The menu features a choice of six appetizers and a large number of seafood, meat, and poultry entrées.

The guest rooms are decorated with equal care and include many brass beds and attractive wallpapers. Air conditioning has been added in deference to some modern tastes, but never will a telephone or television jar you from your sleep. Personal touches are the rule here; do not hesitate to ask for an extra pillow or two if you wish.

Accommodations: 22 rooms, all with private bath. *Driving Instructions:* Take exit 3 from Route 9 (exit 69 on the Connecticut Turnpike) to Essex Village.

Glastonbury, Connecticut

BUTTERNUT FARM

1654 Main Street, Glastonbury, CT 06033. 203-633-7197. *Innkeeper:* Donald B. Reid. Open all year.

To the best of our knowledge this handsome home is without peer among New England guest houses with respect to its collection of antiques and the architectural richness. Butternut Farm was built in two stages by Jonathan Hale, beginning in 1720, the year of his marriage. The interior of this classic Colonial house was painstakingly restored to its original condition by innkeeper Donald Reid by exposing the original wide brick fireplaces, uncovering the broad pumpkin-pine floorboards, and removing paint from the paneling on many of the rooms' walls. Hand-hammered hinges, paneled fireplaces, handsome summer beams, and cornice detailing are but a few of the features. Many visitors come simply to see the collection of eighteenth-century Connecticut antiques. A cherry highboy, a cherry six-board chest, ball-foot "hired man" beds, a pencilpost cherry bed, a pine-and-oak gateleg table, early eighteenth-century bannister-back chairs, and a fine collection of English Delft are but a representative sampling. There are several herb gardens, along with a herd of dairy goats and Mr. Reid's flock of prize chickens.

Overnight accommodations are in rooms furnished in keeping with the Colonial period. Breakfast is served in the former kitchen.

Accommodations: 3 rooms with 2 shared baths, plus an apartment with private bath in the eighteenth-century barn. *Driving Instructions:* Take I-91 or Route 2 to Glastonbury. From the center of town drive south 1.6 miles to the inn. Enter from Whapley Road.

Greenwich, Connecticut

THE HOMESTEAD INN

420 Field Point Road, Greenwich, CT 06830. 203-869-7500. *Innkeepers:* Nancy Smith and Lessie Davison. Open all year.

The Homestead began in 1799 as the home of Augustus Mead, a judge and gentleman farmer. It was remodeled over the years in the distinctive "Carpenter Gothic" Victorian style it displays today. The interior has been redone stem to stern. One attractive little bedroom with exposed beams has delicate, original stenciling of robins; hence its name, the Robin Room. The snug Poppy Room is all tans and reds, while the large Butterfly Room is bright and sunny.

The inn is furnished throughout with a fine collection of antiques. Its classic French restaurant, La Grange, is open to both guests and the public. The blue and white Wedgwood plates and formal settings contrast grandly with the rugged barn siding and ancient chestnut beams hung with bunches of dried herbs. A fire burns in the brick hearth on cool evenings.

A favorite retreat for guests is the intimate library with its lush furnishings and working fireplace. The best entertainment at the Homestead is investigating the rooms and narrow staircases. In warm weather the veranda, overlooking the hilly lawn and shade trees, has antique wicker for relaxing in turn-of-the-century style.

Accommodations: 13 rooms with private bath. *Pets:* Not permitted. *Driving Instructions:* Take Route I-95 to exit 3. Turn west toward the railroad bridge, and take a left onto Horseneck Lane. Drive to the end, and turn left onto Field Point Road. The inn is a quarter of a mile uphill on the right.

Ivoryton, Connecticut

COPPER BEECH INN

Main Street, Ivoryton, CT 06442. 203-767-0330. *Innkeepers:* Paul and Louise Ebeltoft. Open all year, closed Mondays.

The Copper Beech Inn is renowned for its restaurant, a recipient of praise from nearly all of the major magazines and newspapers that cover Connecticut. For several years it has been named the best restaurant in the state by the readers of *Connecticut Magazine.*

This Victorian home, dating from 1898, has gained a reputation for its unusually large menu, which can best be described as country-French classical. Meals are served in three well-appointed dining rooms: the Queen Anne Ivoryton Room, the Chippendale Comstock Room, and the Empire Copper Beech Room. Candlelit dining at the Copper Beech features formal service, hand-blown stemware, and silver. Before dinner, guests may enjoy drinks in what was once a greenhouse. Among the dining rooms' specialties are rack of lamb carved at the table, roast clams, Long Island duckling, fresh native fish, lobster bisque, medallions of veal chasseur, and sweetbreads served in brioche in champagne sauce. Beef Wellington is served in a truffle sauce. After the meal, guests may retire to one of the guest rooms, furnished in colonial motif. Each has retained its original cast-iron claw-footed bathtub.

Accommodations: 5 rooms with private bath. *Pets:* Not permitted. *Children:* Inquire before bringing. *Driving Instructions:* The inn is on Main Street, 1½ miles west of Route 9, exit 3 or 4.

TOLLGATE HILL INN AND RESTAURANT

Route 202 and Tollgate Road, Litchfield, Connecticut. Mailing address: P.O. Box 39, Litchfield, CT 06759. 203-482-6116. *Inn-keeper:* Frederick J. Zivic. Open all year.

Innkeeper Fritz Zivic, no newcomer to food service, has owned and managed eleven restaurants in four states. But with the Tollgate Hill Inn, he and his wife, Anna, realized a dream of combining food service with overnight accommodations. The Zivics' found a suitable property when they discovered the former Captain Bull Tavern, built in 1745. In 1983, following a rigorous restoration, the inn reopened to an enthusiastic reception.

One enters the inn through a Federal-style doorway into a long, narrow room with a cherry bar constructed by a local craftsman to match the original paneling. Dining is offered here in the Tavern Room with its wide pine–paneled walls and floorboards and a fire-place with Dutch door. On the other side of the front foyer, a more formal dining room has paneling like the bar's but stripped of paint. Its curved corner cupboard, original to the house, was an important feature contributing to the building's listing in the National Register of Historic Places. Prints of American primitives, a fireplace surrounded by paneling, and painted wainscoting complete the room's decor. Upstairs are the Ballroom and Parlor, the former with a large fieldstone fireplace, hand-pegged Federal sideboard, and three copper chandeliers hanging from a vaulted ceiling. Indian shutters cover the windows in this room, which is often used for dinner or for private parties. The inn's dinner menu offers such specialties as seafood pie, seafood chowder, veal Dijon, and breast of chicken with cream cognac sauce. Lunch is also served to guests and the public, and breakfast is included in the room charges for overnight guests. Many guest rooms at the Tollgate Hill Inn have working fireplaces, and all are decorated with fabric and wall-coverings created for the new American wing of The Metropolitan Museum in New York. Some have four-poster beds; others have canopied double beds. When guest rooms were created from the attic space on the third floor, under the gambrel roof, the original beams and chimney were left exposed.

Accommodations: 6 rooms with private bath. *Driving Instructions:* Take Route 202 to Litchfield and the inn.

Madison, Connecticut

MADISON BEACH HOTEL

94 West Wharf Road, Madison, CT 06443. 203-245-1404. *Innkeepers:* Mr. and Mrs. Henry Cooney and Mr. and Mrs. Roben Bagdasarian. Open mid-April to early November.

On a curve of sandy beach overlooking Long Island Sound stands the Madison Beach Hotel, a handsome unpainted clapboarded building. Public lodging has been on this spot since the late eighteenth century, when there was a stagecoach stop here on the old Boston Post Road. A boardinghouse, built in the heyday of whaling ships in the mid-nineteenth century to house shipbuilders and their families, underwent many additions and changes. In the Roaring Twenties it was a summer resort for stars of stage and screen, who came with their maids and chauffeurs in tow. In an extensive 1982 renovation, rooms were enlarged, private baths were added, and cable television and air-conditioning were installed. Old-fashioned print wallpapers above the original wainscoting capture a Victorian flavor, as does turn-of-the-century wicker, rattan, and golden oak furniture. The Wharf, the hotel's restaurant, serves lunches and dinners to the public (seafoods and steaks) and a Continental breakfast to overnight guests.

Accommodations: 32 rooms with private bath. *Pets:* Not permitted. *Driving Instructions:* From I-95 take exit 61 (right from New Haven, left from New London). Turn right at the second light and then left at the Exxon station. The inn is at the end of the road.

THE INN AT MYSTIC

Routes 1 and 27, Mystic, CT 06355. 203-536-9604. *Innkeeper:* Jody Dyer. Open all year.

On 15 acres of land in historic Mystic is a complex of buildings the jewel of which is a Colonial Revival mansion built in 1904 that overlooks the harbor and Pequoitsepois Cove. It was bought by the innkeepers of the Mystic Motor Inn and Flood Tide Restaurant, a new and highly rated establishment built in an old peach orchard. The inn adjoins this property and sits amid 8 acres of attractive formal gardens. Wide porches with towering columns offer views of the gardens and Mystic's harbor in the distance.

The guest rooms at the inn are decorated with antique furnishings, and some have canopied beds and working fireplaces. The English pine-paneled drawing room with its baby grand piano also offers somewhat formal Victorian charms. Bathrooms at the inn are sheer self-indulgence with luxurious whirlpool soaking tubs and "thermacuzzi" spas.

The formal dining room, drawing room, and gardens are popular for weddings and formal functions, and the grounds offer swimming, boating, and tennis.

In addition to the five period guest rooms in the inn, there are four rooms in the Gatehouse. Built in the early 1950s as a guest house, this building has English paneling, fireplaces, imported mantels, and a quiet setting overlooking the orchard. All other accommodations in the Inn at Mystic are modern motel rooms.

Accommodations: 70 rooms with private bath. *Pets and children:* Not permitted in the inn or Gatehouse. *Driving Instructions:* The inn is at the corner at Routes 1 and 27.

RED BROOK INN

10 Welles Road, Old Mystic, Connecticut. Mailing address: Box 237, Old Mystic, CT 06372. 203-572-0349. *Innkeepers:* Verne Sasek and Ruth Keyes. Open all year.

The Red Brook Inn is an eighteenth-century New England Colonial complete with traditional center chimney and working fireplaces in each room. The barn-red inn stands on a bluff and is surrounded by woodlands and masterfully crafted stone walls. Although it is just 2 miles from Mystic Seaport and the Long Island Sound, it is secluded and peaceful. It is furnished throughout with country New England antiques, handwoven rugs, and the innkeepers' large collection of antique lighting devices. The hardware, woodwork, pineboard floors, and fireplaces are original to the house. On chilly evenings guests are treated to a fire in their own hearths. Two fireplaces have beehive ovens, including the one in the keeping room, where breakfasts are served by the fireside. Innkeepers Ruth and Verne bake something special each morning, perhaps cornbread one day and walnut waffles the next. The front parlor is casual, with cable television, table games, and leather lounge chairs.

Accommodations: 3 rooms, 1 with private bath. *Pets and children under 8:* Not permitted. *Driving Instructions:* From I-95 take exit 89 and drive north 1½ miles to Route 184. Head east on 184. The inn will be on the left side, at the intersection with Welles Road.

New Preston, Connecticut

BOULDERS INN

Route 45, Lake Waramaug, New Preston, CT 06777. 203-868-7918. *Innkeepers:* Carolyn and Jim Woolen. Open all year.

Up in the Berkshire Hills, on 30 acres of woods and lake frontage, is the Boulders Inn. Oxen dragged granite lintels and fieldstones like boulders to the building site in 1895. The inn overlooks the hills and Lake Waramaug, which provides year-round scenic interest and offers guests many recreational opportunities. In summer there are swimming, fishing, sailing, and canoeing; with winter comes the ice for skating and ice fishing. The hills are crisscrossed with trails that beckon hikers and cross-country skiers.

The inn was a private home up until thirty-five years ago and has been a hostelry ever since. Its den and living room, both with fireplaces, are furnished with family antiques and upholstered chairs in groupings by picture windows. The terrace with its lake vistas is popular in warm weather for dining and for viewing the sunsets at the cocktail hour. Meals at Boulders offer traditional American and Continental fare, along with some international specialties, such as Kasmir lamb, veal with lemon, and chicken paprikasch.

The five spacious guest rooms have a blend of antiques and comfortable furniture. Four duplex cottages scattered about the inn's grounds are winterized, each has its own deck, and all have fireplaces.

Accommodations: 5 rooms with private bath in the inn, 4 duplex cottages. *Driving Instructions:* Take Route 202 to Route 45 north. The inn is 1½ miles up the road on the right.

Norwalk, Connecticut

SILVERMINE TAVERN

Perry Avenue and Silvermine Avenue, Norwalk, CT 06850. 203-847-4558. *Innkeeper:* Francis Whitman, Jr. Open all year, except Tuesdays from September to May.

Four buildings make up the Tavern group — the Coach House, the Old Mill, the Country Store, and the Tavern itself. The buildings are furnished in antiques, Oriental rugs, and primitive paintings. Each guest room has authentic antique beds (three have canopies). Several rooms have balconies overlooking the millpond. A waterfall contributes to the charm of the 200-year-old building called the Old Mill. Fireplaces going in winter, shade trees in summer, and colorful foliage in autumn create an atmosphere of New England hospitality.

The Tavern has several dining rooms overlooking the swans on the millpond and the wooded banks of the Silvermine River. Decorated with unusual kitchen utensils and primitive portraits, it is very popular with tourists. The menu features traditional New England fare: shore dinners, Boston scrod, steaks, and chicken. The Tavern is particularly proud of its Indian pudding.

Accommodations: 10 rooms with private bath. *Driving Instructions:* Take exit 39 on the Merritt Parkway (Route 15). Proceed south on Route 7 to the first traffic light, then turn right on Perry Avenue. Follow Perry for 1½ miles to the inn.

Old Lyme, Connecticut

BEE AND THISTLE INN
100 Lyme Street, Old Lyme, CT 06371. 203-434-1667. *Innkeepers:* Bob and Penny Nelson. Open all year.

The Bee and Thistle Inn is on 5½ acres along the Lieutenant River in the historic district of Old Lyme. Its bordering stone walls, sunlit porches, inviting parlors, and formal gardens capture the feeling of a traditional New England home. Built in 1756, the inn has many fireplaces, a carved staircase, and antique furnishings typical of the pre-Federal period. Guest rooms have canopied or four-poster beds covered with antique quilts or afghans. Nooks abound where one can curl up with a book or write a letter to a friend.

Breakfast is served on the sunny porches or before the fire in the dining room. Freshly baked muffins and omelets highlight the morning meal. In the evening, candlelight dining focuses on fresh seafood, lamb, veal, duckling, and choice steaks. Many of Old Lyme's galleries, museums, gift shops, and antique shops are within walking distance of the inn.

Accommodations: 11 rooms, 9 with private bath. *Pets and children under 7*: Not permitted. *Driving Instructions:* From the south, take I-95 to exit 70, turn left off the ramp, then right at the stoplight and left at the next stoplight. From the north, take exit 70 off I-95 and turn right off the ramp. The inn is the third building on the left.

Ridgefield, Connecticut

THE ELMS

500 Main Street, Ridgefield, CT 06877. 203-438-2541. *Innkeepers:* Robert and Violet Scala. Open all year except Wednesdays.

The Elms was built in 1760 by Amos Seymour, a master carpenter of his time. Such were his woodworking skills that he also made every piece of furniture in his home. Forty years later Seymour's house was turned into an inn by one S. A. Rockwell.

The Elms survives with a selection of antiques that makes a visit there reminiscent of a stay at grandmother's house. Perhaps this is most evident in the inn's sitting room, with its large Victorian couch. The recently refurbished guest rooms upstairs have four-poster or brass beds.

Downstairs, the bar has exposed beams, a large fireplace, and walls hung with old barometers. Dining is available in two formal dining rooms, one of which has a fine chicken weathervane as part of its decor. A special private dining room, for groups who wish to reserve it, has such luxurious touches as silver candlesticks. The Elms offers Continental cuisine, strongly influenced by French and Italian culinary traditions.

Accommodations: 20 rooms with private bath. *Pets:* Not permitted. *Driving Instructions:* The inn is on Main Street (Route 35).

STONEHENGE

Route 7, Ridgefield, CT 06877. 203-438-6511. *Innkeepers:* David Davis and Douglas Seville. Open all year; restaurant closed Tuesdays.

Stonehenge, an 1832 farmhouse turned country inn, is renowned for its cuisine served in an attractive setting. The white brick and field-stone house is beside a trout pond with its own waterfall and a number of water fowl including mallards, wild and tame geese, and some swans. On a quiet country side road, the inn is surrounded by lawns, shade trees, and a wooded glen with a scenic footpath that leads around the pond. The house is filled with antiques, and its library–living room is presided over by a grandfather's clock and several old barometers. Two large guest rooms are upstairs in the house, and six are in an annex just across the lawn. All are furnished with antiques, and one in the farmhouse has a fireplace.

Stonehenge prides itself on its unusual fare. Some of their special offerings are smoked trout, Stonehenge's own smoked sausage with mustard wine sauce, and shrimp in beer batter with pungent fruit sauce. Main-course specialties include fresh brook trout, rack of lamb, and pheasant and venison in season. Stonehenge, just an hour and a half from New York City, is a perfect spot for a weekend getaway.

Accommodations: 3 rooms in the house, 10 rooms in the annex. *Pets:* Not permitted. *Driving Instructions:* The inn is on a side road off Route 7. A large sign on the road points the way.

Riverton, Connecticut

OLD RIVERTON INN

Route 20, Riverton, CT 06065. 203-379-8678. *Innkeeper:* Mark A. Telford. Open all year; dining room closed Mondays.

The Old Riverton Inn was built in 1796 as a stagecoach stop on the Hartford to Albany Post Road and was completely remodeled in 1940, when a new bridge was constructed in front of it.

The inn's front lounge and dining room have wallpaper by Nancy McClelland, an authority on antique papers. Its design, taken from an old hatbox, is called the "Hampshire Bird." An upstairs lounge where houseguests frequently gather has a paisley design. The room also features a card table and a number of picture puzzles as well as needlepoint chairs to relax in. In the ten upstairs guest rooms, needlepoint is again seen on the luggage racks.

In 1954 the Grindstone Terrace was enclosed to make a room in which about fifty antique wheels make up the floor. The early wheels were mined in Nova Scotia and brought to the mouth of the Connecticut River by boat and subsequently to the inn by ox cart. Other floors in the bar and entrance have polished Vermont flagstone that made the journey from the north on barges down the Connecticut. The Hobby Horse Bar has saddles on wooden kegs. The dining room menu features standard New England fare with a selection of steaks, chops, seafood, and chicken dishes.

Accommodations: 10 rooms with private bath. *Driving Instructions:* Take Route 8 north, and turn right on Route 20.

UNDER MOUNTAIN INN

Undermountain Road (Route 41), Salisbury, CT 06068. 203-435-0242. *Innkeepers:* Al and Lorraine Bard. Open Wednesday through Sunday all year except March.

Under Mountain Inn, set amid Litchfield County's Connecticut Berkshires, is meticulously restored, with a profusion of antiques, attractive wallpapers, and wide-board pine. Under Mountain was fashioned from the ancestral homestead of the Scoville and Fisher families. A large part of the building predates 1740. A clue to its antiquity was found during the restoration; a bundle of very wide pine boards was discovered hidden between the ceiling and attic floorboards. Apparently the result of a pre-Revolutionary silent protest, the boards were probably placed there in disobedience of a colonial law requiring all such lumber to be turned over to the king of England.

The wide pine is now to be seen on the front of the bar in the Tavern Room. This intimate dining room, once the "borning" room of the house, is one of four dining rooms at the inn. When we were there, a fire burned in the hearth, and the aroma of burning pine mingled with that of the food being prepared in the kitchen. The menu posted on the blackboard offered starters of asparagus on artichoke hearts and mushroom caps stuffed with crab. Duckling with a plum glaze is a specialty, and lamb (roast and shanks), sirloin steak, Cornish game hens, and New England meat pies appear with regularity. The inn's comfortable parlor has a blue Oriental rug, rose-colored walls, a profusion of plants, and interesting woodwork around the fireplace. A separate living room is done in soft greens with a rose rug.

The seven bedrooms upstairs are done with equal care. Perhaps the most popular is the one Al Bard laughingly refers to as the "Love Room," because of the size of its claw-footed bathtub and its four-poster bed. A twin-bedded room has old-fashioned rose and blue wallpapers with matching drapes and headboard, a blue woven rug, an antique highboy, and wing chairs. The hall outside the room has a library full of books. Horses graze in a meadow adjoining the inn.

Accommodations: 7 rooms with private bath. *Pets:* Not permitted. *Driving Instructions:* The inn is on Route 41, just south of the Massachusetts border in the northwestern corner of Connecticut.

CURTIS HOUSE

506 Main Street, South Woodbury, CT 06798. 203-263-2101. *Innkeeper:* Garwin Hardisty. Open all year.

Curtis House has been in this pretty colonial village since 1736. One of the oldest inns in the state, it was first operated by Anthony Stoddard in 1754, and its history is evident in its tiny twelve-over-twelve windows, dark green paint, and gently rolling, squeaky pine floors. A big barrel of apples stands by the reception desk with a hand-lettered sign offering the first apple free. The low-ceilinged dining rooms are popular with both tourists and local residents, and lunch and dinner include traditional American dishes such as flaky chicken pot pie. Overnight guests are served a Continental breakfast.

The old-fashioned and appealing guest rooms have tiny-print wallpapers, antique rag rugs on sloping floors, and canopied beds, including some canopied twin beds. The third-floor rooms are homier with room sinks, country antiques, and painted floors. The carriage house across a footbridge houses four modern guest rooms with air-conditioning. Antique lovers will find many shops in Woodbury and the surrounding countryside.

Accommodations: 18 rooms, 12 with bath. *Pets:* Not permitted. *Driving Instructions:* Take I-84 (exit 15) to Route 6 to South Woodbury.

Tolland, Connecticut

OLD BABCOCK TAVERN

484 Mile Hill Road (corner of Cedar Swamp Road), Tolland, CT 06084. 203-875-1239. *Innkeepers:* Barbara and Stuart Danforth. Open all year.

Old Babcock Tavern, one of the oldest inns we have encountered, was built in 1720 and offered food and lodging to travelers on the Bolton Notch, a bumpy road to South Windsor in the eighteenth century. The Danforths saw potential under the dilapidated exterior, purchased the building, and, after years of elbow grease and gallons of paint remover, plaster, wax, polish, and paint, restored it to its original splendor. Barb and Stu, justifiably proud that it is now listed in the National Register of Historic Places, offer guests an opportunity to learn about the restoration with a slide presentation in the evenings. The rooms have wide-board oak floors. The large stone center chimney, its four fireplaces, and its two stone bake ovens offer more than just warmth and a glow to the rooms. The Tap Room, Keeping Room, and parlor are just as they would have looked in colonial times, as are the three guest rooms, the largest of which has a lace-canopied bed. With a bow to convenience, there are two shared bathrooms. A full country breakfast is served, including a wedge of warm pie.

Accommodations: 3 rooms with 2 shared baths. *Pets and children:* Not permitted. *Driving Instructions:* From Hartford, take I-84 east 15 miles to exit 98 and Route 31. Follow Route 31 south for 2 miles to the first stop sign. The Tavern is on the corner.

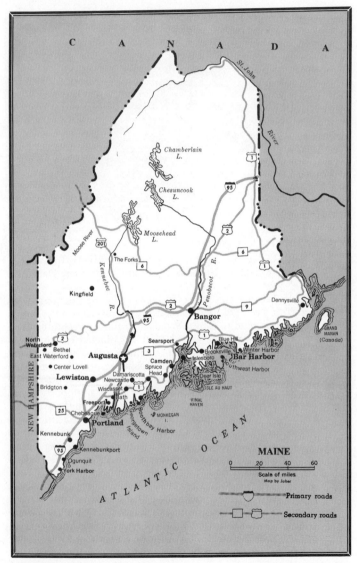

MAINE

Scale of miles

0   20   40   60

Map by Jober

——◯—— Primary roads

——□——◻—— Secondary roads

Maine

Bar Harbor, Maine

BAYVIEW INN

Eden Street, Route 3, Bar Harbor, ME 04609. 207-288-3173. *Innkeeper:* John A. Davis, Jr. Open mid-May through October.

A 1930s Georgian-style manor house, Bayview Inn offers overnight guest accommodations in luxurious surroundings. The handsome thirty-eight-room brick residence was built for Major George McMultry, one of Teddy Roosevelt's Rough Riders, and his society wife, Teresa, and its spare-no-expense elegance seems undiminished. As a private home until 1983, its guest list included Roosevelts, Vanderbilts, and Pulitzers among many of Europe's and America's social glitterati. The current owners, Mr. and Mrs. John Davis, Jr., have carefully maintained the 1930s atmosphere and decor while adding many of their own museum-quality pieces and art objects. The inn is on the edge of Frenchman's Bay, its sweeping lawn extending to a rocky shore dotted with pines. Many of its suites have views of the bay, three have fireplaces, and all have antique furnishings. Decor in the public rooms includes grand pianos, hand-carved Italian furniture, lacquered Oriental pieces, and artwork collected from around the world. Food is served to guests and the public in the dining rooms and paneled hunt room. Working marble fireplaces set the mood, and the menu includes local seafoods, veal, lamb, chicken, and beef. In addition to lunch and dinner, the inn's Sunday brunch is rapidly becoming a Bar Harbor favorite; Continental breakfast is served to guests.

Accommodations: 6 rooms with private bath. *Pets and children:* Not permitted. *Driving Instructions:* The inn is on Route 3.

CENTRAL HOUSE INN AND RESTAURANT

60 Cottage Street, Bar Harbor, ME 04609. 207-288-4242. *Innkeepers:* Jeremiah and Kathleen Jellison. Open May – November.

At the turn of the century, Bar Harbor rivaled Newport in both social prominence and the number of large summer "cottages." Many of these giants were destroyed in a great fire that swept Bar Harbor in 1947, but Central House was one that survived. Built in 1887 as Briarfield, an eighteen-room shingle-and-clapboard country house, it was once the summer retreat of Evalyn Walsh McLean, an owner of the Hope Diamond. The big Victorian house was converted to a hotel during the Roaring Twenties, and many rooms reflect that era today with their Art Deco and Art Nouveau decorative pieces, although most furnishings in the guest rooms, common rooms, and restaurant are Victorian. Large porches overlook herb and flower gardens. The restaurant and cocktail lounge, with indoor and terrace dining, emphasize local seafoods including such specialties as smoked haddock fettucine, Creole bouillabaise, and crab imperial, as well as steaks, chicken, and game. Overnight guests, who are served a Continental breakfast, can visit or curl up and read by the hearths.

Accommodations: 12 rooms, 6 with private bath. *Pets:* Not permitted. *Driving Instructions:* From Ellsworth or Bar Harbor airport, follow Route 3 for 10 miles to Bar Harbor. Turn left on Cottage.

CLEFTSTONE MANOR

92 Eden Street, Bar Harbor, ME 04609. 207-288-4951. *Innkeepers:* The Jackson family. Open mid-May through mid-October.

Cleftstone Manor was built in 1884 for John How, and among subsequent owners were the Blair family, whose name is more familiarly associated with their residence opposite the White House in Washington, D.C. An elegant Victorian inn with a distinctly English flavor, Cleftstone Manor contains a superb collection of antiques and art objects, including a 12-foot dining room table that once belonged to Joseph Pulitzer. The breakfast room is furnished entirely with antique Bar Harbor wicker complemented by the room's Dutch blue Delft collection. The tone of the more formal downstairs rooms is set by tapestries, velvets, heavy lace, and blue Wedgwood. Guest rooms range in size from modest to mammoth. The large Romeo and Juliet room, once part of the ballroom, has a beamed ceiling, a large fireplace, a blue Victorian sitting area, and a white lace–canopied brass double bed. In other rooms are a large French armoire decorated in gold leaf, walnut and marble-topped bedroom sets, a private balcony overlooking the bay, goose-down comforters, hand-crocheted bedspreads, brass or canopy beds, and, in five guest bedrooms, working fireplaces. What aren't in the bedrooms are television and telephones.

Breakfast, the only meal served at Cleftstone Manor, includes a bowl of fresh fruit, several varieties of inn-baked breads, coffee cakes, blueberry, bran, and apple muffins, two kinds of juice, imported teas, and a special-blend coffee. In the afternoon, horseshoes, croquet, and other lawn games are available before tea is served. Guests select their own cup from the inn's private collection, and Mrs. Jackson pours from the silver tea service. Freshly baked Scottish shortbread or pecan tarts are the usual offerings. In the evening, wine, cheese, and crackers are offered with the compliments of the innkeepers. There are libraries for guests on the second and third floors, and a gift shop on the first floor. For a modest fee, guests may obtain privileges for tennis and swimming at the Bar Harbor Country Club.

Accommodations: 18 rooms, 13 with private bath. *Pets:* Not permitted. *Driving Instructions:* Take Route 3 to Bar Harbor, where it becomes Eden Street.

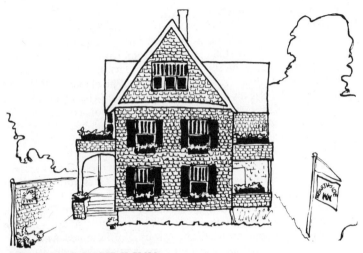

THE HEARTHSIDE INN

7 High Street, Bar Harbor, ME 04609. 207-288-4533. *Innkeeper:* Lois Gregg. Open late June through Labor Day.

The Hearthside Inn is a seaside summer "cottage" built just after the turn of the century by a wealthy doctor to house his family and office. The original waiting room and office are now a guest room with its own private porch and a working fireplace. The living room has comfortable couches and chairs grouped around the hearth, where fires burn on cool evenings. Across the entry hall is the music room, containing a studio grand piano for musically inclined guests, where a Continental breakfast, the only meal served, is set out. Many guests enjoy having their coffee out on the porch or the secluded patio, which are also the settings for afternoon teas and get-togethers.

Guest rooms are furnished with a blend of family antiques and more modern pieces. One room has its own balcony and a leaded-glass bay window, and two others have fireplaces and private porches. The most elegant room is the master bedroom, and the most intimate is the Green Room. The Hearthside Inn is a few blocks from Bar Harbor's shops and restaurants.

Accommodations: 9 rooms, 7 with private bath. *Pets:* Not permitted. *Children:* Under ten not permitted. *Driving Instructions:* Take Route 3 south to Bar Harbor and turn left at the stop sign onto Mt. Desert Street. Turn left at High Street, the third street on the left.

HOLBROOK INN

74 Mount Desert Street, Bar Harbor, ME 04609. 207-288-4970. *Innkeepers:* Richard, Patricia, Alan, and Violet Grant. Open May through October.

Holbrook Inn is an 1878 summer cottage surrounded by trimmed lawns on a quiet residential street just a five-minute walk from town. Organdy-curtained windows are trimmed with black shutters, and hanging pots of flowers and greenery decorate the tree-shaded front porch. Two generations of Grants have worked together restoring the nineteen-room house, papering walls with tiny floral-print wallpapers and painting trim in contrasting colors. The living room and sun room are favorites with guests. Breakfasts of juice, coffee, and blueberry muffins or coffee cakes are served amid lots of greenery and the Grants' basket collection. Everyone tries to get back for the afternoon tea and wine that are a tradition. The rooms' furnishings are a blend of Victorian and colonial family antiques with some comfortable traditional upholstered pieces. Guest rooms have such special touches as an antique mantel clock on a fireplace or a doll or two from one of the inn's collections. Among the antique beds are a few with canopies.

Accommodations: 11 rooms, 2 with private bath. *Pets:* Not permitted. *Driving Instructions:* Take Route 3 from Ellsworth. At the first stop sign, turn left. The inn is on the right.

MANOR HOUSE INN

106 West Street, Bar Harbor, ME 04609. 207-288-3759. *Innkeepers:* Jan & Frank Matter. Open mid-April — mid-November. In the late nineteenth century it was the fashion of the wealthy to build elegant summer cottages at the seashore. Two of the most fashionable summer communities were Newport and Bar Harbor, and it was in the latter that Colonel James Foster built his twenty-two–room Victorian mansion. Listed in the National Register of Historic Places, Foster's "cottage" is now the site of the Manor House Inn, complete with wraparound veranda and beautifully landscaped grounds.

The Manor House Inn has been decorated with antiques appropriate to Colonel Foster's time. Wallpaper patterns characteristic of the last half of the nineteenth century were chosen, and Oriental rugs, high-backed Victorian beds, marble sinks, and formal upholstered period chairs and sofas are the rule. Breakfasts include warm blueberry muffins, freshly baked bread, cereal, fruit, coffee, tea, and juices. Guests may request picnic lunches if they wish to explore the countryside all day. Frank is the publisher of several books about Bar Harbor and the surrounding Mount Desert Island, and it is hard to imagine a question about the area that the Matters will not be able to answer. The Matters recently restored an 1897 chauffer's cottage, which has two suites and a guest room.

Accommodations: 7 rooms, 5 suites, and 2 modern cottages, all with private bath. *Pets and Children:* Not permitted. *Driving Instructions:* West Street runs from Route 3 to Main Street.

MIRA MONTE INN

69 Mt. Desert Street, Bar Harbor, ME 04609. 207-288-4263. *Innkeeper:* Marian Burns. Open early May to late October.

Mira Monte is one of Bar Harbor's summer "cottages," built for a wealthy family back in 1864. It remained a private estate for more than a hundred years until Marian Burns, a native Mt. Desert Islander, purchased the 17-room house, restoring the estate and its grounds. The inn has rooms filled with Marian's collections of antiques and traditional upholstered pieces such as the wing chairs flanking the hearth in the living room. Walls are covered with flowered wallpapers and gilt-framed oil paintings and portraits, and Oriental carpets provide spots of color on polished floors. Four guest rooms have antique Franklin stoves, and others have private balconies or porches. The library is where guests can relax by the hearth. Wine and cheese are served at a get-together in the afternoon, and a Continental breakfast of freshly baked muffins and beverages is set out in the morning. A nearby private club offers Mira Monte guests the use of tennis courts and a large swimming pool for a modest fee. Acadia National Park is just minutes away.

Accommodations: 11 rooms, 9 with private bath. *Pets:* Not permitted. *Driving Instructions:* Take Route 3 from Ellsworth.

STRATFORD HOUSE INN

45 Mount Desert Street, Bar Harbor, ME 04609. 207-288-5189. *Innkeepers:* Barbara and Norman Moulton. Open mid-May through October.

Stratford House was built at the turn of the century by the wealthy Boston publisher Lewis A. Roberts, whose firm brought out Louisa May Alcott's *Little Women*. The house, just a short walk from town, is a handsome English Tudor design styled after William Shakespeare's sixteenth-century birthplace in Stratford-on-Avon. Glassed-and screened-in porches are set below the bold half-timbering of the upper stories. The Moultons have furnished the first floor with Jacobean antiques in keeping with the ornate black oak paneling that recalls the atmosphere of old England. There are several fireplaces, one of which is in the library, where guests may relax. A Continental breakfast is served in the dining room. Three of the guest rooms, whose furnishings include antique four-poster or brass bow-bottom beds, have working fireplaces for added romance.

Accommodations: 10 rooms, 7 with private bath. *Pets:* Not permitted. *Driving Instructions:* Take Route 95 to Augusta, then Route 3 to the inn in Bar Harbor.

GRANE'S FAIRHAVEN INN

North Bath Road, Bath, ME 04530. 207-443-4391. *Innkeepers:* Jane Wyllie and Gretchen Williams. Open all year.

Grane's Fairhaven Inn stands on the bank of the Kennebec River surrounded by 27 acres of meadows, lawns, and dark pine woods. There are outstanding views of the river from its windows. The colonial structure was built in 1790 by one Pembleton Edgecomb for his bride and was the Edgecomb family homestead for the next 125 years. In the mid-1900s its back extension was added, and in 1979 the innkeepers converted it to an inn.

The Fairhaven Inn was an instant success. Its spacious country rooms are decorated with a blend of antiques and comfortable furnishings. The ceilings are low, befitting an inn of its age, and the floors are the original pumpkin-pine boards. Colonial colors chosen for the inn's walls and fires burning in its hearths create an atmosphere of easygoing country tranquillity, a result of the extreme care and hard work lavished on it by the two innkeepers.

It is difficult when here to imagine that the city of Bath with its well-known Maine Maritime Museum and Performing Arts Center is only 3 miles away. The inn offers hiking and cross-country skiing on the property.

The inn is renowned for its country breakfasts of juices; fruits in season; eggs served in many styles; and often scrapple, hash browns, or even Finnan haddie. Accompanying all this are homemade breads and muffins with a selection of jams and jellies put up by Gretchen and Jane. Breakfast is the only meal served and is enjoyed by fireside on chilly mornings. The tavern at Fairhaven offers a "bring your own bottle" wet bar, game table, stereo, color television, and piano for friendly get-togethers. There is a library with a large fieldstone fireplace that is just the thing on cold evenings. This is a "get away from it all" place where the guests and the innkeepers alike have a grand time.

Accommodations: 9 rooms with 4 shared baths. *Pets:* Permitted with advance notice. *Driving Instructions:* Take U.S. 1 north from Brunswick and exit at New Meadows. At the top of the exit turn right and go $\frac{7}{10}$ mile to a stop sign. Turn right for one car length, then turn immediately left. Go $\frac{7}{10}$ mile. The road then turns right, and a golf course is on the left. Continue for $\frac{9}{10}$ mile, make a left turn into North Bath Road, and go $\frac{1}{2}$ mile to the inn.

Bethel, Maine

THE BETHEL INN AND COUNTRY CLUB

Broad Street, Bethel, Maine. *Mailing address:* P.O. Box 26, Bethel, ME 04217. 207-824-2175. *Innkeeper:* Richard D. Rasor. Open all year.

If you were traveling through New England and found any one of the buildings that constitute the Bethel Inn you would be more than pleased. This resort-inn has five outstanding buildings dating from the late nineteenth and early twentieth century. It is, in effect, a village of colonial-style guest buildings set on 85 rolling acres interlaced with shaded paths and gardens. The main inn, built in 1913, has a living room, a music room with a Steinway, a library, a dining room, and a lounge. Each of these rooms has its own fireplace, which is kept going on cool fall and winter days.

The main dining room seats 220, a number in keeping with the resort's size. An Oriental rug before the room's formal fireplace creates an atmosphere of quiet elegance enhanced by the painted beams, swag-draped banks of windows, white linen, and Syracuse china service. Typical menu offerings include Maine lobster, sole baked in wine, stuffed shrimp, haddock au gratin, duck à l'orange, and roast prime ribs.

The inn's sixty-five guest rooms are large and airy with carpeting and simple furnishings that include Windsor chairs, lace curtains, and nubbly white bedspreads. Each has a private bath and direct-dial telephones.

The Bethel Inn faces the village common, a National Historic District with the Moses Mason House and Museum directly opposite the inn. The rear of the inn overlooks the resort's acreage and the White Mountains in the distance. Major resort facilities in summer include swimming, golf on a nine-hole course, tennis, and sailing. In winter there is cross-country skiing on the inn's trails, which crisscross the golf course and surrounding woodland. Rentals and instruction are available at the inn's touring center, which also operates a competitive racecourse. Downhill skiers are drawn to the Sunday River Ski Area with its 5,100-foot chair lift and 19 trails up to 3 miles in length.

Accommodations: 65 rooms with bath. *Pets:* Not permitted. *Driving Instructions:* Take Route 26 (exit 11 on I-95) to Bethel. From New Hampshire, take Route 2 into the village.

NORSEMAN INN

Bethel, ME 04217. 207-824-2002. *Innkeepers:* Jakki and Claus Wiese. Open December 26 through skiing season and June through August.

The Norseman Inn has been fashioned out of a Revolutionary War home by its multitalented innkeepers, Jakki and Claus Wiese. It is a welcoming, family-oriented place that is more than simply a skiing inn, even though there is a strong skiing tradition here. The Wieses are avid skiers, and all of their family are experts; Jakki started the first girls' skiing team in New Hampshire. The family's interest in the sport, as well as the inn's proximity to the Sunday River Ski Area (3 miles) and the New Hampshire White Mountain ski areas at Wildcat, Black Mountain, and Tuckerman Ravine (all within half an hour's drive), means that many skiers stay at the Norseman every winter.

There is a decided Scandinavian atmosphere at the Norseman: Claus was born in Oslo, Norway, and Jakki is of Swedish heritage. Claus is a dedicated gardener whose produce appears regularly on the dinner table. His talents extend to carving, and his gnarled bowls are displayed in the inn as is his excellent artwork.

Dining is a special event at the Norseman. Jakki gets to know her

guests and finds out their preferences and special needs. She respects the differences between adults' and children's palates and often serves children's meals designed especially to appeal to them. Meals, served family-style, center around a daily entrée. Depending on the time of year and the cross-section of guests in residence, the entrée might be a roast leg of lamb, a Scandinavian poached fish dinner, or even a complete Swedish smorgasbord. The traditional fish dinner — a recent addition to Jakki's repertoire that guests have greeted enthusiastically — is poached cod with boiled potatoes, drawn-butter sauce, hard-boiled eggs, and pickled cauliflower and other classic accompaniments.

The guest rooms upstairs are simple and comfortable. Each is wallpapered; some have antique furniture and others have sturdy old-fashioned beds. One front room has twin spool-beds. There is an old spinning wheel in the hall upstairs and, on the wall, a striking photographic portrait of Jakki's grandparents. The inn is very much at home with children and has a special recreation room just for younger guests. While here, don't miss nearby Grafton Notch State Park, with its spectacular gorges deeply cut in stone by the river currents.

Accommodations: 14 rooms, 1 with bath. *Pets:* Not permitted. *Driving Instructions:* From the south take Route 95 to Route 26, which passes the inn near the center of Bethel. From Montreal take either Route 2 or 26, which lead to the inn.

Blue Hill, Maine

ALTENHOFEN HOUSE

Peters Point, Blue Hill, ME 04614. 207-374-2116. *Innkeepers:* Peter and Brigitte Altenhofen. Open May through November.

Altenhofen House is a large mansion built in 1810 on a spit of land surrounded by the tidewaters of the Atlantic Ocean and Blue Hill Bay. The handsome Georgian estate sits amid rolling pasturelands dotted with grazing horses. Verandas look out to the sea or out across the swimming pool to distant Maine hills.

Innkeepers Peter and Brigitte Altenhofen serve breakfast and will steer guests to nearby restaurants for other meals. They will also arrange for deep-sea fishing or sailboat rentals. A large swimming pool is available to guests, and miles of carriage paths offer unspoiled cross-country skiing and horse-drawn sleigh rides in winter and hiking or horseback riding in warmer months.

The mansion has been beautifully restored by the Altenhofens. The rooms are furnished with nineteenth-century antiques, and several are highlighted by working fireplaces, including two in guest rooms and two in the library. Peter and Brigitte are from Germany, speak many languages, and traveled all over the world before settling in Maine.

Accommodations: 6 rooms with private bath. *Driving Instructions:* Blue Hill is reached via Route 172 from Ellsworth or Route 15 from Bucksport.

ARCADY DOWN EAST

South Street, Blue Hill, ME 04614. 207-374-5576. Off-season telephone: 813-254-6104. *Innkeepers:* Tommie and Andy Duncan.
Open Memorial Day to mid-October.

Arcady Down East is a brown-shingled Victorian with turrets, gables,
arches, and a circular tower wing that has a softly rounded dome, all
overlooking Blue Hill Bay and the distant Cadillac Mountain on
Mount Desert Island. Overnight guests have the luxury of relaxing or
visiting with the Duncans and fellow guests in the inn's library or game
room, furnished, as one would expect, with Victorian pieces. The
guest rooms are each unique, with their own special feature; a
romantic, and possibly haunted, turret room or a master suite complete with turn-of-the-century antiques and a sitting area.

Guests are served a Continental breakfast of freshly baked pastries and pots of hot coffee or tea, either in the dining room or out on
the veranda, accompanied by distant vistas of sea and islands.

Accommodations: 8 rooms, 3 with private bath. *Pets and children
under 13:* Not permitted. *Driving Instructions:* From Route 1 and 3,
take either Route 15 or 172 to Blue Hill. At the intersection in
town, turn right toward Deer Isle. About ½ mile, look for South
Street on the left.

BLUE HILL INN

Blue Hill, ME 04614. 207-374-2844. *Innkeepers:* Rita and Fred Boytos. Open all year.

The Blue Hill was built in 1830 and has been serving guests as an inn since 1840. The old building is brick-ended, with white clapboard sides and many chimneys. Large shade trees surround the inn. Window boxes of petunias provide color in the summer months. The inn's central location is a short walk from the park and the harbor.

Inside, the Blue Hill Inn has the atmosphere of a comfortable family home, a feeling enhanced by the Boytos, who go out of their way to make you feel welcome. The bright rooms are cooled in the summer by ocean breezes and are warm and intimate in winter. Colonial wallpapers, white curtains, and many-paned windows add a country ambience.

The Boytos serve a Continental or full country breakfast and a home-cooked dinner with a single entrée, varied daily, along with special chowders and desserts. The public is invited by reservation only. Guests may bring their own liquor, since there is no liquor license at the inn. Blue Hill Country Club extends privileges of tennis, golf, and its beach to guests.

Accommodations: 10 rooms with private bath. *Pets:* Not permitted. *Driving Instructions:* Take the Maine Turnpike (I-95) to Augusta. Take Route 3 past Bucksport to Route 15 to Blue Hill.

Bridgton, Maine

TARRY-A-WHILE RESORT

Ridge Road, Bridgton, ME 04009. 207-647-2522. *Innkeepers:* Hans and Barbara Jenni. Open mid-June to Labor Day.

Intrigued by its old-fashioned name, we were pleased to discover this unusual spot where two historic inn buildings, five cottages, a Swiss chef, and an azure lake are important features.

The resort's oldest building, now called Gasthaus, dates from more than a century ago and was moved to its current spot by sled from a nearby town. The most old-fashioned of the buildings, it has eleven guest rooms, whose furnishings include antique beds. Schloss is a Victorian home built in 1902. Its large rooms also capture the feeling of an earlier era with five-drawer pine chests, natural wood trim, and pine-panel fireplaces. There are five two-bedroom cottages on the 30-acre property. The grounds of the resort slope gently through the pines to the edge of Highland Lake, which offers canoeing, swimming at two sandy beaches, and rowboats and pedal boats as well as lake fishing, sailing, wind-surfing, and waterskiing.

Tarry-A-While has the definite feel of a Swiss resort. Hans is from Davos, and each summer the Jennis fly in a Swiss chef who prepares specialties of his native land. One of our Swiss favorites, *raclette* (melted cheese with potatoes and gherkins), is prepared at the table and is a real treat. Swiss wines are featured on the wine list.

Accommodations: 39 rooms, 26 with private bath. *Pets:* Not permitted. *Driving Instructions:* Take Route 302 to Bridgton. Pick up Ridge Road at the base of Highland Lake and follow the lake road for 2 miles, just past the Highlands Golf Course.

BREEZEMERE FARM INN

Route 176, Brooksville, Maine. Mailing address: P.O. Box 290, South Brooksville, ME 04617. 207-326-8628. *Innkeepers:* Joan and Jim Lippke. Open mid-May to mid-October.

Breezemere has operated as a seacoast farm since the middle of the nineteenth century. In New England style the house is attached to the barn by a series of rooms designed in an earlier time to afford access to the farm livestock in severe weather. In 1917 the farm began to take in guests; by the 1930s the demand for accommodations was so great that eight cottages were built, scattered around the inn. The Lippkes completely redecorated the inn in 1978 and have furnished it with antique early-American furniture. The wallpapers are copies taken from early-American homes.

The first floor consists of a pine-paneled living room, a reading room with a wood-burning Franklin stove, a small dining room, and a dining porch overlooking Orcutt Harbor and the meadow where ponies and sheep graze. A front porch has old wicker furniture. The upper two floors have a total of seven bedrooms and four baths. Rooms have four-poster beds, antique bureaus, and mirrors. White organdy curtains frame their many windows.

In 1948 a recreation lodge was built on the property facing the sea. It has a full-length veranda, a library room, and a recreation room with a large fieldstone fireplace where guests gather to play games, sing, dance, and listen to music.

Breezemere is a friendly, casual place. Guests often spend the day hiking, bicycling, and boating. There are marked trails throughout the inn's 60 acres, and boats are available. The inn has a large blueberry field where guests may pick berries for the next day's breakfast. The Lippkes are happy to point out good spots for clamming, picking mussels, seal-watching, and fishing. Bird-watchers frequently sight bald eagles, blue herons, and loons.

Toward the day's end guests gather at the antique bar for drinks (bring your own liquor), then enjoy five-course dinners centered around organically grown vegetables and home-baked breads. Typical dinners start with choice of appetizer, soup, and salad followed by a choice of two of the inn's specialties, such as coquilles St. Jacques, lemony stuffed cod, bouillabaisse, or sesame-seed glazed chicken.

After dinner you can go outside and peer into the trees with a flashlight. If you are lucky, you will be able to see a porcupine eating an apple in the branches. On Saturday evenings a clambake with lobster and chicken is followed by entertainment in the lodge.

Accommodations: 7 inn rooms with 4½ shared baths; 6 cottages with private bath. *Pets and children*: Permitted in cottages only. *Driving Instructions:* From Bucksport, take Route 175 to Route 176.

AUBERGINE

6 Belmont Avenue, Camden, ME 04843. 207-236-8053. *Inn-keepers:* David and Kerlin Grant. Open May to late fall.

When Aubergine first opened, David and Kerlin Grant put much of their energy into creating the first restaurant in Camden offering "French cuisine the new way." What has emerged since then is all of that and more. Aubergine — very much what its advertising has stressed: a small, romantic inn — is a large silver-gray Victorian home built in 1890 with additions in 1910. A small hand-lettered sign hanging from the horse chestnut tree is the only sign that the house on this quiet back street is actually an inn.

When the Grants purchased Aubergine, they removed some of the modernizing features added in recent decades. In the process they discovered that all of the original lighting fixtures and many of its original furnishings had been stored in the basement. All were restored and re-installed in the house. Aubergine has ninety-nine windows — a fact we are sure the innkeepers knew all too well! Each is leaded in the original (1890) part. The inn's rooms are light, with papers and colors chosen so that the eye travels happily from space to space. An abundance of wicker along with freshly painted white trim give a summery feeling to the navy-blue and white living room–bar. Every evening in the fall there is a fire in both the bar and dining room fireplaces. The latter room is decorated in yellow and gray complemented by white linen, silver, and bouquets of fresh flowers from the inn's garden. The sunny bedrooms are decorated in different color schemes. Each is named for its dominant color, with a single wall of old-fashioned flowered wallpaper surrounded by three painted walls. Furnishings are combinations of family antiques and simply styled contemporary pieces. Handmade quilts cover most beds. Outside are several flower and herb gardens, including one planted in pinks and whites for the special enjoyment of those taking an after-dinner stroll.

David is a professional chef trained in France. His menu applies *nouvelle cuisine* techniques to a number of regional foods as well as to more widely available meats and vegetables. There are only a handful of appetizers, such as fish pâté and duck terrine, followed by the choice of such main dishes as confit of duck with fresh cherries and a Maine bouillabaisse—these offerings change frequently. The wine list is extensive and highly acclaimed by the *Wine Spectator*. Reservations for dining are essential. The innkeepers will also prepare picnics for inn guests and will arrange sailing charters.

Accommodations: 6 rooms, 4 with private bath. *Pets:* Not permitted. *Children:* Under six not permitted. *Driving Instructions:* From the south take U.S. 1 into Camden, stopping at the blinking light and stop sign. A yellow schoolhouse will be on the right. Turn right and go 1½ blocks to Aubergine on the left-hand side. Watch for the sign.

GOODSPEED'S GUEST HOUSE

60 Mountain Street, Camden, ME 04843. 207-236-8077. *Innkeepers:* Linda Goodspeed and Gloria Herrick. Open mid-June through mid-October.

Camden is a scenic, well-cared-for seaport on the coast of Maine where the mountains extend down to the beautiful, snug harbor. The Goodspeeds and their daughter, Linda, fell in love with Camden and decided to open a guest house here. They took one look at an 1879 house on Mountain Street and bought it on the spot. The sale took just one hour. In June 1982 the restored guest house, following a face-lift, installation of an outside deck, and a paint job, opened for business and became an instant success.

Modeled after the inns and pensions of Europe, Goodspeed's Guest House is furnished with antique beds, crisp white linen curtains, and old-fashioned tiny-floral-print wallpapers. Two of the rooms have bay windows. The sitting room, with its Franklin fireplace, is a popular spot with guests. It is airy, with polished spruce floorboards, white antique wicker furniture with soft cushions, lots of plants, and a large stained-glass window. In warm weather breakfast is served on the deck. The dining room and sitting room both display examples from the Goodspeeds' collection of antique clocks.

Accommodations: 6 rooms with shared baths. *Pets and children:* Not permitted. *Driving Instructions:* Take U.S. 1 to Camden and turn west on Route 52. The inn is six blocks farther on.

WHITEHALL INN

52 High Street, Camden, ME 04843. 207-236-3391. *Innkeepers:* The Dewing family. Open late May to mid-October.

The Whitehall Inn occupies a commanding position in the center of Camden. Edna St. Vincent Millay was sixteen years old when she first recited her poetry at the inn, which maintains a special room filled with Millay memorabilia. Additions have grown out from a sea captain's house that was built in 1834 and forms the nucleus of the inn's buildings. In keeping with the inn's history, antiques have been used throughout in a pleasing way and add to the feeling that one is a guest in a large but comfortable country home. Two Victorian homes across the street house additional guest rooms. One of these is open all year.

Meals at the inn feature typical New England food with homemade breads, muffins, pastries, and cakes (frequently with Maine's own famous blueberries), New England chowders, and fresh seafood at the head of a long list of specialties. The innkeepers pride themselves on using local ingredients purchased from the many farmers and fishermen in the Camden area, whenever possible.

Accommodations: 41 rooms, 38 with private bath. *Pets:* Not permitted. *Driving Instructions:* Take Route 1 North to Warren, Maine. Then take Route 90 to the center of Camden. From northern Maine, take Route 1 South to Camden.

THE CHEBEAGUE INN BY-THE-SEA

Chebeague Island, ME 04017. 207-846-5155. *Innkeepers:* Russ and
Helen Brown. Open Memorial Day to Columbus Day.

If you'd like to try an island vacation (or even an overnight stay) in a
country inn with fine Down East cooking, friendly innkeepers, and
fellow guests bent only on unwinding and enjoying the island's
natural beauty, then this inn is certainly the place.

The Chebeague has all the lines of a classic Norman Rockwell
summer hotel. It is on a knoll out in the open with a view overlooking
a couple of fairways of the island's nine-hole golf course and Casco
bay. To get to the inn you first take an hour-and-a-quarter ferry ride
from Portland or a twelve-minute water-taxi ride from Cousin's
Island.

Inside, the inn has a comfortable family-oriented living room with
a large stone fireplace, comfortable wing chairs, and plenty of reading
material. The dining room provides three meals daily, with an evening
menu that features fresh seafood, especially local crab dishes and
Maine lobster. A cocktail lounge opens onto a porch with views of the
bay and sunsets.

The guest rooms have all been redecorated, and the third floor,
completely renovated, including the addition of private baths. There
is golf and tennis, as well as miles of coastline and peaceful island
roads for hiking and bicycling.

Accommodations: 20 rooms, 15 with private baths. *Pets:* Not permitted. *Driving Instructions:* Call the inn to check the latest ferry and
water-taxi schedules and to arrange taxi pickup at the dock.

Clark Island, Maine

THE CRAIGNAIR INN

Clark Island Road, Clark Island, ME 04859. 207-594-7644. *Innkeepers:* Terry & Norman Smith. Open all year except February. The Craignair is an unpretentious seaside country inn. Originally built to house quarry workers, the Craignair is at the end of the road that leads to Clark Island. Ospreys nest on the disused quarry poles. Set above the ocean and Clark Island as well as the local cove, the dining room and many of the guest rooms have an unobstructed view of the sea. A deck at the seaside allows guests to relax in the sun while watching the lobster boats at work. Indoors is a sitting room with a fireplace, as well as a library. This plain white, unshuttered building is not an inn with fancy surroundings or myriad resort-style activities. It is likely to appeal to writers, naturalists, artists, beachcombers, and anyone seeking relaxation and an opportunity to reaffirm one's inherent connection with the sea. Dinner is a single-entrée affair, with the meal of the day chosen from a menu that changes daily.

Accommodations: 16 rooms with shared baths. *Driving Instructions:* From Thomaston, drive south on Route 131 for 5½ miles to Route 73 East, then 1 mile to Clark Island Road and 1½ miles to the inn.

Damariscotta, Maine

DOWNEASTER INN

Bristol Road, Damariscotta, ME 04543. 207-563-5332. *Innkeepers:* Bob and Mary Colquhoun. Open all year.

The Downeaster Inn has one of the handsomest facades of any inn in Maine. Four fluted Corinthian columns rise two stories at the inn's front. When we first spotted the Downeaster from Route 129, we thought that the building might be of modest proportions; but when we rounded the corner of the house to approach the side door, we found that the inn continued back and back.

The original building was constructed in 1810 by Maine's first justice of the peace, who built it to be his home. Sited to provide a view of the Damariscotta inlet, it is now an inn furnished with Victorian antiques, and it is ably managed by Bob and Mary Colquhoun, who have brought a delightful Scottish atmosphere to the place.

In the front hall a grandfather clock greets visitors. The inn's 10-foot ceilings have a number of chandeliers, and on one wall of the living room is a mural depicting a winding country road. Several rococo love seats and period chairs grace this room as well. A door on one side of the inn has blue etched glass. Upstairs and to the rear of the inn, the light and airy guest rooms are comfortably furnished with twin or double beds.

Accommodations: 14 rooms, 8 with private bath. *Pets:* Not permitted. *Driving Instructions:* From Damariscotta, take Route 129 east.

Deer Isle, Maine

PILGRIM'S INN (originally The Ark)

Main Street, Deer Isle, ME 04627. 207-348-6615. *Innkeepers:* Dud and Jean Hendrick. Open mid-May to mid-October.

Built in 1793 and now listed in the National Register of Historic

Places, the Pilgrim's Inn has a true colonial flavor, with its pumpkin-pine wide-board floors, soft colonial tones on the walls, paneled parlor, and numerous working fireplaces. Guests can sit in the common room and gaze out over the millpond nearby. Before-dinner cocktails and hors d'oeuvres are also served in this room. The inn has twelve guest rooms, all with wood stoves and electric bedwarmers and all but three with semiprivate bath.

This is a true restoration in which the original lines and purpose of each room have been altered as little as possible. The result is an almost Shaker-like classic simplicity.

Dining is in the former barn, with its whitewashed walls and open beams. Wide screened doors open to views of the fields and pond behind the inn. Antique chairs are drawn to tables set with white cloths and freshly picked flowers.

Accommodations: 12 rooms with private or shared bath. *Driving Instructions:* Take Route 1 north of Bucksport and turn south on Route 15 to Deer Isle Village. There, turn right on Main Street (the Sunset Road) and drive one block to the inn on the left side.

Dennysville, Maine

LINCOLN HOUSE COUNTRY INN

Dennysville, ME 04628. 207-726-3953. *Innkeepers:* Mary Carol and Jerry Haggerty. Open May through November.

In 1787, General Benjamin Lincoln built a fine country house of fifteen rooms on a piece of the 10,000-acre parcel he had purchased after the Revolutionary War, where some years later, James Audubon was a guest. In 1976, Jerry and Mary Carol Haggerty purchased the old home and returned it to its former splendor. Jerry Haggerty is an expert furniture refinisher, and Mary Carol has designed the menus and supervises all the cooking. Jerry's talent as a furniture builder is clear when one sees the hand-crafted bar in the pub he created from the former woodshed.

There are two dining rooms at Lincoln House where guests and the public, with advance notice, can enjoy dinner entrées that include scallops, poached salmon, roast sirloin, or leg of lamb. From several of the guest rooms, one can see the river below with its family of nesting eagles. Salmon fishing, birdwatching, nature trails, tennis, boating, canoeing, and river swimming are close by. After walking to the river's edge to watch the animals and birds drawn to the water, return and curl up by the hearth in the old summer kitchen, a cozy spot.

Accommodations: 6 rooms with shared bath. *Driving Instructions:* The inn is in sight of the intersection of U.S. 1 and Route 86.

East Waterford, Maine

THE WATERFORD INNE

Chadbourne Road, Box 49, East Waterford, ME 04233. 207-583-4037. *Innkeepers:* Barbara and Rosalie Vanderzanden. Open all year except March and April.

The Waterford Inne is an old country inn in a postcard setting. At the end of a country lane, part of a former stagecoach route, is an 1825 farmhouse complete with shutters, chimneys jutting out here and there, an old red barn, a farm pond, 10 acres of open fields, and dark Maine woods. Barbara and her mother, Rosalie, bought the house in 1978 and lovingly restored and renovated it. The inn still retains its wide-board pumpkin-pine floors and steep narrow stairways.

Five guest rooms are in the main house; four more were recently added to the ell that formerly served as the woodshed. Each room has special touches giving it its own personality and is decorated with antiques and stenciled wallpapers coordinated with the beds' comforters. Such amenities as fresh flowers in summer or electric blankets in winter add to guests' enjoyment and comfort. The downstairs public rooms are decorated with portraits, pewter, copper, and brass pieces, and old wall sconces.

Breakfasts and dinners are always a treat here. Rosalie and Barbara describe their dinners as "country chic," referring to the extra niceties and the gourmet touch the meals receive, and the attention paid to table settings and locations. A couple might be served in an intimate nook, or a table of four might enjoy dining in the library.

Accommodations: 9 rooms, 6 with private bath. *Pets:* Fee charged. *Driving Instructions:* From Norway, Maine, take Route 118 West for 8 miles to Route 37. Turn left onto Route 37 and go ½ mile to Springer's General Store; then take an immediate right turn up the hill and continue another ½ mile to the inn.

Freeport, Maine

HARRASEEKET INN

162 Main Street, Freeport, ME 04032. 207-865-9377. *Innkeeper:*
Penny Gray. Open all year.

Harraseeket Inn is ideal for L.L. Bean buffs—the store is just two
blocks away. A large Italianate-style house built in 1860 with later
additions in the 1920s, the inn is surrounded by flower gardens. Freeport's only surviving dairy farm, which provides pastoral charm next
door, is scheduled to become part of the inn's property. Formal antique furnishings, fireplaces, and half-canopied beds are reminiscent
of an elegant past, while steambaths or Jacuzzis in private bathrooms
and cable television in the rooms provide today's comforts. Full
breakfasts are served in the dining room or out in the garden on the
brick terrace; several restaurants are within walking distance of the
inn. L.L. Bean has attracted many outlet stores and craft shops to
Freeport, including Frye Boots and a Dansk factory outlet. Portland,
with its restored Old Port's shops, restaurants, and museums, is just
15 miles south of Freeport.

Accommodations: 6 rooms with private bath. *Pets:* Not permitted. *Driving Instructions:* The inn is two blocks north of L.L.
Bean on Main Street.

Georgetown Island is one of many islands and peninsulas that extend from the mainland in southern Maine. Just south of the Bath area, the island is noted for *Reid State Park*, the land for which was donated by the builder of the Grey Havens Inn. The area has several fine beaches, picturesque sights of the local lobstering industry, and an Audubon sanctuary.

GREY HAVENS INN

Reid Park Road, Georgetown, Maine. Mailing address: Box 82, Five Islands, ME 04546. 207-371-2616. *Innkeepers:* The Hardcastle family. Open June 15 through Columbus Day.

At Grey Havens you can lie in your turret guest room and have a 180-degree panoramic view of the ocean. The inn is on an island that feels remote but is accessible by road and a short drive from Bath. Four of the rooms are in the inn's twin turrets. The inn was built by Walter Reid in 1904. It has 260 feet of deep-water anchorage and its own dock. It is within rowing distance of an island nature preserve, and an Audubon sanctuary is just down the road.

The lounge at Grey Havens has a big rock fireplace and a 12-foot picture window, the glass for which was hauled to the inn by ice barge from Rockland. At the time it was the largest piece of glass in the state. The inn is noted for its huge wraparound porch, where guests can relax and even have breakfast if they wish. The dining room features a selection of down east cooking including corn and cheddar chowder, pumpkin chowder, and fresh broiled and baked seafood, each accompanied by home-baked breads and followed by fresh desserts.

Accommodations: 14 rooms, 6 with private bath. *Pets:* Generally permitted with advance notice. *Children:* Well-behaved children over twelve permitted. *Driving Instructions:* Just east of Bath take Route 127 South. Drive 10½ miles to Reid Park Road, on the right. The inn is ¼ mile down this road, on the left.

LE DOMAINE RESTAURANT AND INN

Box 496, U.S. 1, Hancock, ME 04640. 207-422-3395. *Innkeeper:* Nicole L. Purslow. Open mid-May through October.

Le Domaine, just north of Mount Desert Island, is a country inn reminiscent of the *auberges* and restaurants that dot the countryside in France and Switzerland. It is run by a talented French lady, Nicole Purslow, who continues the traditions begun in 1946 by her mother, Marianne Purslow-Dunas. Nicole, who earned a diploma from the Cordon Bleu cooking school in France, has received accolades for her restaurant and inn, including praise from *Gourmet* magazine's Terry Weeks, who wrote, "Nicole is a conscientious and gifted chef, and her restaurant would shine anywhere." Her specialties include soups, quail, rabbit, veal and seafood dishes with sauces, and brandade de morue, a rich puree of pounded cod, garlic potatoes, and cream. Breakfast, which is offered daily to houseguests, includes warm scones, muffins, or croissants with honey from Nicole's own hives, plus real French coffee. The restaurant is closed on Mondays.

In the French Provincial dining room, the copper gleams, the table linens are sparkling white, and fresh flowers are everywhere. The public lounge has a grouping of wicker furniture in front of a stone hearth, where a fire burns on cooler evenings. The guest rooms, each named for a garden herb, are decorated in soft colors and have antique prints on their walls, fresh flowers on each bureau, and thick carpeting. Private porches look out to the pine forest.

Accommodations: 7 rooms with private bath. *Driving Instructions:* The inn is 9 miles northeast of Ellsworth on U.S. 1.

Islesboro, Maine

ISLESBORO INN

Dark Harbor, Islesboro, ME 04848. 207-734-2222. *Innkeeper:* Kathleen Waterman. Open late May to November.

The Islesboro Inn describes itself as a converted "summer cottage." This is more than somewhat of an understatement, as this "cottage" has twelve working fireplaces. Seven of these are in guest rooms, and the rest are in various public rooms with views of Penobscot Bay. Even the ride to the island is a treat aboard the *Governor Muskie,* a 24-car, 125-passenger ferry that leaves from Lincolnville Beach. As you watch the mainland slip away, you are easily convinced that a time of relaxation is ahead.

The inn has a terrace often used for luncheon as well as cocktails before dinner. There are four guest-moorings for yachts nearby, as well as a golf course and, at the inn, a clay-surfaced tennis court. Life here is purposely slow, and the separation of the island from the mainland means that guests are more likely to be contented with sailing, bicycling, bird-watching, berry picking, or beachcombing. Day trips to the mainland provide ample opportunity to go shopping or explore.

Accommodations: 15 guest rooms, 6 with private bath. *Pets:* Not permitted. *Driving Instructions:* Take Route 1 through Camden and to Lincolnville Beach. Board the ferry there; upon disembarking on Islesboro Island, take the first three paved right-hand turns in a row.

Kennebunkport, Maine

THE CAPTAIN JEFFERDS INN

Pearl Street, Kennebunkport, Maine. Mailing address: P.O. Box 691, Kennebunkport, ME 04046. 207-967-2311. Open most of the year.

The Captain Jefferds Inn was built in 1804 as the home of sea captain William Jefferds, Jr. Captain Jefferds had eleven children, many of whom followed their father's vocation. With all that seafaring, it would stand to reason that the house would have at least one ghost, although none has been discovered so far. The innkeepers are still listening and hoping. Today the Captain Jefferds is a handsome inn with landscaped grounds, white picket fences, and even an antique shop in an adjoining barn. The inn's lawn adjoins the River Green, a small common. If you climb to the widow's walk on the river side of the inn, there is a splendid view of the river below.

Thanks to the innkeepers' expertise as professional collectors of antiques, the inn is filled with unusual pieces—folk art, quilts, and wicker. There is an air of country elegance throughout. Both a living room and a sun parlor have been comfortably furnished. Of the eleven working fireplaces, four are in guest rooms. Full country breakfasts are served to guests.

Accommodations: 11 rooms with private bath. *Children:* Under twelve not permitted. *Driving Instructions:* In Kennebunkport, take Ocean Avenue. Turn left off Ocean at the "King's Wharf" sign to Pearl Street.

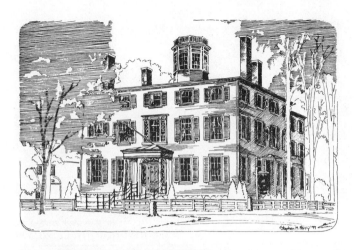

THE CAPTAIN LORD MANSION

Pleasant Street, Kennebunkport, Maine. Mailing address: Box 800, Kennebunkport, ME 04046. 207-967-3141. *Innkeepers:* Beverly Davis and Richard Litchfield. Open all year.

The Captain Lord Mansion is one of the finest examples of nineteenth-century craftsmanship in current use as an inn in the State of Maine. Built in 1812 by a skilled crew of ships' carpenters idled by the British blockade of the harbor, the mansion is an impressive structure with multiple chimneys and a cupola large enough to hold a group of people. Captain Lord clearly could spend as much as he wished to perfect the details of his three-story house. The front door with its elaborate leaded-glass fanlight opens onto an unusual three-story unsupported elliptical staircase of strength and grace. The wide-board pine floors have been restored to their original warmth, and the walls of the mansion's common rooms and guest rooms have been covered with carefully selected reproduction wallpaper.

The entire mansion is carefully appointed with antiques. There are fifteen working fireplaces, eleven of which are in the guest rooms. The beds in the rooms are antiques and include a 10-foot-tall black walnut four-poster and a cannonball king-size bed. Plants, steamer trunks, handmade quilts, and old rugs add personal touches to the rooms.

The romantic qualities and serene atmosphere of this old home are certain to appeal to those who seek a quiet retreat. From the octagonal cupola, guests can enjoy the sunset, gaze at the stars, or watch the boats on the Kennebunk River. Flower gardens and chestnut and elm trees grace the inn's grounds. Guests are served country-style breakfasts around the big kitchen table. No other meals are served.

Accommodations: 16 rooms with private bath. *Pets:* Not permitted. *Children:* Under twelve not permitted. *Driving Instructions:* Take exit 3 off Route I-95 and follow signs to Kennebunkport's Dock Square. At the square, turn right onto Ocean Avenue and go 3/10 mile to Green Street. Take Green Street (left) uphill to Pleasant Street. The inn is on the corner. Parking is behind the mansion.

THE CHETWYND HOUSE

Chestnut Street, Kennebunkport, ME 04046. 207-967-2235. *Innkeeper:* Susan Knowles Chetwynd. Open all year (guests should be sure to check first).

The Chetwynd is a small guest house built in the mid-nineteenth century by Captain Seavey of Kennebunkport and recently redecorated. The blue-shuttered white clapboard house is in the heart of Kennebunkport just a few blocks from restaurants, art galleries, and craft shops on Dock Square. Across the street from the Chetwynd is the busy Kennebunk River, which empties into the ocean one-half mile away. There are two sandy beaches, and the rocks of the breakwater are a good place to sit and watch the parade of fishing boats and sailboats heading for the sea.

Inside, the Chetwynd House has been carefully decorated by innkeeper Susan Knowles Chetwynd. Wide pumpkin-pine boards glow with the patina of age. Victorian antiques mingle with comfortable upholstered furniture. The parlor is filled with books and is a relaxing spot to meet other guests after a day of exploring the village. A handsome staircase leads to the four guest rooms upstairs. Each bears Susan's touch: The Fern Room, for example, has wallpaper imprinted with small green ferns. The quilt on the bed picks up the fern color, and white wicker furniture provides contrast.

Every morning Susan serves breakfast in her breakfast room with its collection of blue and white china. It is a special meal with melon, strawberries, orange juice, and occasionally — if a guest fancies it —

oyster stew! Tea and coffee are available at Chetwynd House at any time.

Accommodations: 4 rooms, 1 with bath. *Pets:* Not permitted. *Children:* Permitted but not encouraged. *Driving Instructions:* From Dock Square take Ocean Avenue two blocks along the river toward the ocean and Chestnut Street.

1802 HOUSE

Locke Street, Kennebunkport, Maine. Mailing address: P.O. Box 774, Kennebunkport, ME 04046. 207-967-5632. *Innkeepers:* Bob and Charlotte Houle. Open all year.

1802 House has come a long way from its days as a boardinghouse for the seamen who worked the locks on the Kennebunk River, enabling ships built locally to get to the sea. Today, innkeepers Charlotte and Bob Houle welcome guests to a comfortable inn decorated with period wallpapers, Colonial antiques and near-antiques, delicate linens, and herbs hanging to dry near on old potbelly stove. Everyone breakfasts together, summoned by the old ship's bell, on a full meal

baked from scratch that day. In the evening, guests frequently gather in the common room, where couches are piled with pillows and a fire burns in the stove. In winter cross-country skiers can take off from the front door and return to hot mulled cider or cocoa. Sometimes the Houles offer sleigh rides or, in the fall, romantic hayrides. In summer there is swimming at the nearby shore, and evenings may be spent at the summer-stock theater.

Accommodations: 8 rooms with private bath. *Pets:* Not permitted. *Driving Instructions:* Take exit 2 (Wells) from the Maine Turnpike, then go left onto Route 1 North. Follow the signs to Route 9 East to Kennebunkport. Go through the lights, over the drawbridge, and through town until you come to a T. Take a left and drive to the third left, next to the church.

ENGLISH MEADOWS INN

Route 35 (RFD 1), Kennebunkport, ME 04046. 207-967-5766. *Innkeepers:* The Kellys. Open April through October.

English Meadows is a turreted Victorian farmhouse with an attached carriage house. Standing on a knoll, the inn is sandy beige with light green shutters, tangerine doors, and white trim. Within its main building are a large living room, dining room, office, and country kitchen. English Meadows, run by antique-lovers who operate a small shop on the grounds, is filled with antique pieces and early art and prints.

The inn's dining room has a large eight-panel bow window with views of nearby meadows (named after the Englishes, who first owned the property). In the morning, deer still come to feed within

sight of the inn. The dining room houses Gene's collection of art-glass baskets and Staffordshire china. The guest rooms in the Carriage House are decorated with old English hunting prints and other art. Remodeled in the 1940s, many of these rooms open off a large gathering room that has a fireplace and a collection of early wicker. Upstairs are four large rooms, with strawberry-patterned wall-to-wall carpeting, that share two connecting baths. Many rooms in the Carriage House contain sinks. Breakfast is a treat with something special every day.

In addition to its antiques, decorative art, and architecture, an appealing feature of the English Meadows Inn is its location. Although within walking distance from the center of the village, it is far enough away from the bustle of this popular tourist spot to retain its country feeling. Available nearby are deep-sea fishing, white sandy beaches (a mile distant), walking tours of the village's historic streets bordered by sea captains' houses, and visits to the Brick Store Museum and to the Seashore Trolley Museum, the largest of its sort in the world.

Accommodations: 15 rooms; 2 suites with private baths. *Pets and children under 10:* Not permitted. *Driving Instructions:* Take the Maine Turnpike (I-95) into Kennebunk and turn left onto Route 35. The inn is 5 miles down the road on the right.

THE HERBERT HOTEL

Main Street on the Corner, Kingfield, Maine. Mailing address: Box 67, Kingfield, ME 04947. 207-265-2000. *Innkeeper:* Bud Dick. Open all year.

The restoration of the Herbert Hotel is a true labor of love. Innkeeper Bud Dick watched the grand old place decline over the decade that he had been coming to Maine to ski at Sugarloaf mountain. In October 1982 he and a group of investors purchased the Herbert and began the long, arduous task of restoring it to the grandeur of 1918, the year it was built. It is said locally that the hotel began as a tax write-off for a wealthy politician, Herbert Wing, who had designs on the governorship, and for that reason had the Herbert built to resemble the state capitol building. Although Wing lost his bid two years later, he had spared no expense in building the hotel. Many features survive, including such furnishings as brass beds, cherry writing desks, and a grand piano in the lobby. There are Italian terrazzo floors, and the deep color of the "fumed" white oak paneling was attained by a time-consuming process: The room was sealed and ammonia pumped in until the desired tone was achieved.

Today the restoration continues. The guest rooms have period wallpapers and retain much of their original decor. A luxury for skiers and white-water rafters are the steambath-spa units installed in each room. The public rooms are furnished mostly with Victorian antiques. Ornate brass fixtures gleam and a moosehead stares sedately from a lobby wall. Two dining rooms offer seafood, chicken, and barbecued ribs. The maple marble cheesecake is an award winner.

Accommodations: 33 rooms with private bath. *Driving Instructions:* Take Route 27 or Routes 201 and 16 to Kingfield. The inn is on Main Street.

THE WINTER'S INN

P.O. Box 44, Kingfield, ME 04947. 207-265-5421. *Innkeeper:* Michael Thom. Open all year.

In the late nineteenth century, A. C. Winter and his friends the Stanley Brothers (inventors of the Stanley Steamer) returned from a day of hunting and, being at a loss for something to do, designed a house to be built on a hill overlooking the lovely little village of Kingfield. The result was Winter's mansion, a fine example of Georgian Colonial Revival architecture. An entrance of etched glass and oak welcomes guests to the Grand Salon, where a fire burns in one of the inn's three matched fireplaces. From here a large staircase ascends to a Palladian window on the landing and continues up to the curved maple bannister on the second floor. The mansion is furnished with antiques and period oil paintings and, in the second-floor guest quarters, big brass beds. The guest rooms on this floor are larger than those on the third floor. Guests are greeted by Balthazar the cat.

Off the Grand Salon are the dining rooms of the inn's restaurant, Le Papillon, serving French specialties by candle- and firelight to guests and the public. These rooms overlook meadows.

The inn has tennis courts and a swimming pool for summer enjoyment. A seasonal ski shuttle is provided to nearby Sugarloaf.

Accommodations: 10 rooms, 7 with private bath. *Pets:* Not permitted. *Driving Instructions:* Take Route 27 north from Farmington to Kingfield. Take a left on Depot Street to the intersection with School Street (at Tranten's General Store). Turn right up the hill to the inn.

Newcastle, Maine

THE CAPTAIN'S HOUSE

River Road, Newcastle, Maine. Mailing Address: Route 1, Box 19, Newcastle, ME 04553. 207-563-1482. *Innkeepers:* Cathy and Kirk Schlemmer. Open all year.

Captain Farley Hopkins picked a fine spot along the old River Road with an excellent view of the Damariscotta River. Here in 1840 he built his home, a refuge from grueling months at sea. The handsome clapboarded Colonial house remained in his family until 1983, when Cathy and Kirk Schlemmer purchased the building and transformed it into a country bed-and-breakfast inn. The spot the captain picked is still quite beautiful, and almost every room has a view of the river. Bedrooms are furnished with antiques that the Schlemmers refinished themselves. A wood-burning stove in the common room beckons guests to gather around. Kathy and Kirk serve a full country breakfast at an old trestle table in the dining room. The Newcastle area offers year-round recreation as well as excellent antiquing and sightseeing, and the Schlemmers are happy to share their expertise with guests.

Accommodations: 4 rooms, 1 with private bath. *Pets:* Not permitted. *Driving Instructions:* Driving north on Route 1, exit at Newcastle/River Road, and bear left 8/10 of a mile to The Captain's House. Driving south on Route 1, exit at Newcastle, turn left at the stoplight, and go a mile to River Road exit, then go left ⅛ of a mile to the Captain's House.

NEWCASTLE INN

24 River Road, Newcastle, ME 04553. 207-563-5685. *Innkeepers:* Sandra and George Thomas. Open all year.

Newcastle Inn is a comfortable Maine inn of indeterminate vintage. The rooms throughout the inn are filled with antiques, folk art, and Victoriana, thanks to the antiquing prowess of the owner. Many of these pieces are for sale; so if something takes your fancy, ask about it. There are several intimate sitting rooms; but the favorite gathering spot seems to be the living room, where a fire burns nightly in the large hearth. The guest rooms are appealing with their varied antiques and wallpapers. A gourmet breakfast, the only meal served, is offered to guests in a room with vistas of a tidal river and the twin towns of Newcastle and Damariscotta. Rocky beaches are nearby, as is a particularly fine lighthouse. Sailing is available to guests.

Accommodations: 20 rooms, 11 with private bath. *Driving Instructions:* Take River Road off Route 1 into Newcastle, 6 miles north of Wiscasset.

OLDE ROWLEY INN

Route 35, North Waterford, ME 04267. 207-583-4143. *Innkeepers:* Michael and Debra Lennon and Peter and Pamela Leja. Open all year, except March and April.

The great appeal of the Olde Rowley Inn, built in 1790, is that it preserves, with few modifications, a roadside stagecoach inn much as it appeared in the early nineteenth century. A carriage house was added in 1825 to connect the barn to the inn. As soon as you enter the inn's keeping room, you are back in early America. Here are low exposed-beam ceilings, pumpkin-pine and hemlock floors, and a large open-hearth fireplace complete with bake oven and two warming cupboards above. A rocking chair, an old basket of firewood, and a high-backed bench are drawn up to the hearth.

Three dining rooms have about a dozen candlelit tables. One room has king's-pine wainscoting and rose and blue pineapple stenciled wallpaper. Another dining room, in the carriage house, has plaster walls and exposed-beam ceilings festooned with drying herbs and old baskets. The third dining room has a hand-stenciled mustard and red Christmas-candle pattern and is lit by copper wall lanterns. The Olde Rowley's menu includes starters such as salmon mousse and deep-fried cheeses and entrées such as chicken Veronique, steak Diane, and shrimp amandine. Meals may be concluded with heaping portions of sherry trifle, walnut bourbon pie, fruit parfait, or brownie hot-fudge sundae.

Guest rooms, reached by climbing the narrow tight-winder staircase, all have period wallpapers and furniture. Some have four-posters and all have nice touches such as nightcaps, dried-flower arrangements, tin-lantern lighting, and reproductions of old children's book illustrations.

Accommodations: 5 rooms, 1 with private bath. *Pets:* Not permitted. *Driving Instructions:* Take Route 35 from Route 302 to North Waterford.

Ogunquit, Maine

CAPTAIN LORENZ PERKINS HOUSE

North Main Street, Ogunquit, Maine. Mailing address: P.O. Box 1249, Ogunquit, ME 03907. 207-646-7825. *Innkeepers:* Ron and Jean Mullenaux. Open April through October.

Captain Perkins's house, more than a hundred years old when he and his family moved there in the late nineteenth century, remained in the Perkins family until the 1970s.

The house stands on almost 2 acres in the coastal village of Ogunquit. Antiques and country collectibles are set in rooms papered with floral prints. Some of the beds feature handmade quilts that match the colors of the walls and trim. The halls and stairs are covered with colorful wool rugs painstakingly braided by the Perkins women.

Complimentary wine is served in the parlor, and a second-floor sitting room is stocked with magazines and books. Innkeeper Ron Mullenaux is the baker, and his breads and coffee get rave reviews from guests, who eat breakfast family style around the dining-room table.

In the adjoining carriage house there are also several antique-filled bedrooms. Jean's shop, "The Captain's Mistress," specializing in old glass, collectibles, and hand-crafted Maine gifts, is a block.

Accommodations: 13 rooms, 5 with private bath, plus 2 efficiencies. *Pets and children under three:* Not permitted. *Driving Instructions:* Take York/Ogunquit exit from I-95. Follow U.S. 1 north 7 miles to Ogunquit Village.

OLD VILLAGE INN

30 Main Street, Ogunquit, ME 03907. 207-646-7088. *Innkeepers:* Ben Lawlor and Catherine Nadeau. Open all year except January. When we first discovered the Old Village Inn one winter's evening several years ago, we were turned away at the door. The line of eagerly awaiting diners extended past the front porch, and there would be no more dinners available that evening. Such is the popularity of this inn in the center of a most popular southern-Maine coastal village. The Old Village Inn was built as a hostelry in 1833 and has been improved and updated throughout the years, adding to the guests' comfort without detracting from its appeal. Upstairs are eight guest rooms, of which five are suites consisting of bedroom, sitting room, and bath. Several rooms have views of the ocean. The nearby Berwick House houses nine additional rooms, all with private baths, cable TV, and air-conditioning.

One can dine at the Old Village in a diverse group of dining rooms. Views of the ocean can be enjoyed from the greenhouse dining room with its profusion of plants. The center dining room, known as the Keeping Room, has a beamed ceiling, richly stained panel walls, a fine collection of antique porcelain, and a framed copy of the 1947 *Saturday Evening Post* cover depicting the Old Village Inn. Recently the front porches that surround the inn's entrance were completely glassed in and now offer dinner guests a view of Main Street. The dining rooms serve dinner to both guests and the public daily during the summer. They are closed on Mondays in cold weather.

The public parlors at the inn are spacious and decorated with period antiques. One has a fireplace and color television for the use of overnight guests; the other has a piano for those who enjoy playing.

Accommodations: 17 rooms, all with private bath. *Pets:* By prior arrangement only. *Driving Instructions:* Take Route 1 into the center of Ogunquit Village.

Searsport, Maine

HOMEPORT INN

Route 1, East Main Street, Searsport, ME 04974. 207-548-2259.

Innkeepers: Dr. and Mrs. F. George Johnson. Open all year.

The Homeport Inn is a fine example of a wealthy sea captain's home. The atmosphere, high-ceilinged rooms, and fine period antique furnishings from around the world are similar today to when wooden clipper ships ruled the waves. The mansion, built in 1863, stands on a hill just east of Searsport, offering views of Penobscot Bay, to which the inn's property extends. Scalloped picket fences enclose the lawns and the circular drive. The interior, befitting a home port of a world-traveling sailor, is filled with unusual antiques. The Johnsons have been carefully restoring the house to its former glory with the help of a young cabinetmaker, Phillip Nedza, who is truly a master restorer. He constructed and installed a shell-shaped alcove, now housing an Oriental vase, that looks as if it has always been there. The paneled library is another fine example of his work. In many of the rooms and halls, chandeliers hang from elaborate plaster ceiling medallions and

Oriental rugs cover the floors. The front sitting room has a black marble fireplace, Oriental vases, palms, and brass chandelier and fireplace accessories. The dining room has another black marble hearth and a rounded cupboard displaying family antique china. Dr. Johnson's green thumb is evident in the profusion of greenery here. The plants are rivaled only by the number of grandfather clocks. There are so many clocks at the Homeport that virtually no one is able to keep up with all the winding required. One of the most inviting rooms is the Keeping Room with informal rag rugs, country pine cupboards, an old couch, and an iron stove to warm the room on winter days. The inn also has its own antique shop.

It is no small task picking a favorite guest room here. All of them have floor-to-ceiling windows; one has a working fireplace with an elaborately carved oak mantel; another room has a fine old desk. All feature unique antique bedsteads — two each in the front rooms — covered with puffs. Marble-top bureaus, fresh flowers in season, and green plants enhance each room. The Sun Porch is a pleasant spot to plan the day's adventures over a hot cup of coffee served with the full country breakfast. Or if you choose, you may breakfast in the formal dining room.

Homeport is just a short distance from the Penobscot Marine Museum. Also nearby is the town of Searsport, with its streets lined with antique shops. It is centrally located for visits to Bar Harbor, Acadia National Park, and picturesque Camden.

Accommodations: 10 rooms, 6 with private bath. *Pets:* Permitted in the kennels only. *Driving Instructions:* Follow Route 1 northeast from Searsport a short distance to the Homeport Inn on the right.

South Bristol, Maine

THE BRANNON-BUNKER INN

Route 129, South Bristol, Maine. Mailing address: H.C.R. 64, Box 045, Damariscotta, ME 04543. 207-563-5941. *Innkeepers:* Joe and Jeanne Hovance. Open all year.

The Brannon-Bunker Inn, near the Damariscotta River, is on the edge of a meadow, complete with farm pond. The inn consists of an 1820 Cape-style house connected to a big barn, the site of a notorious dance hall in the Roaring Twenties.

The guest rooms, with their old-fashioned print wallpapers, are decorated with Victorian bureaus; a sleigh bed is in one room, two old four-posters are in another. Rayo lamps, needlepoint chairs, and nautical prints in gilded frames in the sitting room all add charm. In addition to the rooms in the inn, there are several guest rooms and an apartment in the little barn just across the lawn. Guests are served a complimentary breakfast of fruits, juice, coffee, and homemade muffins and coffee cakes in the dining area. Setups are provided by Joe and Jeanne in the living room at cocktail hour. (Guests bring their own liquor.)

Accommodations: 7 guest rooms, 4 with private bath, and 1 apartment suite. *Driving Instructions:* Take U.S. 1 through the town of Damariscotta to Route 129. Take Route 129 south about 5 miles.

The Forks, Maine

CRAB APPLE ACRES

Route 201, The Forks, Maine. Mailing address: P.O., West Forks,
ME 04985. 207-663-2218. *Innkeepers:* Chuck and Sharyn
Peabody. Open all year.

Crab Apple Acres is an 1835 farmhouse overlooking the Kennebec
River in a rather remote section of Somerset County. The inn offers
seven guest rooms that share two baths. The farmhouse has many old-
fashioned features, including the original fanlight over the door, a
Dutch-oven fireplace, wide pumpkin-pine floorboards, original
Christian-cross doors, and old hinges and thumb latches. The inn is
popular with people seeking a peaceful retreat and with hunters,
snowmobilers, and those on canoe trips. White-water rafting on the
Kennebec River is the favorite sport here, and the Peabodys can outfit
guests for an exciting run through the gorge.

Meals at Crab Apple are served family style, mostly to guests, but
the public is welcome by reservation. The Peabodys' home-style cooking often includes Chuck's French toast at breakfast and Sharyn's
turkey, roast beef, and lasagna suppers.

Accommodations: 7 rooms, none with private bath. *Pets:* Not
permitted. *Driving Instructions:* Take Route I-95 to the Skowhegan,
Quebec, exit; then take Route 201 to the farmhouse in The Forks.
Quebec City is about 140 miles north of here.

Weld, Maine

KAWANHEE INN

Route 142, Weld, Maine. Mailing address: 7 Broadway, Farmington, ME 04938. 207-585-2243. *Inkeeper:* Marti Strunk. Open June to October.

Kawanhee Inn is a rustic lodge built in the 1920s on the shore of crystal-clear Webb Lake in western Maine. The lodge, designed by an artist to house the wealthy parents of children at nearby Camp Kawanhee, is on a forest slope at the foot of Mount Blue and Tumbledown Mountain. A stand of pines towers protectively over the lodge and eleven cabins. Hefty yellow birch beams, pine paneling, and several fieldstone fireplaces create the atmosphere of an old-fashioned hunting and fishing retreat. A moosehead peers down from its perch over the fieldstone hearth in the lodge living room, which is decorated with rustic peeled-log furnishings and old rockers. Table games and bumper pool are in one corner. Guest rooms are simply furnished with iron beds and colorful quilts. The dining room and screened porch are open to guests and the public for breakfast and dinner. Among the inn's popular dishes are fiddlehead ferns, fresh seafoods, and owner Marti Strunk's award-winning tuna chowder. The inn is an ideal spot for mountain climbers and wind surfers. Many people fly seaplanes in for dinner, pulling up on the beach.

Accommodations: 14 rooms, 6 with private bath. *Pets:* Not permitted. *Driving Instructions:* Take Route 4 to Livermore, Route 108 to West Peru, Route 2 to Dixfield, and Route 142 to the inn.

As you drive north through Wiscasset on Route 1 and you have left the central village, look to the right at the harbor and you will see one of the most eerie yet romantic sights of coastal Maine. There, at the shoreline, lie the remains of two grand old schooners. Gray, shadowy reminders of the glory of sailing days gone by, these majestic giants are now lying on their sides, slowly being reclaimed by the sea they once sailed.

Wiscasset is a much visited and photographed coastal village. There are many antique and craft shops here and several small, pleasant restaurants. Among the museums in the area are the *Lincoln County Fire Museum* with its collection of antique fire trucks, hearses, and carriages; the *Lincoln County Museum* and old *Lincoln County Jail*; the *Maine Art Gallery* with its collection of work by Maine artists, including art for sale; and, finally, the *Music Museum*, displaying a wide variety of old musical instruments.

THE SQUIRE TARBOX INN

Westport Island, ME. Mailing address: RFD 2, Box 2160, Wiscasset, ME 04578. 207-882-7693. *Innkeepers:* Karen and Bill Mitman. Open mid-May through October.

The Squire Tarbox is a rare find in Maine — an old country inn in an incomparable setting. It is on a quiet rural island near Wiscasset, linked to the mainland by a bridge. Westport Island has one main road, Route 144, running the length of it. At the end of this road is an old house, part of it dating from 1763. The larger main building was added later. Today the property consists of a main house and a barn, with connecting smaller sections between. Through these the farmer and his family could walk from their house to the barn to do chores without having to go out into the bitter-cold winter weather.

The house was carefully restored some years ago, and it retains the original floors, carvings, moldings, fireplaces, wainscoting, and old windows so characteristic of a home of the early nineteenth century. This is not a large inn; the nine guest rooms are almost always occupied. Each summer, guests are drawn here by the crisp, clean Maine air. This is a place for people who love old things and do not require the organized activity of larger inns or resorts.

The inn has eight fireplaces and wide pumpkin-pine floors. The beams in the dining room were rescued from old sailing ships and repegged in place at the inn. The ground floor of the attached barn has been made into a sitting room with one wall that is all screen doors that open on warm days. Upstairs are two guest rooms.

Dinner is served every evening, although lobster is not on the menu since the innkeepers believe it is best enjoyed "in the rough" at one of the nearby restaurants. Entrées include flounder, sole, haddock, or any of the native shellfish served in a variety of sauces. Each meal includes three vegetables and unusual soups, such as peach cantaloupe. Dessert might be a chocolate mint pie with whipped cream and almonds or a cheesecake with brandied blueberries. Guests are served a complimentary breakfast.

Accommodations: 9 rooms, 3 with private bath. *Pets and children under 12:* Not permitted. *Driving Instructions:* Take Route 1 north from Bath. Turn right on Route 144, and follow it for 8 miles.

HARBOR HILL

Grindstone Neck, Winter Harbor, ME 04693. 207-963-8872.
Innkeeper: Susan Webber. Open mid-June through Labor Day.
When we rounded the bend of the peaceful road leading out to Grindstone Neck one summer morning, we came upon a stone and shingle-turreted country-estate house that, to our delight, turned out to be Harbor Hill, the inn we had been seeking. This is an inn of great dignity, and the parlor is a perfect introduction to it. The grindstone in the name Grindstone Neck refers to ones cut from the many neighboring quarries and carried by schooner to mills up and down the coast a century ago. One such grindstone is set into the fireplace in the parlor.

Even the lobby entrance has its own fireplace, and to the left a broad staircase rises to the upstairs guest rooms. Light from a skylight filters down the staircase to the lobby below. Of the inn's seven bedrooms, one large one has a granite fireplace, wood paneling, and a bathroom with a marble-topped sink. The tower guest room has curved walls, a granite fireplace, and views of the grounds.

Downstairs, the inn's dining room has yet another large fireplace. An adjoining closed-in porch has soft blue-green wainscoting and five windows surrounded by more woodwork.

Accommodations: 7 rooms, including 3 single rooms. *Pets:* Not permitted. *Driving Instructions:* Take Route 1 to West Gouldsboro, then Route 186 south toward Winter Harbor. Watch for a road branching off to the right and follow the signs to Harbor Hill.

THE YORK HARBOR INN

Route 1A, York Harbor, Maine. Mailing address: Box 573, York Harbor, ME 03911. 207-363-5119. *Innkeepers:* Joe and Garry Dominguez. Open all year.

York Harbor Inn has welcomed travelers since the middle of the nineteenth century, serving in the 1890s as a private club for the area's summer population. In 1980 two enterprising young innkeepers bought the big, rambling seaside inn and, with considerable elbow grease that exposed beams and shored up rolling floors, redecorated it from stem to stern. The inn reopened in 1981, welcoming guests with casual guest rooms—some overlooking the entrance to the habor—three dining rooms with ocean views, and an intimate cellar bar with a poetry corner. Listed in the National Register of Historic Places, the inn is built around a 1637 post-and-beam loft room whose sturdy beams and large stone hearth were used in the eighteenth century to dry heavy canvas sails. It now serves as a guest meeting room. The dining rooms, open to guests and the public for lunch and dinner, offer real Down East cooking emphasizing fresh seafoods. Breakfast is served only to overnight guests. Some guest quarters have stenciled walls and floors.

Accommodations: 10 rooms with shared baths. *Pets:* Not permitted. *Driving Instructions:* From I-95 take the York/Berwicks exit. Turn right at the blinking light and then left at the first traffic light, onto Route 1A about 3 miles. The inn is on the left.

Massachusetts

BEECHWOOD

2839 Main Street, Route 6A, Barnstable, Massachusetts 02630.
617-362-6618. *Innkeepers:* Jeffrey & Bea Goldstein. Open all year.
Beechwood is a definite departure from the Cape Cod Colonials that
dot the peninsula. A big rambling Queen Anne whose core was built
in 1853, the house was enlarged greatly throughout the rest of the
nineteenth century. Current owners Jeffrey and Bea Goldstein moved
here with their two small children from California, where they ran an
antique business. Their dream was to own and restore a Victorian inn,
and the Beechwood proved to be just the thing. Bold yellow, gold,
and jade-green shingles and trim outside, and splashy, large-patterned
wallpapers in authentic 1880s colors within, set the tone of this
valentine to the Victorian era. Afternoon teas and homemade
savories are set out in the parlor with its tiny marble fireplace and
stained-glass windows. The dining room, where freshly baked breakfasts are served around a big mahogany claw-footed table, has an
unusual tin ceiling and wood paneling. On warm days breakfast and
afternoon tea are served on the wicker-furnished veranda. The guest
rooms also capture the atmosphere of the 1880s; those downstairs
have working fireplaces. One room has a queen-size four-poster bed
so high that steps are provided to get up to it.

Accommodations: 5 rooms with private bath. *Pets and children:*
Not permitted. *Driving Instructions:* The inn is ½ mile west of Barnstable village on Route 6A.

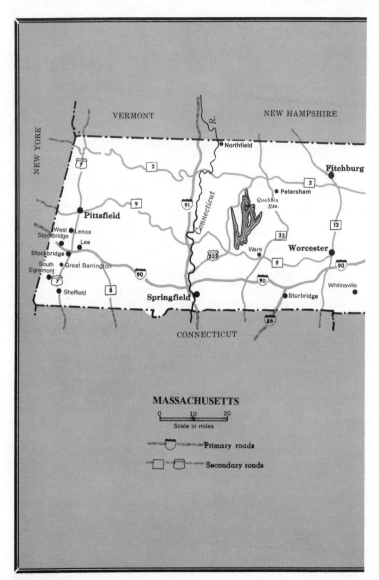

MASSACHUSETTS

```
0        10        20
Scale in miles
```

Primary roads

Secondary roads

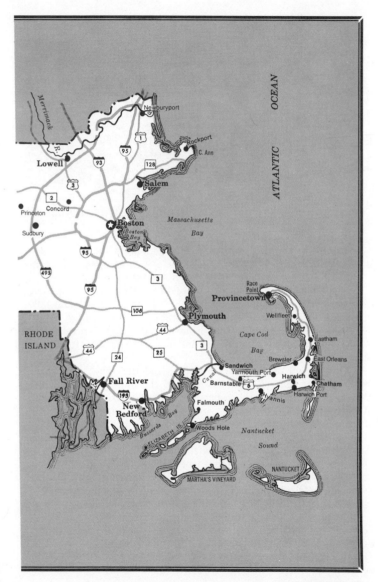

Brewster, Massachusetts

THE BRAMBLE INN

Route 6A, Brewster, Massachusetts. Mailing address: P.O. Box WW, Brewster, MA 02631. 617-896-7644. *Innkeepers:* Karen L. Etsell and Elaine C. Brennan. Open April through December.

The Bramble Inn, in the heart of the Historic District of Cape Cod, comprises two old Cape houses built in 1849 and 1861. Around 1890 the first telephone in Brewster was installed in the inn by W. W. Knowles and connected to what is now the Brewster General Store. The Bramble Inn has offered food and lodging to travelers for almost half a century.

The owners of the inn are artists, and they have created an extensive art gallery, using the walls of the public dining rooms. Works exhibited are by the owners and many local artists working in a variety of media. The Bramble Inn is within walking distance of the ocean, adjacent to tennis courts, and close to other Brewster attractions and the Cape Cod bicycle trail. Guests are housed in three rooms in the main house and five renovated rooms in a Greek Revival house two doors away. The dining room's menu offers wines and cocktails, a choice of clam chowder or a soup of the day, and six entrées. Dessert specialties include the inn's own Cape Cod Bramble and chocolate mint crepes. The public is welcome at both lunch and dinner.

Accommodations: 8 rooms, 3 with private bath. *Pets and children:* Not permitted. *Driving Instructions:* Take Route 6 toward Brewster to exit 10 (Route 124) and drive 4 miles to the dead end at Route 6A. Turn right; the inn is five buildings down on the left.

THE CAPTAIN FREEMAN INN

15 Breakwater Road, Brewster, Massachusetts. Mailing address: Rural Route #2, Brewster, MA 02631. 617-896-7481. *Innkeepers:* Barbara and John Mulkey. Open all year.

Many seafaring families settled in Brewster in the nineteenth century, among them Captain William Freeman, who become wealthy in the clipper trades and built himself a mansion across from the town green. A hardy soul, he survived a mutiny and a fire at sea as well as a 2,100-mile journey in a small open boat. A picture of his ship, the *Kingfisher,* hangs in the main hall at the inn today.

John and Barbara Mulkey recently bought the old captain's home, which had been transformed into a country inn some years back. It is furnished with antiques, including some memorabilia from Captain Freeman's days. Guest rooms, some with views of the bay, have antique beds with quilts and comforters. The common room downstairs is available for guests' use, as is the inn's swimming pool out back. Each day Barbara bakes muffins using seasonal berries from the Cape; blueberries and cranberries are particular favorites. The inn is within walking distance of restaurants, the beach, antique shops, and many recreational activities. The Mulkeys provide bicycles for touring the Cape Cod Bike Trail and Nickerson Park.

Accommodations: 9 rooms, 4 with private bath. *Driving Instructions:* Take Route 6 (Mid-Cape Highway) to exit 10, turn on Route 124 toward Brewster, and go to Route 6A. Turn right on 6A, go about 100 yards, then turn left on Breakwater Road and go about 50 yards.

THE OLD MANSE INN

1861 Main Street, Brewster, MA 02631. 617-896-3149. *Innkeepers:* Sugar and Doug Manchester. Open all year.

The mansard roof on the Old Manse belies its age. The inn was built in the early nineteenth century by a Brewster sea captain. Later the roof was raised and a third floor was added, as well as a new mansard roof. As a result, rooms on the third floor actually have higher ceilings than the floor below. Slave quarters in the back of the house held coolie slaves brought back to Brewster by Captain Knowles during the China-trade era. During the Civil War the house was a link on the underground railroad, and during the 1940s church services were held in the sunroom. It was, in fact, the wife of the minister who first opened the Old Manse as an inn.

The Old Manse is decorated with antiques and hand-braided and Oriental rugs. Many of the rooms have fireplaces, although none of the guest room fireplaces may be used. The decor includes patchwork quilts and old-fashioned print wallpapers.

A Continental breakfast of fruit, cereals, and fresh muffins is served in the dining room. Cocktails and wines are available.

Accommodations: 9 rooms with private bath. *Pets:* Not permitted. *Driving Instructions:* Take exit 9 off Route 6 onto Route 134. Drive north to Route 6A. Turn right on 6A and go 7½ miles to the inn.

OLD SEA PINES INN

2553 Main Street, Brewster, MA 02631. 617-896-6114. *Innkeepers:*
Stephen and Michele Rowan. Open May through October.

How could anyone resist being fascinated by a place called the Sea
Pines School of Charm and Personality for Young Women? Certainly
the Rowans couldn't, and after much careful renovation they opened
their inn in what was once a farmhouse dating from the mid-nineteenth century. From 1907 to the 1970s, the building served as Bick-
ford Hall during the property's tenure as a finishing school.

The inn is on 3½ acres of wooded grounds within walking or biking distance of bayside beaches. Its large sunny rooms are furnished
with pieces from the 1930s and 1940s, and its atmosphere is very much
that of an old-fashioned summer home. One wing has brass and iron
beds, and two rooms have fireplaces. Guests may use the living room
with its fireplace, and rockers are set out on the wraparound porch.
Breakfast and dinner are served to both guests and the public.

Accommodations: 12 rooms, 8 with private bath. *Pets:* Not per-
mitted. *Children:* Under ten not permitted. *Driving Instructions:*
Take exit 10 off Route 6. Turn right at the Brewster General Store.
The inn is 1 mile down Main Street, on the left.

Chatham, Massachusetts

CAPTAIN'S HOUSE INN

369 Old Harbor Road, Chatham, MA 02633. 617-945-0127. *Innkeepers:* Cathy and David Eakin. Open all year except the last two weeks in January.

In 1839, Captain Hiriam Harding, a packet skipper, and two other sailing captains chose this section of mid–Cape Cod for their homes, and although they might now find the Cape a bit too populated for their tastes, they would probably agree they chose one of the finest locations in Chatham. Captain Harding's house, on 3 acres of lawns and gardens shaded by tall hardwoods, was converted to an inn in 1955, and early in 1983, Dave and Cathy Eakin bought it after leaving busy lives in Pennsylvania. After much papering, painting, and polishing, they moved in their extensive collection of antiques and were ready for business. Antique area rugs are set off by wide pumpkin-pine floors. Some guest rooms are furnished with antiques and four-poster beds; others have typical Cape Cod seaside furnishings. The aroma of Cathy's baking breads begins the day, and a sunny dining room overlooking the garden is set up with little tables for breakfast. Both Cathy and Dave are avid sailors, and, with prior arrangements, guests may sail aboard their 35-foot sloop *Tiercel*.

Accommodations: 10 rooms with private bath. *Pets and children:* Not permitted. *Driving Instructions:* On the Cape, take Route 6 to exit 11, then Route 137 South for 3 miles to Route 28. Turn left on Route 28 to Chatham. At the traffic circle in Chatham follow the sign and go toward Orleans (Route 28 South) for ½ mile.

THE QUEEN ANNE INN

70 Queen Anne Road, Chatham, MA. Mailing address: Box 747, Chatham, MA 02633. 617-945-0394. *Innkeepers:* Nicole and Guenther Weinkopf. Open Easter through October.

In the 1840s a young Methodist minister married Captain Howles's daughter. The best of all the wedding presents they received was a house built just for them. Their wedding present is still beautiful today, thanks to the painstaking restoration by innkeepers Nicole and Guenther Weinkopf. The Queen Anne Inn, as their home is now named, is a Victorian hotel with thirty guest rooms and suites and several public rooms, all decorated with many antiques of the period.

The Earl of Chatham, the inn's restaurant, is set up with bentwood chairs, greenery, and formal table-settings lit by the many floor-to-ceiling windows and French doors that line the room's three walls. Fresh seafood from Cape Cod heads the list of offerings here, which include an array of Continental and New England dishes.

The guest rooms are individually decorated with period antiques, have a variety of bedsteads including a canopy or two, and have been totally renovated and updated with modern bathrooms and telephones. Four new tennis courts are on the grounds.

Accommodations: 35 rooms with private bath. *Driving Instructions:* On the Cape, take Route 6 east to exit 11, then Route 137 south. After 3 miles, turn left on Route 28 to Chatham. At the first traffic light turn right onto Queen Anne Road.

THE TOWN HOUSE INN

11 Library Lane, Chatham, MA 02633. 617-945-2180. *Innkeepers:* Russell and Svea Peterson. Open all year except January.

In 1881 Captain Daniel Nickerson commissioned a new home to be built on the site of the old Captain Sears House on Library Street, on a knoll just above Main Street and the harbor. The Town House Inn has been modernized over the years, and all of its guest rooms, including those in an adjacent lodge and cottage, have color television and refrigerators. Nevertheless, the building's high ceilings, original woodwork, and old-fashioned wallpapers capture the mood of the last century. Some of the carved molding and wood trim reveal harpoon and oar motifs. Some of the original walls recently exposed reveal hand-painted scrolling. The Town House is a family-run inn with plenty of personal service and a congenial atmosphere.

Innkeeper Svea Peterson is from Finland, and the menu at their restaurant, Two Turtles, reflects this with a Scandinavian flair in the Continental dishes. Both breakfast and dinner are served to guests and the public.

Accommodations: 21 rooms with private bath. *Pets:* Not permitted. *Driving Instructions:* From Route 6 take exit 11 to Route 137 and go south to Route 28; go east on Route 28 to the center of Chatham. Take the second left after the rotary onto Library Lane.

Concord, Massachusetts

THE HAWTHORNE INN

462 Lexington Road, Concord, MA 01742. 617-369-5610. *Innkeepers:* Gregory Burch and Marilyn Mudry. Open March through December.

The Hawthorne Inn was built in 1870 across the street from a home once occupied by Nathaniel Hawthorne. The inn's grounds were once owned by Ralph Waldo Emerson and Bronson Alcott and then by Hawthorne himself. The famed New England writer planted a number of pines, two of which survive today on the old path to the mill brook beside the Hawthorne Inn.

The Hawthorne, originally a private home, was converted to a small inn in 1976 by Gregory Burch and Marilyn Mudry. The rooms were restored and decorated with antique furniture, handmade quilts, and some of the innkeeper's paintings and other art. Burch inserted leaded-glass transoms over the doorways. The inn is presided over by a striped cat, Ratface. The complimentary breakfasts include a selection of freshly baked breads and turnovers.

Accommodations: 7 rooms, 5 with private bath. *Driving Instructions:* The inn is three-quarters of a mile east of the town center, on Lexington Road, across from the Nathaniel Hawthorne House.

East Orleans, Massachusetts

THE FARMHOUSE

163 Beach Road, East Orleans, MA 02653. 617-255-6654; winter phone: 803-886-6138. *Innkeepers:* John and Nancy Sirigos. Open mid-April through October.

The Farmhouse was built in 1870 by Roland Mayo as a wedding gift for his bride, Mary Clark Snow. The Mayos raised seven children on their self-sufficient farm, and their family kept the property until 1982, when it was bought by John and Nancy Sirigos. The new owners painstakingly restored the Greek Revival farmhouse to re-create the 1870s, installing iron and wooden bedsteads, wardrobes, trunks, washstands, and cupboards. Hand-quilted comforters add color. The dining room at the Farmhouse, where breakfast is the only meal served, has lace-trimmed white curtains and pine, oak, and walnut tables. From its windows guests can see the ocean. In the large public lounge, guests can sit comfortably and read or find a quiet corner to enjoy one of several available table games.

Accommodations: 8 rooms, 4 with private bath. *Pets and children under 8:* Not permitted. *Driving Instructions:* Take exit 12 from Route 6 (the Mid-Cape Highway). At the first traffic light turn right onto Eldredge Parkway. After 2 lights turn right onto Main Street. Follow the signs to Nauset beach.

THE NAUSET HOUSE INN

P.O. Box 774, Beach Road, East Orleans, Cape Cod, MA 02643. 617-255-2195. *Innkeepers:* Diane and Al Johnson. Open April 1 through October.

The Nauset House, built around 1800, is an old Cape Cod farmhouse. This small country inn is furnished with antiques and family memorabilia, and on cooler evenings two fireplaces add their warmth to the atmosphere. There is an afternoon cocktail hour in the common room, with complimentary wine and hors d'oeuvres. The dining room is reminiscent of an old English pub, with a large fireplace and bar where the inn provides setups and ice for the guests (bring your own spirits). A full country breakfast is served by the open hearth. Coffee can be enjoyed out in the ornate Victorian greenhouse. The guest rooms are furnished with antiques, and one has its own fireplace. Nauset Beach is within easy walking distance just down the road.

Accommodations: 14 rooms, 8 with private bath. *Pets:* Not permitted. *Children:* Under twelve not permitted. *Driving Instructions:* Take Route 6 to exit 12; turn right and follow the signs to Nauset Beach. The inn is half a mile from the beach.

SHIP'S KNEES INN

Beach Road, East Orleans, MA 02643. 617-255-1312. *Innkeepers:* Ken and Louise Pollard. Open all year.

The Ship's Knees is surrounded by landscaped lawns with a wide variety of trees and flowers. The original house belonged to an old sea captain and was built more than 150 years ago. It has recently been thoroughly restored and renovated, and a new section was added in 1970. Scenic Nauset Beach is only a short walk away. The doorways are lit by lanterns, and the house is decorated throughout with many antiques. Each guest room has its own special decor with large open beams, counterpanes on four-poster bedsteads, and colonial color schemes. Many of the rooms have ocean views. The favorite is the master suite, which has a working fireplace.

The Pollards have recently added Cove House to the inn complex. It overlooks Orleans Cove and has three guest rooms plus a one-bedroom apartment. The Ship's Knees has its own swimming pool, and other sporting facilities are close by — golf, horseback riding, and ocean and bay swimming. To start the day, the Pollards provide a complimentary breakfast.

Accommodations: 23 rooms, 9 with private bath. *Pets:* Not permitted. *Driving Instructions:* Take Route 6 exit 12 to the first stoplight, turn right, go two stoplights, turn right again. Follow the signs to Nauset Beach.

Eastham, Massachusetts

WHALEWALK INN

169 Bridge Road, Eastham, MA 02642. 617-255-0617. *Innkeepers:* Ginny and Norm de la Chapelle. Open March through November. Whalewalk, named for the widow's walk or "whalewalk" atop the inn, was built more than 150 years ago. Originally a whaling master's home, Whalewalk stands on over 3 acres of lawns and meadows on a quiet country road. Guests can walk or bike to Cape Cod bay, the National Seashore, and Orleans village. Guest accommodations are available in the inn itself, as well as in a renovated barn, in the Guest House, and in a studio cottage. A full breakfast is served daily, and hors d'oeuvres are provided at the cocktail hour. The Ship's Locker, a B.Y.O.B. bar, is equipped with glasses, an icemaker, and mixers.

Accommodations: 6 rooms in the inn, 4 suites in the barn and Guest House, and 1 studio cottage, all with private bath. *Pets:* Not permitted. *Children:* Over 12 permitted in suites. *Driving Instructions:* Take Route 6 to the Orleans Rotary. Take the Rock Harbor exit and follow the sign to Rock Harbor. Bridge Road is the first on the right.

Falmouth, Massachusetts

MOSTLY HALL

27 Main Street, Falmouth, MA 02540. 617-548-3786. *Innkeepers:*
Ginny and Jim Austin. Open all year except part of February.

Mostly Hall, the only house of its kind on the Cape, was built in 1849
by Captain Albert Nye as a wedding present for his New Orleans
bride. The four-story house is topped by an enclosed widow's walk.
The central hallways on each of the four floors dominate the inn's
interior and account for its name—Mostly Hall. The inn sits facing
the village green in Falmouth's historic district, surrounded by homes
dating back to the early eighteenth century.

The rooms are furnished with antiques, and some have 13-foot
ceilings and 10-foot-tall windows. The guest rooms have four-poster
beds, and one has twin antique French sleigh beds. Breakfast is served
in the 45-foot-long living and dining room beside a French fireplace.
Since Ginny Austin has modeled the inn after English bed-and-breakfast establishments, the breakfast menu at Mostly Hall always has a
special dish, perhaps ham-and-mushroom gratinée, stuffed French
toast, or a traditional Cape Cod dish such as homemade codfish cakes
with strawberry soup. The Austins lend guests bicycles to ride on the
paved "shining sea" bicycle path from Falmouth to Woods Hole.

Accommodations: 6 rooms, 5 with private bath. *Pets and children:* Not permitted. *Driving Instructions:* Cross the bridge to Cape
Cod at Route 3 or Route 28. Follow Route 28 to Falmouth. Turn left
on Route 28 South. Follow the signs to Mostly Hall.

Great Barrington, Massachusetts

WINDFLOWER INN

Route 23, South Egremont Road, Great Barrington, MA 01230. 413-528-2720. *Innkeepers:* Barbara and Gerald Liebert and Claudia and John Ryan. Open all year.

We were delighted to hear that our friends Gerry and Barbara Liebert of the Tulip Tree Inn had sold their popular Vermont inn and purchased what had been the Fairfield Inn in Great Barrington. This move to the south will give the Berkshires highly experienced innkeepers who will bring their special style of innkeeping to this attractive inn. Windflower is a Federal-style inn built in 1820, with one addition in the same style built about a century later. Some of the guest rooms have canopied beds. One guest room on the main floor has a stone fireplace that occupies most of one wall. With its own entrance from the terrace, this room is bound to be particularly popular for honeymooning couples. Just outside the door is the inn's swimming pool.

Windflower is the only inn we know of with a full-time mother-daughter chef team. Barbara and daughter Claudia will prepare two or three entrées every evening for their guests and a small number of diners from the public, who must make reservations in advance. A summer dining porch overlooks a small pond.

Accommodations: 12 rooms with bath. *Pets:* Not permitted. *Driving Instructions:* 3 miles west of Great Barrington on Route 23.

Harwich Port, Massachusetts

COUNTRY INN

 86 Sisson Road, Harwich Port, MA 02646. 617-432-2769. *Inn-keepers:* David and Kathleen Van Gelder. Open all year.

The Country Inn, with 6½ acres of farmland, is near the center of Cape Cod on the sound side. Built in 1773, the main building with its eleven fireplaces was once the summer home of the founders of the Jordan Marsh Company in Boston. Through the years several additions have been made to the inn, including three tennis courts and a swimming pool for guests. The fireplaces in the living room, tavern, and dining room are all put into use when the cool weather sets in. Those in the bedrooms are not used but do add to the decor. Dinner is served in the inn's dining room and features fresh seafood dishes, filet mignon, and chicken dishes. The Van Gelders have restored a Victorian guest cottage near the beach, just 1½ miles from the inn. The cottage has five additional rooms.

 Accommodations: 12 rooms with private bath. *Driving Instructions:* From exit 10 on Route 6 take Route 124 to Route 39 (Sisson Road). The inn is about a mile from Harwich center.

DUNSCROFT INN

24 Pilgrim Road, Harwich Port, MA 02646. 617-432-0810. *Innkeepers:* William and Maureen Houle. Open March through December.

Dunscroft consists of two shingled buildings: the two-story gambrel-roofed main inn and a smaller adjacent heated cottage. Built in 1930, Dunscroft takes its name from the Scottish word for "home on the dunes." Although the inn is not literally on the dunes, it is an easy walk to the private beach 300 feet away. Dunscroft is also within walking distance of the town, with its theaters and restaurants. The inn retains its residential feeling with comfortable colonial and traditional furnishings and an abundance of plants and flowers. A television and piano are available to guests in the living room, where the walls are lined with bookshelves and a fireplace is kept going.

The guest rooms are large and airy. In addition to the guest rooms, the Houles have two efficiency apartments and a cottage for rent. A Continental breakfast is served on the sun porch, which opens onto a terrace for sunning. An annual Fourth of July picnic is held for guests, and there are periodic fish-bakes during the season. There is a spacious, shaded picnic area with tables, a shuffleboard court, and horseshoes.

Accommodations: 6 rooms with private bath, 2 efficiencies, and 1 cottage. *Pets:* Not permitted. *Driving Instructions:* The inn is off Route 28 in the center of Harwich Port.

Lenox, Massachusetts

CORNELL HOUSE

197 Pittsfield Road, Lenox, MA 01240. 413-637-0562. *Innkeeper:* Chuck Bowers. Open all year.

In 1980 Chuck Bowers did what many people dream of doing: He quit his job and bought a country inn that needed repair. The new innkeeper closed the inn and labored seven days a week for five months before reopening it as Cornell House.

The inn was built in 1888, and the main building offers the most fully restored rooms with antique furnishings. The inn's carriage house, now called Hill House, also offers freshly redone rooms, but they are somewhat smaller and do not have antique furnishings. A number of the antique pieces in the Main House come from the innkeeper's family. A baby-grand piano graces the music room, and there is also a large living room and library. Continental breakfast including biscuits and muffins baked fresh every morning is served in the dining room. Behind the inn is the 400-acre Kennedy Park, with its miles of cross-country ski trails.

Accommodations: 16 rooms with shared baths. *Pets and children:* Not permitted. *Driving Instructions:* The inn is up a hill from the center of Lenox, just beyond the church.

GARDEN GABLES INN

141 Main Street, Lenox, MA 01240. 413-637-0193. *Innkeeper:* Marie R. Veselik. Open all year except March.

This 190-year-old gabled inn was originally a private estate. Its last owner, Kate Carey, moved the house away from the road, added on, and built a 72-foot swimming pool—the first to be built in Lenox.

The inn is on the Main Street but it has a protected feeling because it is set back on 4 acres of lawns and shade trees. Mrs. Veselik is a great lover of animals, feeding the many birds that come most of the year; in autumn, deer occasionally come to eat fallen apples.

The older parts of the inn have some colonial antiques, while the newer extension is filled with turn-of-the-century antiques. Most of the guest rooms have private baths; others have running water and share hall bathrooms. The comfortable living room has a fireplace with a fire on cool evenings and a good supply of books and magazines as well as FM radio and television. Joining the inn is an interesting gift shop where guests are welcome to browse. Garden Gables accommodates only twenty guests at a time, enhancing its intimate feeling. The one meal served is breakfast, available only to guests, on an optional basis.

Accommodations: 10 rooms, 6 with private bath; and 2 apartments. *Pets:* Not permitted. *Driving Instructions:* The inn is on Main Street (Route 7A), facing Saint Ann's church.

THE VILLAGE INN

16 Church Street, Lenox, MA 01240. 413-637-0020. *Innkeepers:* Clifford Rudisill and Ray Wilson. Open all year.

The Village Inn, built in 1771, is in the center of historic Lenox, a mile from Tanglewood. Its guest rooms are decorated in colonial fashion with country antique furnishings of the period. During the winter, open fireplaces add a glow of warmth to the lounges and dining room. A baby grand piano, available for guests and visiting musicians, graces the front reception room.

Below is the Village Tavern, where guests may enjoy cocktails, beer, and wine and light snacks in a room that has a hand-hewn bar and church pew seating. A breakfast and luncheon menu is offered daily in the inn's dining room. Dinner is served on Friday and Saturday evenings only. The dinner menu changes seasonally and includes beef, chicken, and fish offerings. Breakfast ranges from flapjacks and French toast to eggs Benedict; lunch includes homemade soups, quiche, and crepes. A traditional English afternoon tea is served daily.

Accommodations: 27 rooms and suites, 8 with private bath. *Pets:* Not permitted. *Driving Instructions:* Take Route 7 or Route 20 directly into Lenox.

WALKER HOUSE

74 Walker Street, Lenox, MA 01240. 413-637-1271. *Innkeepers:* Richard and Peggy Houdek. Open all year.

One can look at some inns and tell at a glance that they are owned and run by people who truly love their work. The Walker House is one such place. Guests don't even need to go inside to get the message here. Immaculately cared-for grounds, a tidy, freshly painted home, and pots of flowers brimming with blooms set the mood.

The Federal-style inn was built in 1804, and a large back wing was added in 1906. One of Lenox's oldest buildings, it is set among beautiful pines and cedars. Each of the guest rooms is named for a different composer, in honor of nearby Tanglewood: Chopin, Mozart, Beethoven, and so on, are furnished with pieces appropriate to the period in which the room's namesake lived. There are canopied and brass beds and high oaken headboards. Five guest rooms have working fireplaces. The parlor and dining room, also cheered by fires in old fireplaces, are available to guests. The parlor has a grand piano, and there is usually a jigsaw puzzle in progress. Breakfasts are popular affairs where everyone eats together on the innkeeper's extensive collection of Depression glass, sharing plates of muffins, croissants, and fresh fruit. In the afternoons lemonade or hot tea and cookies are offered.

Accommodations: 8 rooms with private bath. *Pets and children:* Permitted with prior approval. *Driving Instructions:* From exit 2 (Lee) of the Massachusetts Turnpike, take Route 183, which becomes Walker Street, into Lenox.

Martha's Vineyard, Massachusetts

CAPTAIN DEXTER HOUSE

100 Main Street, Vineyard Haven, Massachusetts. Mailing address: Box 2457, Vineyard Haven, MA 02568. *Innkeepers:* Beyer and Lara Parker. Open all year.

In 1843, Captain Rodolphus Dexter built a fine Colonial residence on a shady street just a block from the beach. His house is now a beautifully maintained island bed-and-breakfast inn sharing the Main Street of Vineyard Haven with other homes of the period. Just a block and a half from the ferry depot, the Captain Dexter House is ideal for overnight guests traveling without their cars, although there is ample parking. Beyer and Lara Parker have filled their inn with many fine period antiques, Oriental carpets, and interesting personal mementoes. Long-gone ancestors peer down from portraits hanging above antique sideboards and fireplace mantels. Each bedchamber, as the innkeepers call them, is decorated with antiques, and coordinated linens and freshly cut flowers are the rule. Some rooms have working fireplaces and four-poster canopied beds. A comfortable living room–library is available for guests' enjoyment. Breakfast, served in the dining room, includes fresh juice and homemade breads, muffins, and preserves.

Accommodations: 7 rooms, 5 with private bath. *Pets and children under 6:* Not permitted. *Driving Instructions:* 1½ blocks from the ferry dock in Vineyard Haven. The ferry is from Woods Hole.

THE CHARLOTTE INN

South Summer Street, Edgartown, MA 02539. 617-627-4751. *Innkeepers:* Gery and Paula Conover. Open all year.

The Charlotte Inn is a very special place. It is, in fact, one of the most elegant small hotels in America, unusual for an inn accessible only by ferry, airplane, or private boat. Of course, thousands of visitors find their way to Martha's Vineyard each year. However, only a few are able to stay in the two dozen rooms at The Charlotte. These rooms are found in the main building and three detached structures—the Carriage House, Summer House, and Garden House. One room in the Carriage House is decorated in deep, rich, tiny floral-print papers with deep blues accented by white trim. Polished brass, English and French antiques, plush wall-to-wall carpeting, and original artwork are frequent elements in the decorative themes. Our room was no exception, with its polished brass-duck magazine rack, brass lamps, and tall brass shaving mirror stand. Fresh flowers and a sterling silver brush and mirror were set out on a marble topped bureau. The white four-poster bed was covered with a calico puff and a great pile of lacy pillows. In the sitting area, a plush loveseat sat in front of a well-stocked bookcase and a fire was laid in the fireplace, all ready for a romantic winter's evening.

Within the main building is a gift shop and an art gallery which specializes in the work of Island artists and antique etchings and hunting prints. Just down a few steps from the gallery is Chez Pierre, the inn's repository of haute cuisine, fashioned from the building's many-paned conservatory. The *prix fixe* menu changes almost daily. One could start with a choice of three-squash soup, smoked salmon with Dijon-dill sauce, marinated Montrachet with sun-dried tomatoes or a warm smoked pheasant and leek salad. The day's four entrées could include Nantucket duckling with cranberry glaze, medallions of veal with chanterelles, Island seafoods on hand-rolled pasta, and entrecote with sauce chasseur. In the morning, guests may choose the complimentary Continental breakfast or, for a small surcharge, have a more elaborate complete breakfast which might feature a special omelet, breakfast crepe, or eggs and bacon. On Sunday mornings a special brunch is available.

The Charlotte Inn is just a half-block from Main Street, yet its

side-street location insures quiet during the busy summer months. The staff at the inn goes to great lengths to make guests comfortable.

Accommodations: 24 rooms, 22 with private bath. *Pets and children:* Not permitted. *Driving Instructions:* The inn is on Summer Street in the center of Edgartown, one block from Main Street.

DAGGETT HOUSES

54 North Water Street, Edgartown, Martha's Vineyard, MA 02539. 617-627-4600. *Innkeeper:* Daniel O'Connor. Open all year. The Daggett Houses are a group of historic houses offering a variety of accommodations on the waterfront in Edgartown. The main house, called Daggett House I, was built in 1750, but it incorporates part of the old tavern run by John Daggett and dating back to the early 1660s. Its lawn slopes gently down to a sandy area and a dock in the harbor. The old tavern room is now called the Old Chimney Room because of its fireplace of beehive construction. It has candlelight doors, a brass flintlock blunderbuss, Betty lamps, and a secret stairway. A full breakfast is served in this room, often before an open fire. Accommodations are available in Daggett House I, as well as in the Garden Cottage near the water (a schoolhouse in the last century) and in Daggett House II—formerly Warren House, a whaling captain's home in the early nineteenth century.

Accommodations: 25 rooms (some in suites) in three houses, all with private bath. *Pets:* Not permitted. *Driving Instructions:* From the center of Edgartown, turn left on North Water Street. Go three short blocks to the inn (across from the library).

THE DR. SHIVERICK HOUSE

Pease Point Way, Edgartown, Massachusetts. Mailing address: Box 640, Edgartown, MA 02539. *617-627-8497. Innkeeper:* Tena McLoughlin. Open all year.

Dr. Shiverick House, an island mansion recently transformed to an inn, has museum-quality antiques, canopied beds, and Oriental carpets on honey-colored pine floors. The house was built in 1840 for the town's physician and his family, and an addition soon housed his office. The grand house, a private residence until recently, was purchased by the Rogers family, whose interior designer scoured New England for antiques to re-create its early elegance. There are canopied beds with dainty floral quilts and dust ruffles, romantic print wallpapers, and fresh- or dried-flower bouquets as well as art objects.

Breakfast, served on the patio or in the dining room, includes island jams on freshly baked breads and granola with local honey; on Sundays, special treats include French toast made from sweet bread and served with blueberries.

Accommodations: 11 rooms, 10 with private bath; and a penthouse with 2 bedrooms, 2 ½ baths, living room, dining room, and full kitchen. *Pets:* Not permitted. *Driving Instructions:* The inn is in the center of Edgartown, just off Main Street, at the intersection of Pease Point Way and Pent Lane.

THE EDGARTOWN INN

North Water Street, Edgartown, Martha's Vineyard, MA 02539. 617-627-4794. *Innkeeper:* Susanne Chlastawa. Open April 1 through November 1.

The Edgartown Inn was originally an old whaling captain's home, built in 1798 for Captain Thomas Worth. A few years later it began a long career as a colonial inn. The Edgartown Inn has played host to many notable guests through the years. Daniel Webster was at first denied admittance because he was dark-skinned and thought to be an Indian. He later returned as a guest, as did Nathaniel Hawthorne, who came for a rest but stayed on to write *Twice-Told Tales.* John F. Kennedy stayed here when he was a Massachusetts senator.

The inn is centrally located in the heart of Edgartown. Minutes away by foot is the beach by the old lighthouse; for surf bathing, the South Beach is a short ride by car or bike. Nearby are golf courses, tennis, and fishing. The inn's front porch overlooks North Water Street with its picket-fenced old captain's houses. The rooms at the inn are much the same as they were in Captain Worth's time, but tiled baths and many antiques have been added. Beyond the back patio garden are the "Captain's Quarters," an old barn with guest rooms without private baths for more modest rates. Country breakfasts featuring homemade breads, muffins, and griddle cakes are served in the paneled dining room and in the garden.

Accommodations: 12 rooms in the inn, 6 in Captain's Quarters. *Pets:* Not permitted. *Driving Instructions:* Go to Woods Hole on Cape Cod, then take the ferry to Martha's Vineyard.

THE GOVERNOR BRADFORD INN

128 Main Street, Edgartown, Massachusetts. Mailing address: P.O. Box 239, Martha's Vineyard Island, MA 02539. 617-627-9510.

Innkeepers: John and Mary Kennan. Open all year.

The Governor Bradford Inn began in 1860 as a private residence on Edgartown's Main Street, just a few blocks from the harbor. In 1982 the Kennans expanded the house, creating an inn with sixteen guest rooms and suites in the new addition. These rooms, of recent vintage and with modern tiled bathrooms, are decorated with fresh flowers and many antiques. Guests have a choice of king-size or twin brass beds, and the suites contain Queen Anne or Chippendale pieces. The numerous common rooms in the original section include a formal Queen Anne living room and a cocktail room with greenery and white wicker. Breakfast is served in a blue-and-white breakfast room, the colors picked up from the Willoware displayed in the Sheraton china closet. Sherry is served in the living room in the evening and tea and lemonade are offered in late afternoon.

Accommodations: 16 rooms with private bath. *Pets and children under 12:* Not permitted. *Driving Instructions:* The inn is in the center of Edgartown.

HAVEN GUEST HOUSE

278 Main Street, Vineyard Haven, Massachusetts. Mailing address: P.O. Box 1022, Vineyard Haven, MA 02568. 617-693-3333.
Innkeepers: Karl and Lynn Buder. Open all year.

The Havens Guest House, just a mile from the ferry, is on secluded shady grounds on the road between the village of Vineyard Haven and the affluent summer community of West Chop. The inn, built in 1918 by a wealthy grain merchant as a wedding present for his son, is a classic Craftsman-style bungalow, tidy and symmetrical in design. Karl and Lynn Buder carefully transformed the house from a summer tourist home into a romantic country inn with family antiques, a Victorian parlor, and a turn-of-the-century dining room where they serve full breakfasts. The inn's solitary television is in an enclosed porch where guests may gather in the evenings if they wish. One guest room is furnished with Karl's parents' bedroom set dating from the 1930s; another room has colonial antiques; and a third has a selection of Victorian pieces.

Accommodations: 8 rooms with private bath. *Pets and children under 12:* Not permitted. *Driving Instructions:* Take Route 28 to Woods Hole for boarding on the Steamship Authority Ferry. The inn is located a mile from the ferry dock on Upper Main Street.

POINT WAY INN

Main Street, Edgartown, Martha's Vineyard, Massachusetts. Mailing address: Box 128, Edgartown, MA 02539. 617-627-8633. *Innkeepers:* Linda and Ben Smith. Open all year.

Ben and Linda Smith had just finished a 4,000-mile cruise when they moored their ketch in Edgartown harbor a few years ago. Soon after, they discovered and fell in love with the 150-year-old erstwhile sea captain's home that is now the Point Way Inn. After a winter of seemingly endless toil, the Smiths and their two daughters had created an inn with antique furnishings, ceiling fans, and working fireplaces in most rooms. (The Smiths provide plenty of wood for the fireplaces.) A recent addition to the inn is the living-room library with fireplace, bar, and refrigerator.

Continental breakfast is served in a sunny room complete with its own Franklin fireplace. Both American and English regulation croquet can be played on the spacious lawn, and afternoon lemonade is a warm-weather tradition. During the cooler months, afternoon tea takes the place of lemonade.

Like many East Coast resort areas, Martha's Vineyard is seeing much more year-around activity, and the Point Way Inn now remains open all year. Bicycles or mopeds are logical alternatives to automobiles here, just a short stroll from the center of town and the wharf area.

Accommodations: 12 rooms with private bath. *Driving Instructions:* The inn is at the corner of Main Street and Pease's Point Way.

Nantucket Island, Massachusetts

THE CARRIAGE HOUSE

4 Ray's Court, Nantucket Island, MA 02554. 617-228-0326. *Innkeepers:* Jeanne and Bill McHugh. Open all year.

The Carriage House was built in 1865 for the purpose that its name indicates. In the center of the Old Historic District, it is a nice example of early Victorian architecture now restored and transformed into an inn. Its location offers guests easy strolls to nearby restaurants, shops, and galleries. It has the added benefit of a quiet setting on a country-lane side street.

The interior of the guest house contains a cheerful and simple living room with a deacon's bench, Windsor rocker, floral-pattern area rug, and a profusion of potted plants and fresh and dried flowers. Outside there is an intimate patio bordered by hydrangeas and other flowering plants and shrubs, where a Continental breakfast is frequently served when the weather is good.

Accommodations: 7 rooms with private bath. *Pets:* Not permitted. *Children:* Under five not permitted. *Driving Instructions:* Take the Nantucket ferry from Woods Hole or Hyannis on Cape Cod.

FOUR CHIMNEYS INN

38 Orange Street, Nantucket Island, MA 02554. 617-228-1912.
Innkeeper: Betty Gaeta. Open April through November.
No fewer than 126 sea captains built their homes on this beautiful historic street in Nantucket. Four Chimneys, built in 1835 by Captain Frederick Gardner, is the largest of all.

Innkeeper Betty Gaeta restored and decorated the lovely old house to the glory of the days when whaling ships and China clippers ruled the seas. The center hall takes guests into the past with its curving staircase, elegant wallpaper, and stately grandfather's clock. Betty is an interior designer, and the decor of the inn is her tribute to the whaling days, Nantucket's golden era. The antique porcelains and Persian carpets are typical of the period. The double drawing room features twin fireplaces, a piano, and inviting sitting areas where guests can visit or enjoy a good book. The guest rooms are authentically furnished with antiques of the period, and most have fireplaces and four-poster or canopied beds and patchwork quilts. Many have views of the harbor. A Continental breakfast is available to guests.

Accommodations: 10 rooms with private bath. *Pets and children:* Not permitted. *Driving Instructions:* Take the Nantucket ferry.

JARED COFFIN HOUSE

29 Broad Street, Nantucket, MA 02554. 617-228-2405. *Innkeeper:* Philip Whitney Read. Open all year.

The Jared Coffin House recaptures the spirit and feeling of the days when Nantucket reigned as queen of the world's whaling ports. Built in 1845 by Jared Coffin, one of the island's most successful ship owners, the main house is a classic example of Greek Revival architecture. This house and later additions were restored in the 1960s to their original style. The living room and library are furnished with Chippendale, Sheraton, and American Federal antiques.

Upstairs in the original house are nine restored guest rooms furnished with antiques and locally woven fabrics. The 1857 Eben Allen Wing has sixteen simply decorated rooms with antiques used wherever possible. The eighteenth-century Swain House behind the wing has three bedrooms with canopied beds. The Daniel Webster House across the patio was built in 1964. It has twelve spacious rooms furnished with twin beds. An 1821 Federal house and an 1841 Greek Revival mansion provide additional guest rooms with canopied beds. A sunny sitting room in one converts to a small conference room when needed.

The main dining room, Jared's, features New England and other American foods. The Tap Room, with its outdoor patio, offers luncheon, snacks, and dinner with entertainment nightly.

Accommodations: 58 rooms with private bath. *Driving Instructions:* Take the Nantucket ferry from Woods Hole (January–March) or Hyannis (April–December) on Cape Cod.

MARTIN'S GUEST HOUSE

61 Centre Street, Nantucket, MA 02554. 617-228-0678. Open all year.

Nantucket Island, its homes, and its twisting streets have changed very little from the old whaling days. One seems to step off the ferry or plane and back into the nineteenth century. What better place to savor the atmosphere than in an old Nantucket home? Martin's Guest House fulfills the requirements. Built in 1805 with additions later in the nineteenth century, the house is on a brick-sidewalked street. There are gardens, a lawn, and a side porch for relaxing. It is an easy walk to the beaches and downtown with its many shops and restaurants. Martin's has a large living room with a working fireplace. The guest rooms have old-fashioned print wallpapers, antiques, and four-poster beds. A breakfast of juice, coffee, and home-baked breads and muffins is available. Reservations should be made six to eight weeks in advance.

Accommodations: 14 rooms. *Pets:* Not permitted. *Driving Instructions:* Take the Nantucket ferry from Hyannis (April–December) or Woods Hole (January–March) on Cape Cod.

SHIPS INN

13 Fair Street, Nantucket, MA 02554. 617-228-0040. *Innkeepers:*
Bar and John Krebs. Open mid-March through mid-December.
The Ships Inn was the home of whaling captain Obed Starbuck between voyages. He built the house in 1812 and many of the rooms are
named for the ships he sailed. The furnishings in the inn today date
back to Captain Starbuck's time, and the charm and atmosphere have
changed little. The inn was also the birthplace of Lucretia Coffin
Mott, one of the very first of the women abolitionists. Downstairs the
living room and dining room are attractively decorated and, on chilly
evenings, there are fires in the two fireplaces. The restaurant, The
Captain's Table, features Nantucket's catch of the day, roast duckling, a daily chef's special, and marinated lamb chops. The Dory Bar
is just that: a bar made from an old dory. Backgammon, cribbage,
and darts are played here, entertaining islanders and tourists alike.
The Ships Inn is a very friendly place.

Accommodations: 12 rooms, 10 with private bath. *Pets:* Not permitted. *Driving Instructions:* Walk or bike; almost anyone at the ferry
dock or the airport can direct you.

Newburyport, Massachusetts

THE ESSEX STREET INN

7 Essex Street, Newburyport, MA 01950. 617-465-3148. *Innkeepers:* The Pearson family. Open all year.

In 1879 Lucy's Stable, a nineteenth-century landmark that once stood at 7 Essex Street, was torn down and a lodging was built in its place. It was built in a fairly conservative, eclectic Victorian style. Located just steps away from the waterfront and harbor, the Essex Street Inn today is a handsome restoration. Its guest rooms are furnished with antiques, and the larger suites have working fireplaces and whirlpool baths. Most have love seats, color television, air-conditioning, and private phones. A Continental breakfast is served to guests in their rooms at an additional charge.

The inn is ideally located in the center of this historic seaport, with its many beautifully preserved old buildings. Nearby are the ocean and Plum Island, which offers miles of beaches, rolling dunes, and paths for walking in the Park River Wildlife Reserve. The town of Newburyport contains craft and antique shops and specialty boutiques selling artwork and imported items.

Accommodations: 17 rooms with private bath. *Pets:* Inquire first. *Driving Instructions:* Take U.S. 1, I-95, or I-93 north from Boston to Route 113 and drive east to Newburyport.

MORRILL PLACE

209 High Street, Newburyport, MA 01950. 617-462-2808. *Innkeeper:* Rose Ann Hunter. Open all year.

A number of New England inns once belonged to sea captains. Morrill Place was owned by three. It is no surprise, therefore, to discover a widow's walk atop this three-story Federal home built by Captain William Hoyt in 1806. Thirty years later the house was purchased by Henry W. Kinsman, a junior law partner of Daniel Webster's, and in the years that followed, Webster was a frequent guest there. The name Morrill Place derives from the Morrill family, which made the house at the corner of High and Johnson streets its home from 1897 until 1979, before it became an inn.

Ten of Morrill Place's twenty-two rooms are guest rooms where canopied brass-and-pineapple four-poster beds are the rule. The guest and public rooms are furnished with antiques, mostly of the Federal period, in keeping with the house. There are a formal front parlor and a library, as well as summer and winter porches that enjoy views of the inn's 2.5 acres of landscaped grounds. The inn's music room has both a square grand piano and a 1910 Steinway.

Accommodations: 10 rooms with shared bath. *Children:* Not permitted. *Driving Instructions:* Take I-95 to Route 113, and proceed east toward town. The inn is on the right, about 2 miles from the exit.

Northfield, Massachusetts

NORTHFIELD COUNTRY HOUSE

School Street, Northfield, MA 01360. 413-498-2692. *Innkeepers:* Jan and Paul Gamache. Open all year except Thanksgiving, the second week in January and two weeks in early August.

Northfield Country House is an English manor house built in 1901 by a wealthy shipbuilding family from Boston. Drawn to the area by the evangelist Dwight Moody, the family fell in love with the Northfield countryside and built their eighteen-room home in a secluded spot. A long, tree-lined drive leads to the house with its rambling stone-columned porches.

Within, the inn has stucco walls trimmed with chestnut. Beams are exposed in several rooms, a wide, open staircase leads to a landing lighted by a large leaded-glass window. A fire usually burns in the living room fireplace, one of five in the house. Over the fireplace opening is: "Love Warms the Heart as Fire the Hearth."

Guest rooms are on the second floor, each decorated individually. Down comforters, antique furnishings, and herbal wreaths made by Jan contribute to the rooms' warmth. Jan, a former interior decorator, has used sheets effectively on several of the guest room walls. Three rooms have working fireplaces and velvet fireside chairs or love seats.

Every morning guests awaken to the smell of freshly baking bread.

Accommodations: 7 rooms with shared baths. *Pets:* Not permitted. *Driving Instructions:* Take exit 28A off I-91 and follow Route 10 north to Northfield Center. School Street is in the center of town, at the firehouse. The inn is 0.9 mile down School Street, which becomes a wooded dirt road.

Petersham, Massachusetts

WINTERWOOD AT PETERSHAM

North Main Street, Petersham, MA 01366. 617-724-8885. *Innkeepers:* Robert and Jean Day. Open all year.

The village of Petersham is noted for its many examples of Greek Revival architecture, and Winterwood is no exception. Listed in the National Register of Historic Places, the inn was built as a private summer home in 1842. For a short time at the turn of the century, it served as an annex to the nearby Nichewaug Inn, now a private academy. Robert and Jean Day have restored Winterwood, transforming it into a formal inn, with detailed interior woodwork accented by the use of richly colored designer wallpapers and fabrics. Antiques, contemporary furnishings, crystal and brass chandeliers, and working fireplaces in most rooms add to the appeal. The innkeepers have used color well in creating different atmospheres in the guest rooms. One sunny room has a yellow decor with an antique brass bed and fireplace. Another has an antique sleigh bed and contrasting colors of navy and coral.

Breakfast is served in the rose- and plum-colored dining room. Fine china and silver seem to make the tea breads and freshly baked muffins taste even better. The inn is across from a thirty-two-acre wildlife preserve with views of nearby Mount Wachusett.

Accommodations: 5 rooms with private bath. *Pets:* Not permitted. *Driving Instructions:* Take the Massachusetts Turnpike to Route 32N. The inn is in the center of town.

Princeton, Massachusetts

COUNTRY INN AT PRINCETON

30 Mountain Road, Princeton, MA 01541. 617-464-2030. *Innkeepers:* Don and Maxine Plumridge. Open all year, Wednesday through Sunday.

Don and Maxine Plumridge have left behind, respectively, careers in advertising and the fashion industry to create at the Country Inn at Princeton one of the region's most elegant classic French restaurants, set in formal Victorian trappings. Built in 1890, the 23-room, gambrel-roofed Queen Anne mansion was once the summer home of Worcester industrialist Charles G. Washburn. The mansion numbered among its prominent guests President Theodore Roosevelt.

The four-star menu at the inn changes often. Among the chef's noted presentations are his cream of watercress soup, pheasant with port wine (as an appetizer), salmon fillet stuffed with mousse of scallops and watercress and served en croute, and roast lamb stuffed with chicken livers, ground veal, and pork. Six parlor suites continue the Victorian theme of the inn with antiques and reproductions, fourposters and high-backed beds. Skiing is nearby.

Accommodations: 6 suites with private bath. *Pets and children:* Not permitted. *Driving Instructions:* Take Route 31 north or south to Princeton. In town, take Mountain Road up to the inn.

Provincetown, Massachusetts

ASHETON HOUSE

3 Cook Street, Provincetown, MA 02657. 617-487-9966. *Inn-keepers:* Jim Bayard and Les Schaufler. Open all year.

Asheton House is actually two adjacent houses offering bed and breakfast to guests visiting Provincetown. One was a whaling captain's home built in 1840; the other is an early Cape house built about twenty-five years earlier. Both houses have been faithfully restored and reflect the gracious atmosphere of an earlier era. All rooms and the suite are appointed with American, French, English, and Oriental antiques from the owners' private collections, augmented by some contemporary pieces. Decorative touches reflect Les's twenty-five years as a professional interior designer.

The variety of rooms at Asheton House provides a wide range of choices. For example, a large bed-sitting room has French furnishings, a working fireplace, and a private bathroom and dressing room. Another room's campaign chests, Maharlika chairs, glass-topped wicker traveling trunk, and potted palm create a safari-like feeling. From still another room you can see the Pilgrim Monument as you lie in a large four-poster bed with complementing early-American furniture. From the inn's gardens and walks bordering the houses, you can watch the fishing boats rounding Long Point.

Accommodations: 6 rooms, 1 suite, 1 apartment. *Pets and children:* Not permitted. *Driving Instructions:* Drive on Route 6 (the Mid-Cape Highway) to Provincetown; take the first Provincetown exit and go to the water. Turn right and follow Commercial St. to Cook St.

BRADFORD GARDENS INN

178 Bradford Street, Provincetown, MA 02657. 617-487-1616.
Innkeeper: Jim Logan. Open April to November.
If you love the sea and a good country inn, you'll love Provincetown and Bradford Gardens. Built in 1820, Bradford Gardens is an informal country inn furnished with antiques and art work. In the old inn are eight individually decorated guest rooms, six with working fireplaces, overlooking the garden and, in the winter, the sea. There is the Jenny Lind Room with early spool furnishings and a fireplace, the Yesteryear Room with its brass bed and brass accents, and the Chimney Nook with garden and water views and a fireplace nook.

The Morning Room has a central fireplace and a bay window overlooking the garden. Here guests mingle and enjoy the inn's country breakfasts, the only meal served. No part of town is more than a mile from the inn, so a car is hardly needed. There are special parkland bicycle and walking trails and miles of beaches.

Accommodations: 8 rooms in the inn and 4 in other buildings — all with private bath. *Pets:* Not permitted. *Driving Instructions:* Take Route 6 (the Mid-Cape Highway) to Provincetown.

THE 1807 HOUSE

54 Commercial Street, Provincetown, MA 02657. 617-487-2173.
Innkeepers: Bob Hooper and David Murray. Open all year.

It may be more accurate to call this the 1783 House, because that is the year it was built. It was 1807 when the Cape-style house was moved from the beach to its present location on higher ground. The 1807 House retains its original wide-board pine floors and has been decorated with designer fabrics and wallpapers. Antique furnishings include a four-poster in the Red Room and a Canadian pine armoire in the Master Suite. Other pine antiques and art by local artists grace the Hospitality Room. A brick patio underneath the oldest pear tree on Cape Cod has a bar with an ice machine, and a spiral staircase leads from the patio to the guest rooms above.

Continental breakfast is provided for guests renting inn rooms and includes home-baked blueberry muffins made with berries picked in the early summer on the hill behind the inn. Located in the quiet, historical West End of Provincetown, the 1807 House is within walking distance of the beach and downtown Provincetown.

Accommodations: 3 rooms with shared bath, plus 5 efficiency apartments. *Pets:* Not permitted. *Driving Instructions:* Take Route 6 (the mid-Cape Highway) to Provincetown. The inn is on Commercial Street (Provincetown's main street).

LAND'S END INN

22 Commercial Street, Provincetown, MA 02657. 617-487-0706. *Innkeeper:* David Schoolman. Open all year.

Land's End is a striking contrast to many New England inns we have written about over the years. In a number of ways this Art Nouveau summer "bungalow" is more reminiscent of inns we know in California. Land's End was built at the turn of the century by Charles Higgins, a Boston merchant. On a high dune overlooking Provincetown and all of Cape Cod Bay, the inn still houses part of Higgins's collection of Oriental wood carvings and stained glass. In fact, it is the inn's outstanding period glass—in both windows and in its hanging and table lamps—and its abundance of potted plants and flowers that distinguish it.

Throughout the inn, numerous Victorian pieces intermingle with a collection of more recent pieces including upholstered, bentwood, and caned chairs. Much of its original wainscoting has been retained, and the combination of the eclectic furniture and antique curtains helps to create an atmosphere at once informal, artistic, and in keeping with the mood and style of the Art Nouveau period. No television or radio are in the rooms, but books abound. The house encourages quiet socializing or the enjoyment of the solitude of a spot away from the bustle of downtown Provincetown.

Accommodations: 15 rooms, 10 with private bath. *Pets and young children:* Not permitted. *Driving Instructions:* Take Route 6 or 6A to Commercial Street, following it almost to the end. Stop at the Land's End sign and walk up the hill to the inn.

ROSE AND CROWN GUEST HOUSE

158 Commercial Street, Provincetown, MA 02657. 617-487-3332. *Innkeepers:* Preston Babbitt, Jr., and Thomas Nascembeni. Open all year.

The Rose and Crown is a classic Georgian "square rigger" built in the 1780s. Its orderly design was the model for many other homes in Provincetown. The guest house sits behind an ornate iron fence containing an unusually lush English garden. "Jane Elizabeth," a ship's figurehead, greets visitors from her post above the paneled front door.

During restoration wide floorboards were uncovered, and pegged posts and beams were exposed. Hooked rugs, patchwork quilts, and antique brass and silver accent pieces create a colonial atmosphere throughout the inn. Each guest room has its own special feature. Crown Room has exposed beams and Oriental rugs, while the brick fireplace wall in Rose Room displays a mysterious portrait of a girl holding a single rose. In addition to the rooms in the inn, the Rose and Crown has a cottage and an apartment, both with kitchen facilities. The inn is particularly appealing in the off season, when the pace slows and guests can relax in the living room and enjoy a breakfast of freshly baked breads and the Rose and Crown's special-flavored coffee.

Accommodations: 8 rooms, 3 with private bath, plus cottage and apartment. *Pets:* Not permitted. *Children:* Permitted in cottage and apartment only. *Driving Instructions:* Take Route 6 (the Mid-Cape Highway) to Provincetown.

SOMERSET HOUSE

378 Commercial Street, Provincetown, MA 02657. 617-487-0383.
Innkeeper: Jon Gerrity. Open April to December.

The Somerset House is one of Provincetown's larger old homes, a black-shuttered yellow building behind a picket-fenced front garden facing the town beach a hundred feet away. The original house was built in 1850 by a successful ship chandler, Stephen Cook. An addition in 1890 doubled its size. Today the Somerset is a guest house offering twelve individually decorated guest rooms and two two-bedroom apartments. The furnishings throughout are an eclectic combination of antique and very modern enhanced by many plants, flowers, and original paintings and lithographs. Eleven of the guest rooms have tiled baths, and several rooms have water views of the harbor. The Somerset House serves no food, but the town has a great many unusual (and usual) restaurants, all within a short walking distance. Whale-watching trips can be arranged.

Accommodations: 14 rooms, 11 with private bath. *Pets:* Not permitted. *Driving Instructions:* Take Route 6 to Provincetown, east end exit. Follow Commercial Street (Provincetown's main street) along the water to Pearl Street.

WESTWINDS — ON GULL HILL

28 Commercial Street, Provincetown, Massachusetts. Mailing address: P.O. Box 644, Provincetown, MA 02657. 617-487-1841. *Innkeepers:* Lloyd Salt and Roger Hanzes. Open all year.

Westwinds is a complex of white clapboard buildings overlooking Provincetown Harbor. They sit on a gentle hill in a country setting of lawns, seaside gardens, and woodlands. Although Westwinds is in a residential section, the historic town is just a fifteen-minute walk past lovely old Cape houses. The main house at the inn, a classic full Cape built more than two hundred years ago, has antique-filled rooms with 32-inch-high single board wainscoting. Guests in the three rooms in the main house are served Continental breakfast in the dining room. One guest room is in the building's former kitchen with a large hearth. For guests' enjoyment there is a sitting room with more antiques, and a deck out back overlooks the lawn and woods and has a surrounding tea-rose garden. There are several guest apartments in various settings: One in the ell of the house and others in the cottage, with its grape arbor and screened porch. An appealing dollhouse of a cottage complete with window boxes is set in a quiet woodsy hollow.

Accommodations: 3 rooms with shared baths; 2 apartments; 2 cottages. *Pets and children:* Not permitted. *Driving Instructions:* Take either Route 6 or Route 6A to Commercial Street.

Rockport, Massachusetts

ADDISON CHOATE INN

49 Broadway, Rockport, MA 01966. 617-546-7543. *Innkeepers:* Margot and Brad Sweet. Open mid-February through December. In 1851 this little house was the talk of Rockport. The first bathtub had arrived and was safely ensconced in the kitchen. Today there are seven baths, and although none is in the kitchen, all are most unusual. The inn is decorated with collections of family antiques, such as museum-quality ship models, clocks, and quilts. Each guest room is furnished with antiques of a particular period or theme. The Sweets' enjoyment of innkeeping shows up in their attention to the decor and in the personal amenities they provide guests. Beds are turned down and surprises are left on pillows. There is even an ocean-racing yacht for sailing excursions. A large swimming pool set in the yard is surrounded by gardens and a profusion of tiger lilies. The Stable House is a cottage with a sleeping loft and teak furnishings. Guests are greeted each morning by the aroma of baking breakfast pastries, which are served in the dining room with its working beehive oven.

Accommodations: 7 rooms with private bath, plus the Stable House for two to four persons. *Pets and children:* Not permitted. *Driving Instructions:* The inn is in Rockport at the junction of Routes 127 and 127A.

EDEN PINES INN

Eden Road, Rockport, MA 01966. Off-season mailing address: 8 Cakebread Drive, Sudbury, MA 01776. 617-546-2505; off season: 617-443-2604. *Innkeeper:* Inge Sullivan. Open mid-May through mid-November.

Eden Pines Inn, a gray-shingled building with black shutters, is on the rocky shore of this popular seacoast village. One can sit on its enclosed porch and watch lobstermen hauling their catches, fishermen at work, and ships going to and coming from European ports. In the distance is Thatcher's Island, with its historic twin lighthouses. Also on the ocean side of the house is a sun deck ablaze with red geraniums in season. Below it, water-smoothed rocks lead to the sea. On the street side a Romanesque-arched Palladian window overlooks the flower-bordered brick walk leading to the inn.

The guest rooms are decorated in bright, fresh colors, and each has its own sitting area. All but one has an ocean view; four have private decks. A living room warmed by a fire in the fireplace contains the inn's television. A Continental breakfast served on the porch includes juices, fresh fruit, coffee, tea, and home-baked pastries. In the afternoon, tea and cookies are served two hours before cocktails.

Accommodations: 8 rooms with private bath. *Pets and young children:* Not permitted. *Driving Instructions:* Take Route 128 north to the lights; turn left on Route 127 to downtown Rockport. Turn right on Mount Pleasant (Route 127A to Gloucester) and go a mile to Eden Road. Turn left on Eden and drive to the inn (on the ocean).

THE INN ON COVE HILL

37 Mount Pleasant Street, Rockport, MA 01966. 617-546-2701. *Innkeepers:* John and Marjorie Pratt. Open late February through October.

The Inn on Cove Hill is a classic Federal-period home, New England in appearance with its white siding and black painted shutters. This is one of several Rockport mansions that were built with pirates' gold by the sons of Joshua Norwood, who had watched the pirates bury their loot. A perfectly pieced granite walkway leads up to one of the finest doorways in Rockport. Many of the architectural and decorative features of the house have been carefully preserved or restored, such as its Christian doors bearing their original hand-forged hinges, its wainscoting, wide pumpkin-pine floors, dentil molding, a ceramic-tile Vaughn fireplace, and the striking spiral staircase in the main entrance hall. The staircase was built with thirteen steps, a common tribute to the original colonies.

Guests are offered Colonial and Victorian rooms with antique and reproduction furniture. There are such personal touches as handmade pincushions for emergency mending, handmade afghans and quilts for winter comfort, and vases of marguerite daisies in summer or pumpkins in autumn.

The public areas in the inn include a third-floor porch with a panoramic view of the harbor, where whales can be sighted during their migrations. The living room for guests is furnished with a blend of new and antique furniture handed down through generations of the Pratt family. Among the treasures are a cherry-wood Winthrop desk and a Windsor chair built by a family ancestor 150 years ago. The walls are decorated with original oils and watercolors.

Breakfast at the inn, often served outdoors on umbrella tables, features blueberry, cranberry, pumpkin, or blackberry muffins and fresh coffee and juice. Winter guests frequently enjoy breakfast in bed, and all year one can wake to the smell of baking muffins.

Accommodations: 10 rooms, 7 with private bath. *Pets:* Not permitted. *Children:* Under ten not permitted. *Driving Instructions:* Take Route 127 to Rockport; once in town, take Route 127A to the center; then turn right with Route 127A and continue on it two blocks.

OLD FARM INN

291 Granite Street, Rockport, Massachusetts. Mailing address: Box 590, Rockport, MA 01966. 617-546-3237. *Innkeepers:* The Balzarini family. Open early spring through late fall.

The Old Farm Inn is between Halibut Point and Folly Cove on the northernmost tip of Cape Ann. The date of the farmhouse is estimated to be 1799, but a house has been on the site since 1705. In the early 1900s, Antone Balzarini, an immigrant from Italy, rented the farm and raised dairy cows and twelve children there. The family later moved down the road. In 1964, one of Antone's sons, John, and his family bought the old place. The Balzarinis restored the farmhouse and furnished it with antiques, including the much used big black iron stove. They added on a dining room overlooking a meadow where ponies graze and a glassed-in terrace dining room. Another dining room has beamed ceilings, open hearths, and floor-to-ceiling windows. The Old Farm Inn specializes in roast duckling and fresh seafood. For dessert there are Indian pudding baked in the iron stove and Uncle Charlie's rum bread pudding. Rockport is a dry town, so bring your own spirits and the restaurant will provide setups.

Guests can enjoy the inn's 5 acres of lawns and meadows, with trees and abundant flowers, or hike to the sea through the state park behind the inn. Four guest rooms are in the Guest House, but three with fireplaces are in the inn.

Accommodations: 7 rooms, 5 with private bath. *Pets:* Not permitted. *Driving Instructions:* Take Route 128 to Gloucester, then follow signs to Rockport. Turn left at Railroad Avenue and follow the sign to Pigeon Cove (about 2 miles).

The Inn

ROCKY SHORES INN AND COTTAGES

Eden Road, Rockport, MA 01966. 617-546-2823. *Innkeepers:* Gunter and Renate Kostka. Open April to late October.

Rocky Shores is a substantial building with seven fireplaces, a wide staircase, and handsome detailing on its interior woodwork. The Kostkas furnished the inn with a number of antiques and added touches of greenery here and there to give it a homey feeling. In warm weather the inn's broad porch is a natural gathering place for guests. In any season the sun parlor and large living room are popular spots. Rocky Shores overlooks the twin lights of Thatcher Island. All the guest rooms have television. The larger rooms have ocean views. Rocky Shores also has a dozen two- and three-bedroom cottages with complete housekeeping facilities. Breakfast, the only meal served at Rocky Shores, is included in the charge for rooms in the inn.

Accommodations: 10 rooms in the inn, 8 with private bath; 12 housekeeping cottages. *Pets:* Not permitted. *Driving Instructions:* Take Route 127 to Rockport. Turn right onto Route 127A, and go one mile to Eden Road. Turn left on Eden Road, and go ½ mile along the ocean to the inn.

SEACREST MANOR

131 Marmion Way, Rockport, MA 01966. 617-546-2211. *Innkeepers:* Leighton Saville and Dwight MacCormack, Jr. Open all year except January.

The Seacrest Manor, built as a luxurious private home in the early 1900s, stands on a scenic rocky outcropping of rugged Cape Ann. An easterly wing and sunny deck were added in the 1960s; from here, guests enjoy outstanding panoramic views of the sea, Straitsmouth Island, and the historic twin lighthouses of Thatcher's Island. One can even see the far-off Mount Agamenticus, nearly 40 miles away in Maine. The Manor resembles an English bed-and-breakfast place with its leather club chairs at fireside in the library, afternoon teas in the sunny living room, and large breakfasts in the breakfast room overlooking the old-fashioned gardens dotting the 2 acres of lawns and woodland. On cool days there is a fire in the breakfast-room hearth. Breakfast is included in the room rate, with special choices each morning: one day it might be blueberry buttermilk pancakes; another day, corn fritters or French toast. There is always a choice of seasonal fruit, beverages, eggs, bacon, and spiced Irish oatmeal.

The eight guest rooms are furnished with a comfortable blend of antiques and traditional contemporary furnishings. They are carpeted and decorated in a simple, unpretentious manner. Four have private baths; the others share adjoining bathrooms. In the evenings guests find their beds turned down and mints on the bedside table. Shoes left outside the door will be polished mysteriously in the night and will be waiting outside next to the morning paper. These are just a few of the amenities found at the Seacrest Manor.

Accommodations: 8 rooms, 4 with private bath. *Pets:* Not permitted. *Children:* Under 16 not permitted. *Driving Instructions:* The inn is up the hill (Mount Pleasant Street) from the center of town. Marmion Way is the second left after the Den Mar nursing home.

THE SEAFARER

86 Marmion Way, Rockport, MA 01966. 617-546-6248. *Innkeepers:* Gerald and Mary Pepin. Open April 15 through October 31.

Marmion Way is a horseshoe-shaped road that hugs the coast overlooking the cove near Rockport. Primarily a residential street, it also serves several of the inns we describe in the Rockport area. The Seafarer, an 1893 gambrel-roofed inn, has been in continuous operation since 1900. Originally part of a large inn and cottage complex called the Straitsmouth Inn, the Seafarer stands at the edge of Gap Cove, overlooking Straitsmouth Island. An old-fashioned porch with deck chairs takes full advantage of the ocean view and breezes.

The inn's airy guest rooms display original oil paintings of the area done by local artists. Doors to the rooms bear brass Lloyds of London certification plates with names like Captain's Quarter, Chart House, or First Mate's Quarters instead of numbers. Every room has an ocean view. Two rooms on the third floor, with breakfast nooks and efficiency kitchenettes, have the finest views but are rented on a weekly basis in season.

The inn's living room has a fireplace that is used on cool evenings. Soft music blends with the gentle sound of the foghorn and seagulls over the water. Throughout the inn the Pepins have utilized many pieces of authentic and reproduction ship paraphernalia, including ships' lamps, paintings, pieces of brass, and teak in the nautical motif. This is a quiet inn where the land merges gently with the sea and its

shore and water activities. Other than a Continental breakfast no meals are served.

Accommodations: 8 rooms, most with private bath. *Pets:* Not permitted. *Children:* Inquire about bringing as most guests are adults. *Driving Instructions:* Take Route 127 into Rockport. At the traffic light, turn right and follow Route 127A one mile to Marmion Way. Turn left and proceed to the inn.

SEAWARD INN

Marmion Way, Rockport, MA 01966. 617-546-3471. *Innkeepers:* Roger and Anne Cameron. Open mid-May to mid-October.

The Seaward is a group of several cottages and a central inn set on land surrounded by lilacs, roses, high-bush blueberries, and stone walls overlooking the rocky shore stretching out from Marmion Way. Each of the six cottages—including The Breakers, whose nine rooms belie the term "cottage"—are perched on granite outcroppings and surrounded by small gardens and lichen-covered ledges. The Breakers, a popular choice, is directly above the surf on orangey-pink granite ledges. From its windows guests can enjoy views across the water of Sandy Bay to the village of Rockport.

The main inn has a glass-enclosed terrace that runs across the front of the building. This is a pleasant spot from which to watch the

changing light on the ocean, join other guests in conversation, or put together an intricate jigsaw puzzle. Anne Cameron has decorated the inn's rooms in colonial style ranging from homespun to elegant simplicity. Guests may choose to take their meals in the long main dining room with its ocean view or in the smaller room that looks out on the lilac bushes where goldfinches at the feeder frequently entertain guests. Each evening guests have a choice of two entrées. Specialties include fresh seafood, salads made from vegetables grown in the Camerons' gardens, and freshly baked rolls and breads. Guests arriving on Saturday can enjoy their weekly boiled lobster dinner. Mrs. Cameron has been supervising the kitchen since 1945 and recently compiled a collection of her recipes, published as the *Cook's Book from the Kitchen of Seaward Inn*.

Roger Cameron has created a sanctuary where rhododendrons are in full bloom in June. Many of the plantings in the sanctuary are gifts from grateful guests over the years. On the property is a swimming pool that the Camerons developed from a small duck pond.

Accommodations: 33 rooms with private bath. *Pets:* Not permitted. *Driving Instructions:* From the center of Rockport, go ¾ mile east on Route 127A and then north ½ mile on Marmion Way.

Salem, Massachusetts

COACH HOUSE

284 Lafayette Street, Salem, MA 01970. 617-744-4092. *Innkeeper:* Patricia Kessler. Open all year.

The Coach House was built by Captain E. Augustus Emmerton, who was a central figure in the development of the Far East trade in Salem. Emmerton, born in 1827, followed the footsteps of his father, who had owned and sailed numerous cargo ships. The junior Emmerton became master of the barque *Sophronia* and other ships that sailed to Far Eastern ports bringing back treasures to Americans thirsty for the newly discovered Oriental arts. Many of these items were built into the Coach House, adding to its Victorian atmosphere.

Detailing within the inn is in keeping with the sea captain's era. There are seven marble fireplaces and rooms with French hand-screened wallpapers, Oriental rugs, stencil-painted furniture, and period antiques. In many ways the interior is reminiscent of a series of Victorian stage sets. Each room is simply furnished, in some cases with four-poster beds topped with pineapple finials.

Accommodations: 15 rooms, suites, and efficiency apartments, 11 with bath. *Driving Instructions:* From Boston, take Route 1A to Salem State College (junction of Routes 114 and 1A). Turn left onto Lafayette Street. The Coach House is two blocks north on the left.

SALEM INN

7 Summer Street (Route 114), Salem, MA 01970. 617-741-0680. *Innkeepers:* Diane Pabich and Jeanne Jensen. Open all year.

Historic Salem has undergone extensive renovation in the past ten years, and part of that restoration includes the Salem Inn, now in the National Register of Historic Places. The inn, which occupies three Federal-style town houses built in 1834, was restored under government guidelines for historic preservation. The original Federal details are evident, and the rooms are decorated with period antiques that blend with modern conveniences such as air-conditioning, telephones, and color television sets. Several rooms have kitchenettes, and each has its own sitting area. Breakfast, the only meal served, is set in the dining room or out in the courtyard with its flower garden.

Innkeepers Diane Pabich and Jeanne Jensen will help guests find the many area attractions including the Witch Museum, Salem Witch House, and the House of the Seven Gables. Whale-watching trips leave from Salem Harbor, and the many recreational water sports here include fishing, boating, water skiing, and wind surfing. Chestnut Street, with its mansions and town houses, is just a block away.

Accommodations: 21 rooms with private bath. *Pets:* Not permitted. *Driving Instructions:* From Boston, take Route 1A north to Route 114 west to Summer Street in Salem. From the Massachusetts Turnpike, take Route 128 north to Route 114 east to Summer Street.

Sandwich, Massachusetts

CAPTAIN EZRA NYE HOUSE

152 Main Street, Sandwich, MA 02563. 617-888-6142. *Innkeepers:* Lynette and Bob Helms. Open all year.

This bed-and-breakfast inn, built in 1829, was once the home of a sea captain. Captain Nye had previously built the Daniel Webster House across the street, but he did not like it, so he built this second home and moved in. His home now has freshly painted and stenciled walls, light polished floors, and a blend of antique and more recent furnishings. On the first floor is a blue and white dining room where guests gather for a breakfast of home-baked breads and muffins. Also on this floor is the front parlor, which serves as the guests' living room. The guest rooms in the front of the house have private baths, while those in the rear have shared baths, but enjoy the extra quiet that results from being set further back from the road. Each of the guest rooms has its own special touch—one has an oak bedroom suite, another has a canopied bed, and a third has a Jenny Lind spool bed. In some, stenciling has been effectively used. In all, soft pastel colors create a restful mood.

Accommodations: 6 rooms, 4 with private bath. *Pets and children under 6:* Not permitted. *Driving Instructions:* The inn is in the center of Sandwich, on Route 6A.

THE SUMMER HOUSE

158 Old Main Street, Sandwich, Massachusetts. Mailing address: P.O. Box 341, Sandwich, MA 02564. 617-888-4991. *Innkeeper:* Pamela J. Hunt. Open May through October.

Among many historic and handsome colonial buildings in Sandwich stands the Summer House, one of the town's nicer examples of a Cape Cod Greek Revival home. The big white house, with its black shutters outlining wavy panes of original glass, was constructed around 1835. In 1877 the Hiram Dilloway family purchased the property, and it remained in the family until innkeeper Pamela Hunt bought it in 1981. Mr. Dilloway and his son-in-law James Lloyd were prominent glassmakers at The Boston & Sandwich Glass Company.

Pamela has done a remarkable restoration of both the house and its grounds, including the English-style perennial flower gardens, and she is in the process of restoring the old rose garden. Inside the house are colorfully painted floors, summery Victorian furnishings, and antiques grouped around the inn's many fireplaces, several in guest rooms. The breakfast room has a fireplace, lots of greenery, and a well-stocked library. Nearby is a sitting room with another fireplace. Among the many personal touches throughout are an antique mirror collection, a silver pot filled with fresh flowers, and a scrolly Victorian stand hung with a fanciful collection of hats.

Sandwich offers visitors numerous attractions, among them the Sandwich Glass Museum, Heritage Plantation, historic houses, and antique and handicrafts shops.

Accommodations: 4 rooms with shared baths. *Pets:* Not permitted. *Driving Instructions:* Take exit 2 off Route 6 (Mid-Cape Highway) to Route 130. Turn left to Sandwich Village and bear right onto Old Main Street for about 500 yards.

Sheffield, Massachusetts

IVANHOE COUNTRY HOUSE

Route 41, Sheffield, MA 01257. 413-229-2143. *Innkeepers:* Carole and Dick Maghery. Open all year.

The Ivanhoe Country House, built in 1800, is alongside the Appalachian Trail at the foot of one of the Berkshire Mountains. Actually this peaceful country inn is in the heart of the famed mountain chain, with its combination of excellent hiking and cross-country ski trails. Ski areas and Lenox's Tanglewood Music Festival are quite nearby.

The inn is a comfortable, quiet retreat furnished with antiques. Guests enjoy lounging by the fireside in the Chestnut Room. Here the Magherys offer a library, games, and television. A special Continental breakfast including homemade blueberry muffins magically appears by each guest-room door in the morning. The inn has nine guest rooms, three with kitchenettes. The 25 acres of grounds provide cross-country skiing and sledding in winter and a swimming pool and hiking in summer.

Accommodations: 9 rooms, 6 with private bath. *Driving Instructions:* The inn is 4 miles south of Route 23, on Route 41.

STAGECOACH HILL INN

Route 41, Sheffield, MA 01257. 413-229-8585. *Innkeepers:* Ann and John Pedretti. Open all year; restaurant closed Tuesdays.

The Stagecoach Hill Inn is a handsome brick building constructed in the early nineteenth century as a stagecoach stop. Its public rooms are reminiscent of an old English inn. The dining room has red walls with lanterns, chintz curtains, portraits of the royal family, and old English hunting prints. The pub, which predates the rest of the inn, is a dark-paneled room with a blazing fire in season. In keeping with the pub atmosphere, English beer is on tap. Dining at the inn features food prepared by John and Ann, both fine cooks. The menu features fresh seafood, veal dishes, and steaks. Roast beef with Yorkshire pudding is available on Saturday evenings. Also popular are the traditional steak and kidney or steak and mushroom pies, as well as New England oyster pie.

The guest rooms, in the main house, barn, and cottages and chalets on the grounds, are all decorated in a country style.

Butternut Basin and the Catamount Ski Area are just a few minutes away, and mountain climbing and cross-country skiing start at the doorstep. In the summer Tanglewood and Jacob's Pillow are an easy drive away. At the inn is a swimming pool.

Accommodations: 17 rooms with private bath. *Pets:* Not permitted. *Driving Instructions:* Take the Massachusetts Turnpike to the Lee exit, Route 7 to Great Barrington, then Route 41 South for 10 miles.

South Egremont, Massachusetts

THE 1780 EGREMONT INN

Old Sheffield Road, South Egremont, MA 01258. 413-528-2111.
Open all year; restaurant closed Mondays.

The 1780 Egremont is an old stagecoach inn built beside the Albany-Boston Post Road in 1780. The inn's grounds slope down to a brook just down the road from the site of Shay's Rebellion, a famous tax-payers' revolt in 1786–87. The oak-beamed living room–lobby was once the inn's stables, reflecting a day when housing the horses was as important as housing the people they served. Fires burn in the curving brick hearth that once served the blacksmith's forge.

Over the next hundred years the inn was greatly enlarged, incorporating guest rooms with private baths, porches, and a combined dining room and tavern. Here, before a central exposed-brick hearth, diners can sit on antique benches and enjoy apertifs. Another popular spot for sipping a drink while waiting for a table is the parlor, with its Oriental rugs on polished pine floors, formal nineteenth-century antiques, and chintz-upholstered antique furniture. Beyond this room is the living room–lobby, where decorator fabrics brighten the old woods in its beams and in the antique desks, the high-backed benches, and the paneled door doing service as the coffee table in front of the fireplace. Out on an enclosed porch is a formal dining room with blue trim and white walls and curtains. The tables are set with stemware, white napery, and arrangements of millinery flowers in antique containers.

The two upper floors house the inn's guests in individually decorated, old-fashioned–looking rooms with antique beds and bureaus and floral-print wallpapers. Our room contained a Victorian bedroom set, its scrolly woodwork painted with sprays of flowers. The bath stood on old-fashioned claw feet. Other rooms feature high bedsteads of walnut or oak as well as other Victorian antiques. A grandfather clock stands sentry by the ground-floor landing.

Guests and the public are served two meals a day. The dinner menu features American food simply presented. We began with cheese wrapped in pastry. The fresh trout was served in a butter sauce along with julienned carrots and zucchini cooked until barely tender and served with the same sauce. Other offerings were roast duck with fruit sauce, veal with champagne sauce, fresh lemon sole, and rack of lamb.

The inn has a swimming pool and tennis courts on its grounds. Tanglewood and the year-round offerings of the Berkshires are within an easy drive.

Accommodations: 21 rooms with private bath. *Pets:* Not permitted. *Driving Instructions:* Go 100 yards east of the center of South Egremont and turn onto Old Sheffield Road. The 1780 Egremont Inn is within sight of the village.

WEATHERVANE INN

Route 23, South Egremont, Massachusetts. Mailing address: P.O. Box 388, South Egremont, MA 01258. 413-528-9580. *Innkeepers:* Anne, Patricia, and Vincent Murphy. Open all year.

The Weathervane Inn comprises three buildings, all dating from the first third of the nineteenth century. The main inn is a typical sprawling New England building that has seen several additions. It houses the inn's "fireside room" with its bar, a comfortable living room, and the dining room, which, like the screened-in deck, is open to the public for dinner on Thursday through Sunday. Breakfast is served all week.

Six guest rooms are within the main inn, and two larger apartments are in the Coach House. All are Colonial in decor. The inn's barn, dating from 1820, has a massive stone fireplace and is home to the Murphys' antique shop. The Weathervane Inn is surrounded by 10 acres of lawns and woods, and the grounds include a swimming pool and places to play volleyball, badminton, and croquet.

Accommodations: 8 rooms, 6 with private bath. *Pets:* Not permitted. *Driving Instructions:* Take Route 23 west from Great Barrington about 3 miles.

South Lee, Massachusetts

MERRELL TAVERN INN

Route 102, Main Street, South Lee, MA 01260. 413-243-1794. *Inn-keepers:* Charles and Faith Reynolds. Open all year except December 24 and 25.

General Joseph Whiton built this brick building in 1794. The historic structure was purchased by its current owners from the Society for the Preservation of New England Antiquities with a historic covenant to preserve the building.

Merrell Tavern is on the Housatonic River, and the lawn extends to the river's edge. Beartown Mountain is directly in back, and gardens have been established among the old stone foundations of barns and livery stables that once graced the property.

Within are working fireplaces in five guest rooms and the old tavern room, which is used for full gourmet breakfasts and as a sitting room. It remains virtually unchanged from the days when William Merrell wined and dined drovers and their passengers there. Lighted by candlebeam sconces and chandeliers, it has what is believed to be the only remaining complete circular colonial bar in America. Seven rooms have canopied beds; two have four-posters. Most furnishings are in the Hepplewhite and Sheraton styles and are set off by authentic paint colors of the period.

Accommodations: 9 rooms with private baths. *Pets and children under 11:* Not permitted. *Driving Instructions:* From the Lee exit off the Turnpike, take Route 102 about 3 miles to the inn.

Stockbridge, Massachusetts

THE INN AT STOCKBRIDGE

Route 7, Box 2033, Stockbridge, MA 01262. 413-298-3337. *Innkeepers:* Don and Lee Weitz. Open all year except for two weeks in November.

Just a mile north of the Stockbridge Village center, on 12 secluded acres, stands a Georgian Colonial, the Inn at Stockbridge. Built as a summer estate in 1906 for the Blagdon family of Boston, the large, white clapboard house remained in that family until the early 1970s. After a brief stint as a bed-and-breakfast establishment, the inn was bought and restored by Lee and Don Weitz. Before entering the inn-keeping profession, Lee had operated a test kitchen used in the development of recipes for new cookbooks. Her prior training in food preparation is evident when one samples the full country breakfasts served at the inn. Favorites are Lee's egg dishes such as soufflés, omelets, and eggs Benedict.

Each living room has a fireplace, and the guest rooms are furnished with antiques. On the grounds are a swimming pool and four cross-country ski trails for beginners and intermediate skiers. Instruction in cross-country skiing is available and equipment may be rented nearby.

Accommodations: 7 rooms, 5 with private bath. *Pets:* Not permitted. *Children:* Under eight not permitted. *Driving Instructions:* The inn is on U.S. 7 north of Stockbridge and the Mass. Turnpike.

THE RED LION INN

Main Street, Route 102, Stockbridge, MA 01262. 413-298-5545.
Innkeeper: Betsy M. Holtzinger. Open all year.

The Red Lion is the grande dame of old Colonial inns. First built in 1773 as a small tavern and stagecoach stop for vehicles serving the Albany, Hartford, and Boston runs, the inn was greatly enlarged in 1862. Although the Red Lion has had several owners, it was owned from the Civil War until the early 1960s by members of the Treadway family. Over the years, various modernizations have been accomplished without disturbing the basic charm of this long-term resident of the Berkshires.

The inn has an extensive collection of antiques that grace its public rooms and greatly add to the feeling of the past. The tavern is paneled in old wood with the warm patina of age. There is a feeling of grandeur in both the dining room and the parlors with their Oriental rugs and grand pianos. In its long history the inn has been host to five presidents of the United States.

Meals are served to the public. Dinner at the Red Lion features twenty or so entrées, including such specialties as entrecote with herb butter, veal à la Oscar, stuffed pork chop, three different lobster dishes, or scallops in mushroom and wine sauce. There are also a modest list of appetizers and a good selection of desserts.

Accommodations: 103 rooms, about half with private bath. *Pets:* Not permitted. *Driving Instructions:* Take exit 2 on the Massachusetts Turnpike to Lee. Follow Route 102 to Stockbridge.

Sturbridge, Massachusetts

The town is most famous for *Old Sturbridge Village*, a re-created town of the 1790–1840 period. As they do the work of early New Englanders, costumed personnel talk with tourists. In addition to the actual working farm village, there are craft work, exhibit galleries, a visitors' center, and shops selling the craft products and period merchandise. *Wells State Park*, off Routes 20 and 49, offers swimming, boating, horseback riding, cross-country skiing, and other recreational activities.

THE COLONEL EBENEZER CRAFTS INN

Fiske Hill, Sturbridge, Massachusetts. Mailing address: c/o Publick House, Sturbridge, MA 01566. 617-347-3313. *Innkeepers:* Patricia and Henri Bibeau. Open all year.

At the top of Fiske Hill, with its vistas of the surrounding hills, stands the Colonel Ebenezer Crafts Inn. The restored farmhouse was built in 1786 by Mr. Fiske, a local craftsman-builder (the hill was named in honor of his grandfather). The Bibeaus are justifiably proud of the house and gladly show interested visitors around its rooms furnished with a blend of colonial antiques and reproductions. The Cottage Suite, furnished by the Sturbridge Yankee Workshop, is attached to the inn by an arched breezeway. The Ebenezer Crafts is named in honor of the Revolutionary War officer who founded the Publick House (below), and the flavor of the inn's beginnings is well preserved.

In the morning there are complimentary juice, coffee or tea, and freshly baked muffins. At teatime, sherry, wine, cookies, fresh fruits, and tea are set out for guests. Other meals are available a mile or so down the hill at the "mother" inn, the popular Publick House where guests at the Ebenezer Crafts should check in. The small swimming pool on the inn's grounds is a treat for summer visitors.

Accommodations: 10 rooms with private bath. *Driving Instructions:* From Hartford, take I-84 or I-86 east to exit 3, bear right and then left along the service road to the back entrance of the Publick House. From Albany or Boston, take the Massachusetts Turnpike to exit 9. The Publick House is on the Common at Sturbridge on Route 131. Stop at the main desk to register and ask for directions.

PUBLICK HOUSE INN AND COUNTRY MOTOR LODGE

On the Common, Sturbridge, MA 01566. 617-347-3313. *Innkeeper:* Buddy Adler. Open all year.

The Publick House was built two hundred years ago to serve coach travelers on the colonial Post Road. The tavern and barn were constructed by Colonel Ebenezer Crafts, an officer who drilled his cavalry troops on the Common during the Revolutionary War. The inn, completely restored and expanded in 1937, is listed in the National Register of Historic Places. The Publick House itself offers twenty-one guest rooms, each with the furniture and decor of the colonial period. Some have beamed ceilings and wide plank flooring, and all have modern bathrooms and air conditioning.

Visitors to Old Sturbridge have a choice of two other accommodations offered by the Publick House. Both the Colonel Ebenezer Crafts Inn (which see) and the Chamberlain House have the atmosphere of yesteryear that adds continuity to the village experience. The Chamberlain House quite near the Publick House has been fully renovated and restored and is also listed in the National Register of Historic Places. Each formal guest room has its own patio overlooking the pasture where sheep graze only a few feet from the door. Most of the rooms are in the six buildings of the inn's modern motor lodge, in a nearby orchard. The five dining rooms and two cocktail lounges that serve the many tourists who come to the historic inn and Old Sturbridge Village are furnished with antiques and reproductions of the period.

Holidays and winter weekends are festive here. Guests are treated to horse-drawn sleigh rides through the village, with hot buttered rum

and roasted chestnuts by a fire at the end of the ride. Wild-game dinners, including venison, mince pie, and apple pan dowdy, top off the day. Arrangements should be made well in advance for these weekends, especially those of Thanksgiving and the twelve days of Christmas. The winter weekends continue from January through March. Be sure to state your room preference when making a reservation.

Accommodations: 21 rooms with private bath in the Publick House; 4 suites in the Chamberlain House and 70 rooms in the motor lodge. *Driving Instructions:* Take the Massachusetts Turnpike to exit 9 or Route I-86 to exit 3. The Publick House is on the Common on Route 131.

Sudbury, Massachusetts

LONGFELLOW'S WAYSIDE INN
Wayside Inn Road (off Route 20), Sudbury, MA 01776. 617-443-8846. *Innkeeper:* Francis Koppeis. Open every day except Christmas.

The Wayside Inn is now a designated national historic landmark. To stay here is to stay at a great museum: It is the oldest inn in America. Originally the Red Horse Tavern, the name was changed following the publication of Longfellow's *Tales of a Wayside Inn*, which were based on his knowledge of the Red Horse. This inn was run by four generations of the Howe family for almost two centuries. It was purchased, along with 5,000 surrounding acres, in the 1920s by Henry Ford, who completely restored it and reproduced a water-powered gristmill that operates today grinding meal for the breads served at the inn. Ford later built a replica of a typical New England chapel nearby, and it is currently popular with members of every faith for weddings. In 1928, Ford purchased a one-room schoolhouse, which had been the real school of Mary and her little lamb in the early nineteenth century. He moved the school from its original site at Sterling, Massachusetts, to its present location near the inn.

Built in stages, starting in 1702, the inn is an extraordinary collection of exposed-timber rooms with original paneling and museum-quality antiques. There is no television or radio. The ten guest rooms, each different and special, have been modernized to add private baths. When you are here, it is hard to remember that the center of Boston is only forty minutes away. The rural quality is made possible by the tract of surrounding land that Ford purchased to protect the inn. For the day visitor, the common rooms of the inn are open for inspection daily, although there is a very small fee to help support the museum. Shortly before his death, Ford deeded the entire property to the Wayside Inn Corporation.

The Wayside Inn dining room is one of the most popular eating places in this area. House specialties include roast duckling, stuffed fillet of sole with lobster sauce, and deep-dish apple pie. A reminder: the New England fall foliage season (late September through October) brings a deluge of travelers. Those wishing country-inn rooms should make reservations well in advance!

Accommodations: 10 rooms with private bath. *Pets:* Not permitted. *Driving Instructions:* Take the Massachusetts Turnpike to Route 495, go north to Route 20 East, then 8 miles to the Wayside Inn (1 mile after the turn at the Wayside Country Store). From the east, take Route 128 North to exit 49 and go 11 miles west on Route 20.

THE WILDWOOD INN

121 Church Street, Ware, MA 01082. 413-967-7798. *Innkeepers:* Margaret and Geoffrey Lobenstine. Open all year.

Wildwood is a rambling Victorian inn with a classic wraparound porch and grand carriage house. It is on a maple-lined residential street on 2 acres of grounds surrounded by stone walls, within an easy drive of many area attractions, including Old Sturbridge and Old Deerfield villages. There is a brook with a swimming hole. In the forested park behind the inn, a river winds. A canoe is provided for guests' use.

Inside Wildwood the Lobenstines have created a warm and inviting inn, where Margaret and Geoff work together to make guests feel at home. The rooms contain pine antiques, braided rugs, and such special items as a collection of classic New England cradles, a cobbler's-bench coffee table, and an old carpenter's chest filled with games.

The inn's guest rooms are decorated to show off the Lobenstines' collection of handmade afghans and heirloom quilts. Each room has its own unique piece—an old washing-machine wringer as a luggage rack, an oak armoire, a wicker cradle at the foot of a bed. In the morning Margaret's homemade bread baking creates tantalizing aromas. A Continental breakfast is included in the room rates, with some extras available at nominal additional charges. Margaret tries to make things that people don't often have at home, such as soufflé-type puff pancakes, Norwegian noodle pudding, or gingerbread and cornmeal surprise. Breads are served with her homemade peach butter, and popovers are often available with morning coffee, tea, and juice. This is the kind of inn where guests frequently feel at home enough to sit before the fire in their flannel nightgowns enjoying the warmth of the hearth.

Accommodations: 5 rooms with 3 shared baths. *Pets:* Not permitted, but there is a heated kennel in town. *Driving Instructions:* Take Route 32 from exit 8 of the Massachusetts Turnpike into Ware. Take Main Street (Route 9) to Church Street (at the traffic light by the fountain opposite South Street). Turn on Church and drive to the inn, ¾ mile up the road on your right.

Wellfleet, Massachusetts

THE HOLDEN INN

Commercial Street, Wellfleet, Massachusetts. Mailing address: P.O. Box 816, Wellfleet, MA 02667. 617-349-3450. *Innkeepers:* The Fricker family. Open late June through Labor Day.

Like many inns on the Cape, the Holden is actually three buildings on one piece of property. The main inn was built in 1840 as a sea captain's house. The building has wide-board pumpkin-pine floors and is furnished with antiques and wicker furniture. Behind the main house is the larger building known as the Lodge, which has both a view of the bay and a large screened porch. The remaining rooms are in the white clapboard cottage next door. Although the inn serves no meals, there are many fine restaurants nearby. The Holden is a five-minute walk from one of the largest Cape Cod marinas. The area abounds with good fishing spots. Guests who prefer to spend time on the ocean rather than the bay can take any of the meandering back roads 4 miles across this narrow part of the Cape to the oceanside.

Wellfleet is one of the headquarters of the Cape Cod National Seashore and a wonderful spot for bird-watchers and hikers.

Accommodations: 24 rooms, 6 with private bath. *Pets:* Not permitted. *Children:* Under ten not permitted. *Driving Instructions:* Take a left (west) off Route 6 at the sign reading Wellfleet Center and a left at the sign to The Pier; continue to the inn on the right.

THE INN AT DUCK CREEK[e]

Main Street, Wellfleet, Massachusetts. Mailing address: Box 364, Wellfleet, MA 02667. 617-349-9333. *Innkeepers:* Robert Morrill, Judith Pihl, and Anne Fortier. Open mid-May to mid-October.

The Inn at Duck Creek[e], a collection of early buildings in a woodland setting, has its own resident family of pet ducks in a pond fringed with tall rushes. The inn overlooks a salt marsh and tidal creek with views of the duck pond from the back porch and dining room. Most guest rooms are in the 1830 Captain's House; five more are in the Saltworks, a 1910 gambrel-roofed building; and three are in a small carriage house. The rooms, with wide-board floors, wainscoting, and a variety of wallpapers, have a country look maintained with painted furniture, spool beds, and Boston rockers. Guests can get acquainted in the common room or over a light Continental breakfast in the breakfast room. The inn's restaurant, Sweet Seasons, and its more rustic, informal Tavern Room both serve local seafoods, steaks, and poultry to the public for dinner. Brunch is served on weekends, and there is often live entertainment in the evening.

Accommodations: 26 rooms, 18 with private bath. *Pets:* Not permitted. *Driving Instructions:* Take Route 6 (Mid-Cape Highway) to the Wellfleet exit (Main Street). The inn is on the right.

West Harwich, Massachusetts

THE LION'S HEAD

  186 Belmont Road, West Harwich, Cape Cod, Massachusetts.
  Mailing address: Box 444, West Harwich, MA 02671. 617-432-
  7766. *Innkeepers:* Laurie and Djordje Soc. Open all year.
The Lion's Head is a Cape Cod inn, half a mile from the beach. It was
built early in the nineteenth century as a Cape half-house and has been
enlarged over the years. The old house, once the home of sea captain
Thomas Snow, has the original "captain's stairs" and pine floors. The
entire house has recently been restored and redecorated with many
antique and traditional pieces. A hearty breakfast is included in the
room charge. Home-baked breads and muffins are a specialty. In the
late afternoon, complimentary wine is served by the hearth in the living room, where chess and backgammon are available to guests. On
the grounds are two cottages available for weekly rental.

  Accommodations: 4 rooms, 2 with private bath, in the inn, plus 2
cottages. *Pets:* Not permitted. *Children:* Under twelve permitted in
cottages only. *Driving Instructions:* The inn is half a block from
Route 28 in West Harwich.

West Stockbridge, Massachusetts

WILLIAMSVILLE INN

Route 41, West Stockbridge, MA 01266. 413-274-6580. *Innkeepers:* Carl and Elizabeth Atkinson. Open all year except the first three weeks in November and three weeks after Easter.

The Williamsville Inn was built by Christopher French in the eighteenth century. Today, one can stay in the Christopher French Room, one of nine antique-filled rooms that have nooks and crannies created by their angled walls. There are eight working fireplaces, one of which is in the Christopher French Room, along with an antique four-poster bed with long curtains tied back to the posts. There are also rooms in the barn, which have Victorian furnishings, including marble-top bureaus and walnut bedsteads. Attic bedrooms are more rustic, with wide floorboards, exposed beams, and skylights.

The inn's parlor is the perfect spot to curl up on the camelback settee and enjoy a before-dinner drink. Three dining rooms offer well-prepared dishes such as rough country pâtés, salmon mousse with sauce verte, roast duckling with Grand Marnier sauce, and steaks. One of the dining rooms is in the former library, with its richly designed wallpaper, books, and a working fireplace. Breakfast is served in a sunny back room.

Accommodations: 9 rooms in the inn; 4 in the converted barn and 2 cottages; all with private bath. *Pets and children under 12:* Not permitted. *Driving Instructions:* The inn is on Route 41, 4 miles south of West Stockbridge.

Whitinsville, Massachusetts

THE VICTORIAN

583 Linwood Avenue, Whitinsville, MA 01588. 617-234-2500. *Innkeeper:* Martha Flint. Open all year.

The Victorian is an old dowager of an inn presiding over a 50-acre woodland estate. Built in 1871 by a wealthy mill owner, this mansion has been impeccably restored and maintained by the innkeeper.

Today the inn houses one of New England's finest restaurants, whose popularity is enhanced by the Victorian setting. The inn is striking in appearance with its dark walnut and mahogany woodwork set off by the wallpapers and draperies of the period. From the finely etched glass doors to the turn-of-the-century furnishings the total effect is one of formal elegance. The guest rooms are all spacious, in keeping with the period. The master bedroom, with its dressing room, is probably the most coveted. One of the guest rooms has a working fireplace, and most have king-size beds.

Meals are served in the inn's well-stocked library and drawing room. The menu features an interesting collection of Continental dishes. Appetizers might include a crab Veronique, blinis with caviar and sour cream, a country pâté, and a crepe du jour. A recent sampling of entrées included scallopini al pesto, a poached salmon Nantua, and several fresh seafood dishes. You might even dine on a classic pheasant dish if you make prior arrangements. The Victorian is a mansion where one can dine, relax, and sleep in a bygone era.

Accommodations: 8 rooms, 6 with bath. *Driving Instructions:* Take 122 south from Worcester and turn right at Linwood Avenue.

Woods Hole, Massachusetts

THE MARLBOROUGH BED AND BREAKFAST INN

320 Woods Hole Road, Woods Hole, MA 02543. 617-548-6218.
Innkeeper: Patricia Morris. Open all year.

Patricia Morris refers to herself as "The Woman Who Came to Dinner." On a two-day stay at The Marlborough she fell in love with the inn, purchased it a few days later, and took occupancy in time to welcome the Fourth of July with a fully booked country inn — and she's never looked back. "The M," as Patricia calls it, is a recent-vintage replica of a traditional full Cape Cod house. It is reminiscent of an English bed-and-breakfast inn with its steep, narrow staircase leading to guest rooms decorated in the style of English designer Laura Ashley, emphasizing romantic ruffles and tiny-floral-print fabrics. There are a selection of antiques and beds with handmade coverlets. The parlor with its Edwardian touches is a popular gathering spot with guests, who get to know Patricia and fellow guests over sherry and cheeses. Breakfast is served amid fresh flowers and starched linen cloths on Patricia's collection of china. The inn's ½-acre of grounds has a swimming pool and tall maples, and an old hammock sways invitingly between two trees.

Accommodations: 7 rooms, 3 with private bath. *Pets:* Permitted by prior arrangement only. *Driving Instructions:* The inn is just off Route 28, 2½ miles from Falmouth.

Yarmouth Port, Massachusetts

COLONIAL HOUSE INN

277 Main Street, Yarmouth Port, MA 02675. 617-362-4348. *Innkeeper:* Malcolm J. Perna. Open all year.

In the 1730s the Josiah Ryder Family built a hip-roofed colonial home on the Old King's Highway on Cape Cod. It was later sold to Captain Joseph Eldridge, and for the next hundred years the Eldridges added on here and there. One addition was floated over from Nantucket in 1820, and in the 1860s a third floor complete with mansard roof and Doric portico transformed the house into a stylish Victorian.

Today, as a Cape Cod inn, the Colonial House sits on 3 acres of land with extensive gardens and a small pond and fountain. The guest rooms, named for former owners, are furnished with antiques and reproduction pieces. Three dining rooms, each with a working fireplace, offer New England fare emphasizing fresh local seafood. The three rooms have distinct personalities. The Oak Room features tiger- and golden-oak tables; the more formal Colonial Room has hand-stenciled walls; and the Common Room is a glassed-in veranda overlooking the gardens and town green. The inn is open seven days a week for lunch and dinner, and brunch is served on Sundays.

Accommodations: 22 rooms with private bath. *Pets:* Not permitted. *Driving Instructions:* The inn is on Route 6A.

THE VILLAGE INN

92 Main Street, Yarmouth Port, Massachusetts. Mailing address: Box 1, Yarmouth Port, MA 02675. 617-362-3182. *Innkeepers:* Mac and Esther Hickey. Open all year.

The Village Inn is a small, family-operated inn housed within what was once the private home of a locally renowned sea captain. In the Yarmouth Port Historic District, the inn has ten guest rooms, of which six have private baths and the other four are really family suites that share baths. There are two comfortable lounges, a spacious porch, and more than an acre of landscaped grounds.

Mac and Esther Hickey have made the Village Inn one of the finest on the Cape by their attentive service to their guests and with their comfortable rooms. We have been privileged to read many of the letters sent by their overnight guests heaping praise on them for their helpfulness and warmth. Here is an inn where you can expect more than to be shown to your room. Many are the times that the Hickeys have gotten an absentminded guest a tube of toothpaste or an extra toothbrush, lent an author a typewriter, or obtained last-minute reservations at a crowded summer theater or a popular restaurant. No meals are served at the inn, except for the unusually generous breakfast cooked "as you like it" every morning, but many nearby restaurants are highly regarded.

Accommodations: 10 rooms, 6 with bath. *Driving Instructions:* The inn is on Route 6A.

THE WEDGEWOOD INN AND GALLERY

83 Main Street (Route 6A), Yarmouth Port, MA 02675. 617-362-5157. *Innkeepers:* Jeff and Jill Jackson. Open all year.

Wedgewood Inn, built in 1812 for a prominent Yarmouth Port attorney who served the prosperous shipping industry, was the first house in Yarmouth Port to be designed by an architect. In 1983 artist Jill Jackson and her husband, Jeff, opened the restored house to overnight guests. The inn stands on 2 landscaped acres of shade trees, rose gardens, and brick terraces.

The inn's original pine floors are polished, and antiques, period print wallpapers, and old English sporting prints create an atmosphere of colonial times. The furnishings that are not antique were made by a local craftsman who fashioned three cherry pencil-post beds in the guest rooms as well as the Windsor chairs in the dining room. Four guest rooms have working fireplaces. A European-style breakfast of freshly baked muffins and croissants as well as fresh fruits is served in the dining room, which is also the common room for guests. The Jacksons offer lunch and dinner by reservation only.

Accommodations: 6 rooms with private bath. *Pets and children under 10:* Not permitted. *Driving Instructions:* From Boston take Route 3 South to Route 6 South. From Route 6 take exit 7 (Willow Street), turning right and going a mile to Route 6A. Turn right on 6A and enter the first driveway on the right.

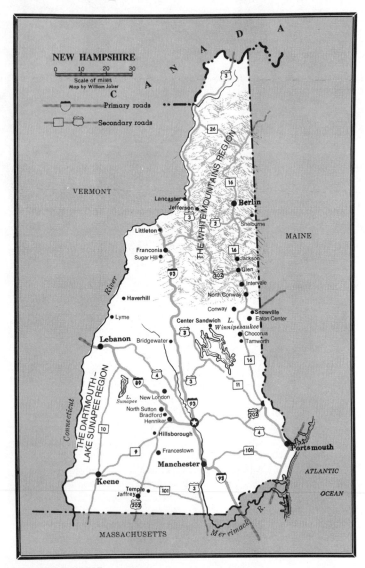

NEW HAMPSHIRE

0   10   20   30
Scale of miles
Map by William Jober

C

Primary roads

Secondary roads

CANADA

VERMONT

MAINE

THE WHITE MOUNTAINS REGION

THE DARTMOUTH – LAKE SUNAPEE REGION

Connecticut

River

Lancaster
Jefferson
Berlin
Shelburne

Littleton

Franconia
Sugar Hill

Jackson
Glen
Intervale
North Conway
Conway
Snowville
Eaton Center

Haverhill

Lyme

Center Sandwich
L. Winnipesaukee
Chocorua
Tamworth

Lebanon
Bridgewater

L. Sunapee
New London
North Sutton
Bradford
Henniker

Hillsborough

Francestown

Manchester

Keene
Temple
Jaffrey

Portsmouth

ATLANTIC

OCEAN

Merrimack R.

MASSACHUSETTS

New Hampshire

Bradford, New Hampshire

THE BRADFORD INN

Main Street, Bradford, NH 03221. 603-938-5309. *Innkeepers:* The Mazol family. Open all year.

Bradford, settled in 1776, has been a summer resort since the early nineteenth century. In 1890 the Bradford Inn was built, complete with a shady front porch for its wicker rockers. It is still welcoming guests. The lobby, parlors, and halls are furnished and decorated with antiques, Oriental rugs, easy chairs, and sofas. Fires are kindled in the front-parlor fireplace from the first autumn chill through the spring ski season. Tom is the chef who oversees the two dining rooms, open both to guests and the public.

Lake Sunapee and the town beach on Lake Massasecum offer all manner of recreational activities. There are bikes at the inn for exploring the area. In winter three downhill ski areas and cross-country skiing are within 10 miles.

Accommodations: 13 rooms, most with private bath, and 2 suites. *Pets:* Not permitted. *Driving Instructions:* Take I-89, exit 9, then Route 103 to Bradford. The inn is near the junction of 114 and 103.

THE PASQUANEY INN

Newfound Lake, Bridgewater, New Hampshire. Mailing address: Star Route 1, Box 1066, Bridgewater, NH 03222. 603-744-2712. *Innkeepers:* Marge and Roy Zimmer. Open mid-May through mid-October and Christmas through March.

The Pasquaney has been welcoming guests on this spot since 1840. The inn retains the flavor of a turn-of-the-century lakeside resort with its many antiques, comfortable couches and lounge chairs, and relaxing pace. The dining and living rooms have fireplaces. The piano is tuned up for anyone wishing to try his hand at entertaining the rest of the guests. The main attraction is still Newfound Lake, reputed to have the clearest water in New England. The inn has more than 600 feet of lakefront and 6 acres of gardens and lawns. There are many lawn games available and on rainy days or in the evenings the recreation barn affords space for square dances, basketball, and table tennis. And the lake is there for swimming and boating as well as fishing, another popular pastime in season. In winter there is cross-country skiing, as well as downhill skiing nearby.

The inn serves hearty country breakfasts and dinners. Homemade soups include cream of broccoli, New England clam chowder, and sometimes even dill-pickle soup. A variety of special dieters', vegetarians', and children's meals are available. The rooms have views of the lake and the sunset over the surrounding mountains.

Accommodations: 28 rooms, 10 with private bath, in summer; 18 rooms, 10 with private bath, off season. *Pets:* Not permitted. *Driving Instructions:* From I-93 North, exit 23, follow Route 104 west to Bristol. Then go north 5½ miles on Route 3A.

Center Sandwich, New Hampshire

THE CORNER HOUSE INN

Routes 109 and 113, Box 204, Center Sandwich, NH 03227. 603-284-6219. *Innkeepers:* Don Brown and Jane Kroeger. Open all year.

Corner House Inn has continuously served travelers for more than one hundred years. It is in the center of a tranquil, unspoiled New England town in the White Mountains, on the shore of Squam Lake, the setting for the movie *On Golden Pond*. Don Brown and Jane Kroeger recently took on the task of renovating the downstairs rooms and barn, transforming them into appealing dining rooms complete with fireplaces and a wood cookstove, painted wide-board floors, and old-fashioned print wallpapers. A full country breakfast is served to guests, and lunch and dinner are available to the public as well.

Center Sandwich is the home of the original shop for The League of New Hampshire Craftsmen (1925), and the town remains highly committed to the encouragement of local craftspersons and artists. The inn reflects this commitment through its use of handmade quilts, appliqués, and artwork. Guests stay in rooms with ruffled curtains, plants, the colorful quilts, and antique furnishings. Tiny-floral-print wallpapers decorate the guest-room walls, and seasonal fresh flowers add a personal touch.

Accommodations: 4 rooms, 1 with private bath. *Driving Instructions:* Take exit 23 off I-93. Follow Route 25 to Moultonboro, then Route 109 north to Center Sandwich.

Chocorua, New Hampshire

STAFFORD'S-IN-THE-FIELD

Route 113, Chocorua, NH 03817. 603-323-7766. *Innkeepers:* Ramona and Fred Stafford. Open all year

At the end of a country lane is Stafford's-in-the-Field overlooking fields, forests, and a brook. Built about 1778, the Federal-style house had several additions made between 1880 and 1905. Stafford's is one of the most handsomely redecorated inns in New Hampshire; each of its guest rooms is special. An attic bedroom, for example, has exposed barnboard and the original hand-hammered nails as well as a brass bed and a hooked rug.

Downstairs the Staffords' collection of antiques is visible everywhere. There are sitting rooms, a library, and a large dining room. In the last, bold blue-and-gold wallpaper extends up to the original tin ceiling. Here guests eat family-style.

To work off these meals, guests can square-dance in the Staffords' barn, swim in the old swimming hole in summer, or hike the long, winding road that leads to Lake Chocorua, with its view of Mount Chocorua. A small golf course surrounds the inn. In the winter there is cross-country skiing on the property or at other, nearby touring centers.

Accommodations: 14 rooms, 8 with private bath. *Pets and small children:* Not permitted. *Driving Instructions:* The inn is on Route 113, a mile west of the intersection of Routes 113 and 16.

Conway, New Hampshire

THE DARBY FIELD INN

Bald Hill, Conway, New Hampshire 03818. 603-447-2181. *Innkeepers:* H. Marc and Maria Donaldson. Open all year except April and early November.

A thousand feet above Mount Washington's valley is the Darby Field Inn. On top of Bald Hill in the White Mountains, the inn commands an outstanding view of the famous mountain and the surrounding peaks and valley. The inn was named for Darby Field, the first white man to climb Mount Washington.

Each of the guest rooms is decorated in country style, with quilts, four-posters, and a mixture of antique and newer furniture. Downstairs, guests have the use of the living room, with its stone fireplace.

The pub and the dining room at the Darby Field are open to the public in the evenings but only to guests for breakfast. The dining room has a view of Mount Washington; its candlelight dinners, presented with an almost Japanese simplicity and best described as "country gourmet."

In summer guests can swim in the inn's pool, and in winter they can ski at least 10 miles of trails that lead from the inn.

Accommodations: 15 rooms with private bath. *Children:* Permitted if closely supervised. *Driving Instructions:* Off Route 16, a half mile south of Conway, turn onto Bald Hill Road. Turn right 1 mile up the road, at the inn's sign. Follow this road a mile.

Eaton Center, New Hampshire

PALMER HOUSE

Route 153, Eaton Center, NH 03832. 603-447-2120. *Innkeepers:* Frank and Mary Gospodarek. Open all year.

The Palmer House, a two-and-a-half-story balustraded inn just south of Conway, is named for Nathaniel Palmer, who built it overlooking Crystal Lake in 1884 as his home. Soon after its completion, Palmer began to take in summer lodgers, and it has been known as the Palmer House ever since and is now noted for its family-style country-casual atmosphere. Except for a plethora of modern paneling, the inn is furnished much as it was a century ago.

An attached New England–style barn has been remodeled to serve as the lounge and dining room. A single entrée is prepared each evening and might be veal Zuricher Art, dilled salmon pie, turkey with oyster stuffing, or beef Stroganoff. The Palmer House is noted for its country breakfasts — bacon or sausage and blueberry pancakes with real maple syrup or eggs and toast.

A deer head presides sedately over the granite fireplace in the guest lounge, with its piano, dartboard, and abundance of overstuffed furniture. Owing to its proximity to many ski areas, the inn is a popular gathering spot in the winter for the many skiers who use Palmer House as a base. Several cross-country skiing trails depart right from the door. In the summer, guests may use the sandy beach at Crystal Lake, which also offers sailing and fishing.

Accommodations: 6 rooms with 3 shared baths, 1 family room with bath, and a dormitory sleeping area. *Driving Instructions:* The inn is 6 miles south of Conway on Route 153 (at Crystal Lake).

Francestown, New Hampshire

THE INN AT CROTCHED MOUNTAIN

Mountain Road, Francestown, NH 03043. 603-588-6840. *Innkeepers:* Rose and John Perry. Open Memorial Day weekend through October 31 and Thanksgiving to the end of skiing.

Originally built as a farmhouse by James Wilson in 1822, the inn served as a stopping point on the underground railway — slaves were hidden in a secret tunnel that connected the cellar to the Boston Post Road. During its first century, the inn was used as both a farm and a boardinghouse. Purchased by Sidney Winslow in 1929, the property was named "Hob and Nob Farm" and became one of New England's most renowned farms, with prize-winning sheep, champion horses, Angora goats, and numerous other farm animals. In the mid-1930s, a tragic fire destroyed most of the farm. The Winslows rebuilt it in its present state. John and Rose Perry purchased the property in 1976.

The ivy-covered inn sits on the northern side of Crotched Mountain with a 40-mile view of the Piscataquog Valley. The inn is a relaxing place with fireplaces including working ones in four of the guest rooms. Dinner and breakfast are available to guests and public alike. The inn offers guests two clay tennis courts, a mountainside pool, and the Winslow Tavern with a fireplace for chilly evenings. Nearby there are fishing in mountain streams and ponds, hiking and mountainclimbing, three golf courses, and, of course, skiing.

Accommodations: 14 rooms, 5 with bath. *Driving Instructions:* In Francestown, turn off Route 47 onto Mountain Road for a mile.

FRANCONIA INN

Easton Valley Road, Franconia, NH 03580. 603-823-5542. *Innkeepers:* The Morris Family. Open Memorial Day weekend to the third weekend in October and mid-December through March.

The Franconia, a family resort, has something for everyone. The sprawling inn is in the Eastern Valley on 117 acres surrounded by the Franconia mountain range, including nearby Cannon Mountain. At the inn are clay tennis courts, a small stream for canoeing, a riding stable, a swimming pool, and even a 3,300-foot airstrip with a glider operation in warm weather. In winter there is a cross-country ski center with 65 kilometers of trails connecting with other inns. The public rooms are of generous proportions, some with old oak paneling. Fires blaze in four hearths, and plants are everywhere. A Ping-Pong room, a children's room, a well-stocked library, and screened verandas provide activities for all, and a hot tub awaits returning skiers. The open dining room with views of moonlit fields serves dinner to guests and the public from a menu stressing Continental cuisine with such dishes as rack of lamb, chicken Florentine, and tournedos King Henry VIII. Breakfast is also served to guests and the public. Guest rooms are simply furnished with colonial reproductions and a selection of real antiques.

Accommodations: 28 rooms, 22 with private bath. *Pets:* Not permitted. *Driving Instructions:* From Franconia take Route 116 south 2½ miles to the inn.

THE HORSE AND HOUND INN

Franconia, NH 03580. 603-823-5501. *Innkeepers:* The Larson family. Open Christmas through the end of skiing and Memorial Day to late October.

This secluded White Mountain inn is a little off the beaten track, on the side of a quiet road under Cannon Mountain. The core of the inn, the dining room, was originally a farmhouse, built in the early nineteenth century. The balance of the inn was built just after World War II. The bar, paneled in thick New Hampshire pine, is the library of the house and has the feeling of an intimate English pub. It looks out onto the inn's gardens.

The two dining rooms are noted for their food. The larger one,

which occupies the original farmhouse, and its smaller counterpart are set with white linens and tall white dinner candles. Every evening the dinner menu includes a half-dozen starters and ten or so entrées that reflect a variety of Continental cooking traditions.

The inn is near many area attractions, including the Cannon mountain ski area and the Robert Frost homestead.

Accommodations: 6 rooms with private bath and 2 suites. *Pets:* Occasionally permitted if well behaved. *Driving Instructions:* From Franconia village, take Route 18 south toward Franconia Notch. The inn is halfway up the 3-mile-long hill. From Route 93, take Route 18 a mile and a half south of the turnoff.

SUGAR HILL INN

Route 117, Franconia, NH 03580. 603-823-5621. *Innkeepers:*
Carolyn and Richard Bromberg. Open all year except November
and the week before Christmas.

The Sugar Hill Inn is on a hillside overlooking pastures and the Cannon and Lafayette mountains. Built as a farmhouse in 1789, it began
taking guests in 1929. It is furnished throughout with antiques. The
living room, with its wood stove, is decorated in the Queen Anne
style. The dining room offers views of the mountains. A full country
breakfast and dinner for guests are served here. The dinners feature a
different single entrée each evening. A typical meal might start with
shrimp mousse, continue with baked stuffed beef tenderloin, and
conclude with a praline and cream torte.

The guest rooms have tiny-floral-print wallpapers, stencilling, and
antiques. Six are in the little motel just down the hill. During the day
there is plenty to do in all seasons; downhill and cross-country skiing,
swimming, hiking, and golf are all nearby.

Accommodations: 16 rooms, all with private bath. *Pets:* Permitted only in the separate motel unit. *Children:* Under six not
permitted. *Smoking:* Not permitted. *Driving Instructions:* The inn is
on Route 117, about half a mile west of Route 18.

Glen, New Hampshire

BERNERHOF INN

Route 302, Glen, NH 03838. 603-383-4414. *Innkeepers:* Ted and
Sharon Wroblewski. Open Christmas to April 15 and Memorial
Day to mid-November.

The Bernerhof Inn was built in the early 1890s by a local businessman
to serve travelers on their way to the Mount Washington Hotel. Since
then it has been in continuous service as a hostelry, and even today a
trail to the peak of Mount Washington originates at the inn.

The inn is furnished with a number of antiques; an intimate dining
room and the oak-paneled Zumstien Room (the lounge) contain Swiss
and other European artifacts.

Dinner at the inn is distinctly European, with such specialties as
delice de Gruyère, escargots bourguignon, and Wiener schnitzel. In
the spring and fall the innkeepers run a cooking school here.

Upstairs, the ten guest rooms vary from those with simple country
furnishings and 1940s furniture to the recently completed sitting-room
suite with private bath. The Tower Room has its bed tucked under the
eaves in the building's turret. Floral striped wallpaper and a small
stained-glass window complete the decor of this popular room.

Accommodations: 10 rooms, 1 with private bath. *Pets:* Not permitted. *Driving Instructions:* The inn is 6 miles north of North
Conway (1 mile north of the intersection of Routes 302 and 16).

Haverhill, New Hampshire

HAVERHILL INN

Dartmouth College Highway, Haverhill, NH 03765. 603-989-5961. *Innkeepers:* Stephen Campbell and Katharine DeBoer. Open all year.

The Haverhill Inn, built as a private residence, is a fine example of classic New England Federal architecture. Set on a rise amid towering sugar maples, the house looks across lawns and an old granite-post-and-board fence to the oxbow bends of the Connecticut River and beyond to the Vermont mountains.

The building was the home of Arthur Carleton, a wealthy eccentric whose impending birth in 1810 had forced a hurried completion to the construction of his future home. Local speculation has it that the two iron rings set into the ceiling of the study held a swing where Arthur sat during the Civil War, gun in his lap, protecting himself and the family fortune. Successfully, it is presumed.

One enters a world of fires in open hearths, New England country antiques, and the aroma of freshly baked breads and pastries. The Haverhill Inn breakfast would do a New England farm wife proud.

All rooms at Haverhill Inn, including the guest rooms, have antique furniture and working fireplaces. Afternoon tea is served in the parlor downstairs, or guests may help themselves to a glass of sherry from the desk in the front hall and bring it to the hearth.

Accommodations: 4 rooms with private bath. *Pets and Children:* Not permitted. *Driving Instructions:* The inn is on Route 10, just south of the Common.

Henniker, New Hampshire

COLBY HILL INN

Colby Hill Road, Henniker, NH 03242. 603-428-3281. *Innkeepers:* The Glover family. Open all year.

Colby Hill Inn is a white country house built around 1800. Once a working farm, with 5 acres remaining, the many barns, sheds, and old stone walls offer a glimpse of the farm life of a hundred years ago. The inn has ten spacious guest rooms comfortably furnished with antiques; eight have private baths. Looking out the many-paned windows, one is treated to open vistas of the surrounding hills and mountains. Guests can waken to the smell of freshly baked bread coming from the farm kitchen. The Glovers' menu features traditional New England fare using locally produced ingredients when available, including vegetables fresh from the farm garden. The inn serves breakfast to guests only but is open to the public for dinner. Homemade soups and desserts are specialties of the house. There is a selection of wines, spirits, and lagers available with dinner. Colby Hill Inn also has a lounge for its guests.

Year-round and seasonal activities abound here, from canoeing and fly fishing in the many ponds and lakes in summer to white-water canoeing and ice fishing in other seasons. Of course, there is skiing — downhill at nearby areas plus 10 miles of local cross-country trails.

Accommodations: 10 rooms, 8 with private bath. *Pets:* Not permitted. *Children:* Welcome if over six years. *Driving Instructions:* Take the Henniker-Bradford exit off routes 9 and 202. Take Route 114 south to the town center. Turn right on Main Street about half a mile to The Oaks. The inn is on the right, just off West Main.

Hillsborough, New Hampshire

STONEBRIDGE INN

Route 9, Hillsborough, NH 03244. Mailing address: Star Route 3, Box 82. 603-464-3155. *Innkeepers:* Nelson and Lynne Adame. Open all year.

Stonebridge Inn is a traditional white clapboard New England farmhouse at the road's edge behind a tidy stone wall. The Federal-style house was built in 1830 as a private home and remained so until Nelson and Lynne Adame renovated it, transforming it into an inn complete with three dining rooms. The inn is furnished in a casual and comfortable manner. A first-floor sitting room is reserved for houseguests as a place to relax and visit with the other guests and the innkeepers. The dining rooms are open to the public for dinner and, in summer and fall, for lunches as well; houseguests are also served a Continental breakfast. Dinners feature nightly specials along with inn favorites such as veal Gruyère, seafood-stuffed shrimp, and fried chicken.

Upstairs are four guest rooms; two of these have a country-farmhouse feeling, another is furnished in Victorian mahogany, and a fourth has reproduction colonial maple pieces. The town of Hillsborough, birthplace of Franklin Pierce, fourteenth president of the United States, is in the Monadnock region with downhill and cross-country skiing within 10 miles of the inn. The many other recreational activities include horseback riding, swimming, tennis, and golf.

Accommodations: 4 rooms with private bath. *Pets:* Not permitted. *Driving Instructions:* From Keene, take Route 9 east for approximately 28 miles to Hillsborough. From Concord, take Route 9 west for approximately 26 miles.

Intervale, New Hampshire

HOLIDAY INN

Route 16A, Intervale, NH 03845. 603-356-9772. *Innkeepers:* Lois and Bob Gregory. Open May 30 through fall foliage (mid-October) and December 26 through the skiing season (mid-March).

The Holiday Inn — no relation to the big chain — has been in continuous operation since the nineteenth century. Situated in the heart of Mount Washington Valley, with spacious grounds, mountain views, and a heated swimming pool, this small inn is a comfortable place. A meandering stream runs through the inn's property. The woodland behind the inn offers 8 miles of hiking and cross-country skiing trails. Inside, the welcoming atmosphere of the Holiday Inn is immediately evident in the parlor–living room. A fireplace glowed when we were there, and several guests had gathered for before-dinner drinks (bring your own bottle) and a chance for some get-acquainted conversation. Dinner is served in the inn's dining room at tables set with white cloths. A different single entrée is served each evening to house guests only.

Upstairs, the rooms are furnished in the style of an old New Hampshire home, with flowered wallpaper, spindle beds, and white curtains. One of our favorites has pale blue flowered wallpaper, organdy tiebacks, a blue rug, and white spreads. The room has pine antique furniture including even an antique towel-rack. The room's washstand comes with a bowl and pitcher set. On the third floor a bedroom has been tucked under the eaves of the inn's mansard roof. There is also a separate stone cottage that was once the law office of Marion W. Cottle, one of the area's first woman lawyers. The cottage has two guest rooms, one with a stone fireplace. The Holiday Inn has something for everyone: swimming and hiking in the summer, skating on the inn's lighted rink and cross-country skiing from the front door in winter.

Accommodations: 10 rooms with bath. *Pets:* Not permitted. *Driving Instructions:* Take Route 16 out from the north end of North Conway; go 1½ miles on Route 16A toward Intervale.

THE NEW ENGLAND INN

Intervale, NH 03845. 603-356-5541. *Innkeepers:* Linda and Joe Johnston. Open all year.

The New England Inn matured slowly over 170 years. It began its life as the Bloodgood Farm, taking in road-weary travelers en route from Boston to Montreal. It provided them with a good bed, substantial meals, and a place for their horses. By the mid-nineteenth century, the travelers were replaced at the farm by artists and other summer visitors. The White Mountain School of Art developed nearby, and even today the inn has paintings swapped for room and board. It has been modernized over the years, and most of the farm buildings have been converted into additional residences, but the modernization is not intrusive within the buildings. The farm grounds now offer a number of sports facilities, including several excellent clay tennis courts and swimming and wading pools. The inn has a complete Cross Country Learning Center with EPSTI certified skiing instructors.

As soon as you enter the New England Inn you know you are in a place rich in history. The lobby area was once the inn's country kitchen and the original fireplace with its black kettle-hook is still there today. A springer spaniel was curled up on the braided rug before the hearth as we checked in. The inn's living room has traditionally low ceilings (built to conserve fireplace warmth). Family antiques including an old desk, an elaborately carved cupboard, and several family portraits set the tone of this room. Several staircases

lead to the upstairs guest rooms, indicating how the house has grown in fits and starts over the years. Our large bedroom had a painted Victorian country bureau, a now unused fireplace, and its own bath.

In addition to the main building at the New England Inn there are five duplex cottages, four single cottages, the meeting house (a building in traditional style across the street offering lodging and small conference facilities), a motel unit, and the sports facilities. All cottages have working fireplaces, with one daily wood delivery included in the room rate.

The inn serves a full country breakfast and offers complete dinners in Anna Martin's Restaurant, which occupies the ground-floor portion of one wing of the main building. Breakfasts include eggs and blueberry pancakes. Dinners feature such American foods as pumpkin bisque, Shaker cranberry pot roast, Indian pudding, and blueberry grunt.

Accommodations: 40 rooms in several buildings, all with private bath. *Driving Instructions:* The inn is on Route 16A, 3½ miles north of North Conway.

Jackson, New Hampshire

DANA PLACE INN

20 Pinkham Notch Road, Jackson, NH 03846. 603-383-6822. *Innkeepers:* Betty and Malcolm Jennings. Open mid-May to late October and mid-December to late March.

Before a backdrop of the White Mountains and Mount Washington, alongside the clear Ellis River, is the 1890 farmhouse-turned-inn, Dana Place. It is surrounded by 300 acres of orchards, gardens, meadows, and deep woods that adjoin the White Mountain National Forest. Cross-country skiing and hiking trails are nearby, while in summer the natural swimming hole formed at the base of a small waterfall is the hands-down favorite spot with visitors. A hot spa, two tennis courts, and trout fishing are also available.

The inn's interior has been renovated and updated. Some parts have been modernized, and others retain the old-fashioned air of a country farmhouse. Two dining rooms are quite contemporary, with picture-window walls looking out at Mount Washington in the distance. The third dining room, the original one, has deep blue flowered wallpapers and decorative touches contrasting with the bright white of the working fireplace's mantel. The menu features a wide selection of Continental dishes.

The Dana Place Inn has a friendly atmosphere enhanced by sunny rooms. The sitting room has a cathedral ceiling and a large airtight wood-burning stove. The guest rooms are papered with old-fashioned flower prints and furnished with farmhouse antiques. Downstairs is a piano bar with a performer on weekends.

Accommodations: 14 rooms, 6 with bath. *Pets:* Not permitted. *Driving Instructions:* Take Route 16 north from Jackson.

NESTLENOOK INN

Dinsmore Road, Jackson, New Hampshire. Mailing address: P.O. Box Q, Jackson, NH 03846. 603-383-9443. *Innkeepers:* Thomas and Patti Burns. Open all year.

This pastoral, early-nineteenth-century inn is reached by traveling 50 yards past a barn-red covered bridge. The farmhouse, the oldest in Jackson, is part of a working farm that includes 65 acres of woodlands, meadows, a river, and high ledges that afford views of Mount Washington. The living room is warmed by fires in the hearth, and there is a video library of more than 125 movie classics. Presiding over all this are two friendly innkeepers who make sure there is plenty of iced tea available in summer and hot cider brewing on the wood-burning stove in winter.

The rooms are decorated with stenciled or country print wallpapers, antique furniture, and many whimsical collections—dolls, cameras, hats, and whirligigs. There is even a guest room with an antique muff collection. If there is no room at the inn, guests can stay in the Manger, the farm's former carriage house, which has five rooms decorated with equestrian antiques. Three rustic cottages are also on the grounds. For breakfast, adventurous guests can take the basket out to the hen house and pick out their own eggs. Tom bakes breads to accompany the bacon, sausages, and eggs, all produced on the farm. The innkeepers run a ski-touring center and take guests on evening sleighrides in winter and hayrides in the summer. There is also a full-scale equestrian program at the farm.

Accommodations: 15 rooms, 6 with private bath; and 3 cottages. *Pets:* By prior arrangement only. *Driving Instructions:* Take Route 16 to the Jackson covered bridge and turn right at Dinsmore Road (just past the bridge).

Jaffrey, New Hampshire

MONADNOCK INN

Main Street, Jaffrey Center, New Hampshire. Mailing address: Box 103, Jaffrey Center, NH 03454. 603-532-7001. *Innkeeper:* Sally Roberts. Open all year.

The Monadnock was built in the early nineteenth century; in the 1870s, Mrs. Sarah Lawrence began taking in summer visitors. She named the placed "Fairview" and later "The Monadnock." The Monadnock has changed hands many times since then but has been operating as an inn ever since (with a short rest in the early 1900s). The Roberts family took charge several years ago, and now the inn contains a comfortable mixture of early American, colonial, and Victorian furniture, a large living room with a fireplace, and an old-fashioned lounge and bar warmed in winter by a wood stove. Lunch and dinner are served to the public and guests; breakfasts are Continental-style, for guests only. Featured in *Gourmet* magazine, the inn's dining room offers delicacies that include oysters baked with Parmesan cheese, saltimbocca, gratin of scallops, sautéed pork in mustard sauce, and steak Diane. These and many other dishes are complemented by a good selection of wines.

Accommodations: 14 rooms, 7 with private bath. *Pets:* Not permitted. *Driving Instructions:* Take Route 124 to Jaffrey Center. The inn is on Main Street.

Jefferson, New Hampshire

THE COUNTRY INN ON JEFFERSON HILL

Route 2, RFD 1, Box 68A, Jefferson, NH 03583. 603-586-7998.

Innkeepers: Greg Brown and Anne Lederhos. Open all year.

The turn of the century was a golden age for large summer resort hotels in the mountains. Jefferson was then a vacationer's paradise, dotted with many such hotels and surrounded by the Presidential range of the White Mountains. The wooden giants are long gone, but the beauty of the mountains remains. Greg and Anne's Country Inn recaptures the flavor of those days on a more intimate scale. The Victorian house was built in 1897 in the resort's heyday but has survived to our time. It overlooks the mountains, its wraparound porch set with many comfortable rocking chairs. The inn's rooms are furnished with antiques, many brought over from England, where Anne and Greg lived for several years. Two rooms in the Victorian cupola have rounded alcoves. In the evening, guests may join the innkeepers for complimentary hot teas, chocolate, or iced beverages served with freshly baked desserts. In the morning a full country breakfast is offered at an additional charge. The inn is near many of New Hampshire's year-round attractions, including the Cannon, Bretton Woods, and Wildcat ski areas, and an old swimming hole is just across the street.

Accommodations: 6 rooms with shared baths. *Pets:* Not permitted. *Driving Instructions:* The inn is on Route 2.

Lancaster, New Hampshire

MORSE LODGE AND INN

39 Portland Street, Lancaster, NH 03584. 603-788-2096. *Innkeepers:* Walt and Judy Johnson. Open all year.

Morse Lodge was originally built in 1858 as a carriage barn to serve the main house. The barn was remodeled and converted in 1936 to include six guest rooms, a dining room, and a guest sitting room. One is greeted by the fieldstone fireplace that dominates the sitting room. In one corner are games and books, chairs grouped for quiet conversation, and a piano. In another corner is a gift shop the Johnsons have named "The Handmaiden." On the two upper floors, six individually decorated guest rooms have antique beds and country-style furnishings. A second-floor balcony opens onto the sitting room below, and at Christmastime a large tree is cut that extends upward toward the second floor.

Just off the sitting room is a dining room with views of the flowers and gardens outside. Breakfast served here includes the innkeepers' special grilled cinnamon bread. On many evenings, according to the season, a single-entrée dinner is prepared for guests and the public by reservation; specialties include Hungarian chicken with spaetzle, beef Stroganoff, and seafood Newburg. In addition to the carriage house, there are two rooms with private entrances in the main house.

Accommodations: 8 rooms, 3 with private bath. *Pets:* Not permitted. *Driving Instructions:* Take Route 2 to Lancaster, where it becomes Portland Street.

Littleton, New Hampshire

BEAL HOUSE INN

Main Street, Littleton, NH 03561. 603-444-2661. *Innkeepers:* Doug and Brenda Clickenger. Open all year.

Beal House Inn was built in 1833 as a farmhouse at the edge of the tiny town of Littleton. In traditional New England fashion, the house was connected to the barn by a carriage house. Today the inn sits on 4½ acres of land; its carriage house and main building house romantic, antique-filled guest rooms, while the barn, an antique shop, over-flows with country antiques. Most of the antiques and decorative pieces in the inn are for sale.

The Clickengers scoured New England for just the right country inn before settling on Beal House. That they love their new profession is evident in their warm welcome and their attention to guests' comfort, and in the relaxed visiting-a-friend-in-the-country atmos-phere. Fireside breakfasts are special occasions where the harvest table is set with candles and Blue Willow china on a soft antique red cloth. One might find waffles topped with local maple syrup or hot popovers and scrambled eggs served in antique Hens-on-Nests china. For winter holidays, Doug and Brenda have special celebrations, in-cluding dinners and sleigh rides.

Accommodations: 14 rooms, 9 with private bath. *Driving Instruc-tions:* From I-93 take exit 42 and drive to the intersection of Routes 18 and 302 (Main Street).

EDENCROFT MANOR

RFD 1, Route 135, Littleton, NH 03561. 603-444-6776. *Innkeepers:* Barry and Ellie Bliss and Bill and Laurie Walsh. Open all year except two weeks in early spring.

Edencroft Manor is a large white country inn with a view of the White Mountains to the east. Built as a farmhouse in the 1890s, it was greatly enlarged in the years following the Depression. The estate became known for its lavish parties and elaborate gardens. As an inn, it now features candlelit dining rooms offering fireside meals where everything, from the basket of warm breads to the rich tortes and trifles, is made from scratch in the inn's kitchens. Specialties of the house are veal and duck dishes and prime rib. Guests and the public may choose to enjoy desserts, coffee, and after-dinner drinks in the living room by the fireplace. The common room has an extensive library for guests, and there is even a children's corner. Baroque and other classical music plays softly in the background, or one can crank up the old Victrola for a livelier session.

The guest rooms are decorated with antiques and new, firm beds. The wallpapers and thick handmade comforters add bright touches to the decor.

Accommodations: 6 rooms, 4 with private bath. *Driving Instructions:* At the end of I-93 in Littleton, turn left onto Route 18. Drive 0.2 mile and turn right on Route 135.

1895 HOUSE COUNTRY INN

74 Pleasant Street, Littleton, NH 03561. 603-444-5200. *Innkeeper:* Susanne Watkins. Open July to November.

1895 House is a perfectly preserved Victorian building that retains its impressive front door with inset beveled glass. The oaken woodwork inside glows with the patina of age. There are oaken wall panels, smooth oaken floors, and an oaken staircase rising three stories. Through tall sliding wooden doors one enters a parlor where guests relax in Victorian spendor on Queen Anne chairs or a Chippendale camelback sofa. The bay windows offer views of the town and surrounding White Mountains. Another set of doors leads to the dining room with its carved oak mantel with the head of Old Man Winter in bas-relief. Breakfast is served here, and the hands-down favorite with houseguests is Susanne's zucchini muffins with cinnamon butter and raspberry jam. Eggs, bacon, and pancakes are served as well.

Guest rooms are also a celebration of Victorian oak brightened by Oriental or colorful braided rugs and Susanne's hand-made quilts and tie-back curtains. The house is on a half acre, with maples and lilacs.

Accommodations: 6 rooms, 2 with private bath. *Pets:* Not permitted. *Driving Instructions:* Take I-93 to exit 41, continue across the bridge to the traffic light, then turn west on Main Street and take the first street on the right (Pleasant Street).

Lyme, New Hampshire

LYME INN

Lyme, New Hampshire. Mailing address: P.O. Box 68, Lyme, NH
03768. 603-795-2222. *Innkeepers:* Fred and Judy Siemons. Open
all year except the day after Thanksgiving through Christmas.

When the Lyme Inn first opened in 1809, it was known as the Grant
Hotel. Over the years it saw service as an inn, a tavern, and a grange
hall and gradually fell into disrepair before being saved and restored
by its three previous owners. The result is an on-the-common inn
whose face and interior show the love bestowed on it by skillful
restorers. The job of transforming it into an exceptional place to stay
was done with such care that even the fire escape—which often mars
the beauty of other inns—has been hidden behind a columned
portico.

One enters the inn through double doors that open onto a full-
length glassed-in porch, which retains its original painted pressed-tin
ceiling. In summer the porch is cool and inviting with bright yellow
cushions on its wicker furniture. In winter a collection of sleds
replaces the wicker. Rooms at the Lyme Inn are decorated individually. Each bed is of particular interest, be it a hand-painted Vic-

torian highback, a scrolly iron one, or one with a canopy. Each of the fifteen rooms has wallpapers ranging from floral patterns and pinstripes to traditional colonial prints. Accessory furnishings and antique prints complement the period of the room established by the bed. Most of the pieces of furniture and the prints are for sale.

The inn has three dining rooms, which are closed on Thursdays. The decorative theme of one is based on early samplers; the second has old Currier and Ives prints; and the third contains the inn's map collection. In the small tavern is a collection of early hand-tools. The dinner menu's diverse offerings include hasenpfeffer, filet au poivre, Wiener schnitzel, Cape scallops, and loin lamb chops among many others. Dinners (not served on Tuesdays) may start with escargots, quiche, smoked salmon, or rumaki (chicken livers wrapped in bacon). For those who prefer lighter supper-style meals, there are veal Marengo and seafood crepes. Breakfast is served to guests only; lunch is not available.

The area surrounding the inn offers year-round activities such as Alpine and cross-country skiing, canoeing, tennis, and fishing. At Dartmouth College, 10 miles away, there is theater and other entertainment.

Accommodations: 15 rooms, 10 with private bath. *Pets:* Not permitted. *Children:* Under eight not permitted. *Driving Instructions:* The inn is 10 miles north of Hanover on Route 10.

Moultonboro, New Hampshire

KONA MANSION INN

Moultonboro Neck Road, Moultonboro, New Hampshire. Mailing address: Box 458, Center Harbor, NH 03226. 603-253-4900. *Innkeepers:* The Crowleys. Open May through October.

The Kona Mansion Inn, commanding a fine view of Lake Winnipesaukee from the highest point above the lake, was built at the turn of the century by Eben Jordan of the Jordan Marsh Company as a wedding present for his daughter, Dorothy, and her fiancé, Herbert Dumeresq, a self-proclaimed count. The Kona mansion originally stood on 1,500 acres of New Hampshire farmland, including 10 miles of lakefront. Today the grounds encompass 130 acres.

The Crowleys are maintaining the property as a tribute to the elegant life-style of the early 1900s. The mansion was built of local fieldstone with English Tudor-style half-timbering above, and the English look is still evident in the carriage house, stables, sheep and hay barns—even the chicken house and repair shed. The fine paneling has not been painted over, nor have the elaborate ceiling murals. Two of the rooms are unchanged from their original state—the bridal suite and the "countess's" sewing parlor. The formal dining room, library, and living room now house the dining rooms of the inn's restaurant. Guests may choose among a variety of antique furnished rooms in the mansion or the cottages on the lake. The inn has its own private beach, tennis courts, and a par-three golf course, all of which help to create the impression that one is staying at a private country club.

Accommodations: 16 rooms with private bath. *Driving Instructions:* From Center Harbor drive east on Route 25, turn right onto Moultonboro Neck Road, and follow signs to the inn.

HIDE-AWAY LODGE

New London, NH 03257. 603-526-4861. *Innkeepers:* Lilli and Wolfgang Heinberg. Open mid-May through October.

Hide-Away Lodge is one of those places that make you think "I shouldn't really be sharing this." It is literally hidden away down an unpaved country lane just past Little Lake Sunapee. The lodge is not a romantic old-fashioned inn, nor is it historic. It was built in the 1930s as a summer retreat for poet-author Grace Litchfield and retains the flavor of a private home that just happens to have five intimate dining rooms. These rooms and the food served in them is what all the fuss is about. Wolfgang and Lilli Heinberg, the innkeepers, run a restaurant that has achieved national acclaim.

The dining rooms are decorated with old-fashioned oak furniture, Oregon fir–paneled walls, and simple country pieces. The tables are set more formally with starched tablecloths and soft napkins arranged with polished silver and attractive glassware. The menu features an array of unusual and original dishes created from fresh seasonal fish, game, vegetables, and berries. Dinner begins with cocktails out on the porch and proceeds to a selection of at least six appetizers, and perhaps ten or eleven entrées, accompanied by a wine from the Heinberg's excellent selection.

Overnight guests are welcome to relax on the wide sun porches or settle down next to a fire in the living room's granite fireplace. The inviting rooms are paneled throughout with Oregon fir. There are four comfortable guest rooms on the second floor and four more in an adjoining guest house. Each has a private bath. The lodge is set on landscaped grounds with trees, lawns, and a mountain brook complete with a fieldstone bridge. The beach on Little Lake Sunapee is just a short walk down the lane. The lake has a rowboat and sailboat.

Accommodations: 8 rooms with private bath. *Driving Instructions:* The inn is 2 miles from New London. Take Main Street out past Colby-Sawyer College. Main Street becomes Little Sunapee Road. Follow signs on the unpaved road past the lake to the inn.

NEW LONDON INN

Main Street, New London, NH 03257. 603-526-2791. *Innkeepers:* Clara and George Adame. Open all year.

The New London Inn is a classic old New England inn with two stories of wide verandas overlooking the main street of this serene New Hampshire town. The white clapboard structure, built in 1792, is furnished throughout with antiques spanning the years.

Each guest room is furnished in its own special style, with four-posters, and other country-Colonial items. Many guests return year after year, trying out different rooms each time. Working fireplaces are in the lobby and the sitting room, which has a wall of books and groupings of floral-upholstered chairs and couches.

The New London Inn has two dining rooms. The main one offers a menu of seafoods and steaks with house specialties of roast duckling with fresh peach glaze, shrimp scampi flamed in anisette, and veal with fresh mushrooms and shallots. Nelson's Tavern serves from a moderately priced menu in a casual atmosphere. The inn is near Colby-Sawyer College and the town's many antique and craft shops.

Accommodations: 27 rooms with private bath. *Pets:* Not permitted. *Driving Instructions:* Take I-93 to I-89, exit 11. The inn is in the village.

PLEASANT LAKE INN

North Pleasant Street, New London, New Hampshire. Mailing address: Box 1030, New London, NH 03257. 603-526-6271. *Innkeepers:* Grant and Margaret Rich. Open all year.

On the shores of Pleasant Lake, this inn was originally built as a farmhouse. Although the earliest parts of the inn date from 1770, its main portions were constructed in 1868. In the days when the property was a farm, the countryside surrounding the lake was shared by the farmers with the Penobscot Indians, with whom the families had friendly relations. The conversion to an inn was done by a Civil War veteran who operated it first as a summer and fall inn.

All but two of the guest rooms share several baths (no more than two rooms to any bath), and much of the inn is furnished with country antiques. The dining rooms, where breakfast and dinner are served, offer views of the lake and Mount Kearsage. Dinners reflect seasonal foods, including several of the Rich's own original entrées.

Accommodations: 13 rooms, 2 with private bath. *Pets:* Not permitted. *Driving Instructions:* Take Route 11 to New London, turn onto North Pleasant Street at the New London Bank, and go 1½ miles to the bottom of the hill at the lake.

North Conway, New Hampshire

CRANMORE INN

Kearsage Street, North Conway, NH 03860. 603-356-5502. *Inn-keepers:* Christopher and Virginia Kanzler. Open Memorial Day weekend through October and December 26 through March.

During the golden age of railroading, up to twenty-six trains daily brought passengers to North Conway from most major cities in the Northeast. At that time, the Cranmore was one of five inns on Kearsage Street. Today the Cranmore is the only one that has survived. When the Cranmore was built in 1863, it was known as the Echo House. Over the years the building has been renovated and modernized, but what remains is a homey, old-fashioned place.

Typical of many Victorian mountain inns, the living room is particularly spacious. Across the hall is a smaller sitting room with its original tin ceiling. It is here that the inn's only television set resides. Beyond are a card room and the dining room. In the mornings the inn serves a full country breakfast. Dinner is served to both guests and the public.

Some of the guest rooms at the Cranmore are in a relatively new wing. Many of the rooms have nice wallpapers and simple but comfortable furniture. The Kanzlers are redecorating many of the rooms to reflect the inn's Victorian atmosphere. All of this adds up to a happy and unpretentious place likely to appeal to those who come to this mountain village for its surrounding natural beauty rather than to find urban sophistication in the country.

Accommodations: 25 rooms, about half with private bath. *Pets:* Not permitted. *Driving Instructions:* Take Route 16 to North Conway. Turn east on Kearsage Street, and drive one block to the inn on the left.

CRANMORE MT. LODGE

Kearsage Road, North Conway, New Hampshire. Mailing address: Box 1194, North Conway, NH 03860. 603-356-2044. *Innkeepers:* Bob and Dawn Brauel. Open all year.

Bob and Dawn Brauel came to innkeeping as a retreat from the more hectic lifestyle of earlier careers as a certified public accountant and a social worker, respectively. Their contentment in their new profession is evident in their enthusiasm for their work.

Cranmore Mt. Lodge was built in several sections, the earliest of which dates from the mid-nineteenth century. First a farmhouse, the early building was converted into an inn in the late nineteenth century by the addition of an octagonal wing. Later additions have included a main dining room, added in the 1930s, and tennis courts, swimming pool, basketball court, and an outdoor Jacuzzi. At one time, the lodge was run by Babe Ruth's daughter. The Babe was a frequent

guest, using the inn as his hunting and fishing retreat. His room was furnished with oaken twin beds, and it continues to be the favorite room of many guests.

The guest rooms have various bed arrangements that can accommodate small or large families. There are eight new guest rooms with cable television and air conditioning in the old barn. These are used most frequently for larger groups of skiers during the winter months. The main floor of the inn has a sitting room with fireplace, a television and game room, and a dining room serving home-cooked single-entrée meals (to guests only). The inn has an alpine ski rental shop.

Accommodations: 10 rooms in the inn with shared baths; 8 rooms in the barn with private baths. *Pets:* Not permitted. *Driving Instructions:* Take Route 16 to North Conway. At the traffic light turn east on Kearsage Street, which dead-ends as Kearsage Road. The lodge is 1 mile to the north.

STONEHURST MANOR

Route 16, North Conway, New Hampshire. Mailing address: P.O. Box 1900, North Conway, NH 03860. 603-356-3113. *Innkeeper:* Peter Rattay. Open all year.

Stonehurst Manor is a turn-of-the-century mansion that looks as if it should have a thatched roof and be in the English countryside. One part of the ground floor is built of fieldstones, accounting for its name. Once the home of the Bigelow Carpet family, it now contains guest rooms and a dining room serving both guests and the public.

The manor's interior has turned spiral columns, baronial-size fireplaces with detailed mantelpieces, and intricate stained glass in many windows and doors. The lounge has thick pile rugs, seats built into the arched-top windows, and modern rattan furniture whose bent-wood curves echo the curves of the window tops. The main dining room's round tables are covered with print fabrics topped with white linen and are surrounded by high arch-back wicker chairs. There is additional dining on the sunny glassed-in porch where hanging plants thrive. Evening menu selections include about thirty entrées, stressing veal, seafood, and steaks. Before dinner, cocktails are served in the Manor library by the fire.

The most appealing rooms are within the Manor itself, although there are an additional ten rooms in a motel unit. Here, as in the rest of the inn, the innkeepers have used rattan and wicker as the basic

furnishings with plush wall-to-wall carpeting and print wallpapers the rule. The inn is set back from the highway on 30 acres of pine trees. On the grounds are a large swimming pool and a clay tennis court.

Accommodations: 25 rooms, 23 with private bath. *Pets:* Not permitted. *Driving Instructions:* Go on Route 16 for a mile north of North Conway to the inn.

WILDFLOWERS GUEST HOUSE

North Main Street, North Conway, NH 03860. 603-356-2224. *Innkeeper:* Eileen Davies and Dean Frank. Open all year except occasional off-season weeks; call first.

Wildflowers is a cottage that was built about a hundred years ago under the direction of the respected Boston architect Stephen C. Earle, who broke with local tradition by facing the house away from the main street. Thus the building takes full advantage of both morning and afternoon sunlight. The intriguing exterior has both board-and-batten and cedar shingling and a porch.

When Eileen Davies bought the building in 1978 it needed a total renovation. She stripped endless layers of paint off the beaded door and window trim, steamed off tired old wallpapers, and then set out to create a decor that would carry out the theme suggested by the inn's name. Eileen clearly had fun selecting the papers for the six guest rooms and the dining room on the first floor. Each is printed with a different flower or grain. A corner bedroom (a favorite of hers and ours) has bold poppy and miniature-flower patterns on a black background. Furnishings in the rooms are an eclectic blend of antique pieces and "vintage yard sale" items. The living room is heated by a wood stove.

Accommodations: 6 rooms with shared bath. *Pets:* Not permitted. *Driving Instructions:* The guest house is on Route 16, north of the village of North Conway.

North Sutton, New Hampshire

FOLLANSBEE INN

North Sutton, NH 03260. 603-927-4221. *Innkeepers:* Larry and Joan Wadman. Open all year except parts of December and April. Like so many New Hampshire inns, the Follansbee has grown over the years to accommodate an increasing number of overnight guests. The lake-front inn was originally a two-story farmhouse built in the early nineteenth century, and two stories were added in 1928–30. The result is an imposing structure with full lounge and dining facilities. The innkeepers shed earlier careers in the states of Delaware and New Jersey and came to the inn filled with enthusiasm for their new family venture. The inn is popular with cross-country skiers because trails lead right to its door.

The talented young chef prepares a wide variety of dishes, the best known being the "drunken bird" and "pig Bee." Dinner is not served on Mondays.

Accommodations: 23 rooms, 11 with private bath. *Pets:* Not permitted. *Driving Instructions:* The inn is 4 miles south of New London on Route 114, behind a white church.

Plainfield, New Hampshire

HOME HILL INN AND FRENCH RESTAURANT

River Road, Plainfield, New Hampshire. Mailing address: RR #2, Box 235, Cornish, NH 03745. 603-675-6165. *Innkeeper:* Roger Nicolas. Open all year.

On his first visit to New England, Roger Nicolas fell in love with this 1818 white brick Federal mansion and its pastoral country setting along the banks of the Connecticut River. He left his highly acclaimed French restaurant, La Potinière, in California to fulfill a dream: An establishment capturing the spirit and style of a chateau of his native France and the warmth and friendliness of a New England inn. Home Hill, after two years of restoration, blends French ambience with early-American charm. The dining rooms have Toile de Jouy–papered walls as backdrops for the formal table settings, as well as country pine pieces, brass lanterns, and working fireplaces. The furnishings and decor of the rooms include French and American antiques alongside reproduction pieces and whimsical touches such as a carousel horse or a twig loveseat. Polished pine floors have Oriental carpets, and fresh flowers are used extensively. The guest rooms' antiques are set off by richly colored wallpapers and handmade quilts. Several rooms have hand stenciling, including the country kitchen, where a Continental breakfast is served. The dining rooms are open to the public for dinner Wednesday through Sunday, offering Roger's innovative French cooking using fresh ingredients and sauces.

Home Hill is on 20 acres of landscaped grounds with a brick terrace, a swimming pool, a clay tennis court, and cross-country trails.

Accommodations: 5 rooms with private bath and a 3-bedroom private guest cottage with kitchen. *Pets:* Not permitted. *Driving Instructions:* From I-89 take exit 20 (Route 12A) south 3 miles to River Road, the first right. Turn right and drive 3 miles to the inn.

Portsmouth, New Hampshire

INN AT CHRISTIAN SHORE

335 Maplewood Avenue, Portsmouth, New Hampshire. Mailing address: P.O. Box 1474, Portsmouth, NH 03801. 603-431-6770. *Innkeepers:* Charles Litchfield, Louis Sochia, and Thomas Towey. Open all year

Portsmouth, a shipbuilding and fishing community settled in the early seventeenth century, was originally named Strawberry Banke. It had its heyday around 1800, a period that saw the construction of many Federal homes, including the building now known as the Inn at Christian Shore—a name derived from the Christian Shore area.

The guest rooms are furnished in keeping with the period, with a few concessions to guests' comfort, such as wall-to-wall carpeting, air conditioning, and color television in the rooms.

Downstairs, a comfortable sitting room is furnished with period and reproduction Federal furniture. The walls are papered with a bold floral print, and a fireplace is faced by wing chairs and a Sheraton settee. The breakfast room is reminiscent of an early tavern room, with its long center table surrounded by eight bow-back Windsor chairs. Several smaller tables are located around the room's periphery, and a large fireplace dominates this low-ceilinged exposed-beam room. Breakfast includes a variety of traditional foods.

Accommodations: 5 rooms, 2 with bath. *Driving Instructions:* Take exit 5 from I-95. At the traffic circle take Route 1 north. Exit by Lum's restaurant. The inn is the sixth house on the left when you are headed downtown.

THE INN AT STRAWBERRY BANKE

314 Court Street, Portsmouth, NH 03801. 603-436-7242. *Inn-keepers:* Mark and Kerrianne Constant. Open all year.

This little bed-and-breakfast inn was built in 1800 for Captain Holbrook. The antiques in its rooms are typical of those made during Portsmouth's early days as a prosperous seaport town. The inn is ideally located just around the corner from the waterfront and Strawberry Banke, Portsmouth's historic restoration. After a day of exploring Strawberry Banke's living museums and the narrow winding streets of this beautiful old seaport with its tiny shops and dockside restaurants, it would seem appropriate to preserve the atmosphere of yesteryear by staying in a house of the same vintage. Complimentary sherry is served in the inn's sitting room, and strawberry sweets (of course) are set out on pillows in the guest rooms. Light breakfasts of coffee, juices, and muffins start the day. Innkeepers Mark and Kerrianne provide bicycles for sight-seeing tours and will gladly steer guests to area restaurants, art galleries, and the city's many antique shops.

Accommodations: 6 rooms, 2 with private bath. *Pets and young children:* Not permitted.

PHILBROOK FARM INN

North Road, Shelburne, NH 03581. 603-466-3831. *Innkeepers:*
Nancy Philbrook and Constance P. Leger. Open May 1 to October
31 and December 26 to March 31.

The Philbrook Farm Inn is a typical New Hampshire building that,
like so many others, has expanded gradually over the generations.
The first section was built in 1934, and the Philbrook family has lived
here since 1861. The Philbrooks have always been proud of their
relaxed atmosphere: an inn "filled with peace, quiet and contentment
in a world turned upside down." The Philbrook survives as the only
inn in an area that used to abound with inns. Some guests are now the
fourth and fifth generation from their families to visit Philbrook
Farm.

The inn is furnished with family antiques and with paintings done
by guests, old maps of the area, and Currier and Ives prints. There are
several fireplaces, including ones in the two living rooms and the dining room with its knotty pine paneling. The playroom has table
tennis, a pool table, and a collection of old farm tools and kitchen
things, as well as its own fireplace. Meals are served family-style from
a menu that changes daily. Much of the food served in the summer
months is raised in the inn's garden. Meals generally include a homemade soup followed by a roast meat or poultry, vegetables, potato,
and dessert. On Saturday nights there is a New England baked bean
supper, and Sunday morning breakfast traditionally consists of fish-
balls and corn bread.

The nineteen guest rooms are in the inn's main building and the
Lodge, the Little House, Undercliff, the Casino, and Birch Cliff.
Most of the last are rented by families or larger groups.

Accommodations: 19 rooms, 7 with bath. *Pets:* Permitted in
summer cottages only. *Driving Instructions:* The inn is 1½ miles off
Route 2. Look for the direction sign, turn, cross the railroad tracks
and bridge, then turn right at the crossroads and drive for ½ mile.

Snowville, New Hampshire

SNOWVILLAGE INN

Foss Mountain Road, Snowville, NH 03849. 603-447-2818. *Innkeepers:* Pat and Ginger Blymyer. Open all year except April.

For many years Pat and Ginger Blymyer had careers in filmmaking, he as a lighting designer and she as a hair stylist. In 1977 they realized they longed for a place in the mountains where they could have animals and welcome people as guests coming to relax and renew themselves, just as the Blymyers would do. They left Los Angeles and toured New England searching for the country inn of their dreams, and when they drove up the mountain road from Snowville, New Hampshire, they found Snowvillage Lodge, a 1916 summer estate house large enough for themselves and their three daughters.

Today the lodge overflows with dogs, cats, and even a pet pig, who lives in "Gracie's Mansion." Fourteen guest rooms decorated in country New England style are in the main house, over the Swiss chalet–style dining room, and in the Barn. On the inn's covered porch one can sit and view fields, woods, and the White Mountains.

Meals at the Snowvillage Inn are special occasions. Tables are laid with linen tablecloths and napkins and crystal glasses. From the kitchen come carefully prepared dishes such as veal piccata, chicken Veronique, roast beef with Yorkshire pudding, or coq au vin.

Accommodations: 14 rooms with private bath. *Driving Instructions:* From Conway take Route 153 for 5 miles south to the Snowville Road. In Snowville, take Foss Mountain Road to the inn.

Sugar Hill, New Hampshire

Sugar Hill is quite near all the attractions of the White Mountains region. The town has several antique and gift shops, including The Sugar Hill Sampler, Colonial Cottage Antiques, Harman's Country Store, the Hildrex Maple Sugar Farm, and Miss Lynn and Miss Monahan's, and there are many antique shops in the surrounding countryside. There are country auctions by the dozen in the warm months—several each week. Golf and cross-country skiing are available at the *Sunset Hill House*. Sugar Hill Historic Museum is in the town.

THE HOMESTEAD

Sugar Hill, NH 03585. 603-823-5564. *Innkeeper:* Esther T. Serafini. Open Memorial Day to November 1, Thanksgiving weekend, and Christmas through April 15.

The Homestead has been in Esther Serafini's family since the Teffts, her grandparents, first opened the old farmhouse to guests in 1880. The original house was built, using hand-hewn beams, in 1802 by Sugar Hill's first settler. Many of the handmade antiques at the Homestead today were brought here in ox-drawn carts by the settlers.

Mrs. Serafini's grandparents enlarged the farmhouse to its present size in 1898. In 1917, the inn's property was expanded again with the addition of the Chalet, built entirely of stones gathered in the surrounding meadows and logs hauled here in horse-drawn sleds.

The Homestead offers ten guest rooms in the inn and seven in the other three buildings on the property. The Family Cottage and the Early Family Home are both small farmhouses containing rooms with private baths. They have porches and verandas with views of rolling meadows and the White Mountains. The Chalet can be rented as a unit. It has a 44-foot living room with a cathedral ceiling and an unusual brick-and-fieldstone fireplace. From the balcony porch one can see three mountain ranges. The Chalet also has a kitchen, a dining room, and two bedrooms. It is decorated with antiques, and handmade threshing equipment is displayed on its walls.

All the rooms in the inn are filled with antiques and family memorabilia. The inn has two floors for occupancy, each with five guest rooms and two hall bathrooms. Mrs. Serafini points out that although the rooms are full of antique dressers, lamps, and beds, the mattresses are definitely *not* antique. There are many up-to-date comforts here that in no way detract from the character of the old inn.

Downstairs, the hand-hewn ceiling beams are exposed to view, and there is an entrance hall, a reading room, a Victorian parlor with a fireplace, and the pine-paneled dining room. The cupboards in the dining room are filled with Mrs. Serafini's extensive glass and china collection. Dinners are hearty and a real New England farm treat. Everything is homemade, from the relishes and conserves to the pies, parfaits, and sauces, and there are no steam tables. Breakfasts are the kind grandmother would make. The public may eat here for dinner but only with a reservation. Gentlemen must wear jackets.

Accommodations: 17 rooms, 7 with bath. *Pets and children:* Not encouraged. *Driving Instructions:* Sugar Hill is off I-93 (exit 38 coming north or exit 39 coming south).

Tamworth, New Hampshire

TAMWORTH INN

Main Street, Tamworth, NH 03886. 603-323-7721. *Innkeepers:* Ron and Nancy Brembt. Open all year except late fall.

The Tamworth was first constructed in 1830, with additions made from 1870 through 1900; it has been an inn since 1888. The tavern and the living room both have working fireplaces and many antiques. The Tamworth has its own pool, and there is excellent trout fishing in the stream behind the inn. This is a fine base for using the many cross-country skiing trails nearby. The Barnstormers summer stock theater is nearby.

The inn's menu features a variety of items ranging from fettucini with chicken to beef and seafood dishes. In summer, guests may have luncheon and cocktails on the outdoor patio.

Accommodations: 22 rooms, 10 with private bath. *Pets and children under 7:* Not permitted. *Driving Instructions:* Take Route I-93 to exit 23, Route 104 East to Route 3, Route 3 a short distance to Route 25, then drive northeast to Whittier and Route 113, which runs north to Tamworth.

Temple, New Hampshire

THE BIRCHWOOD INN

Route 45, Temple, NH 03084. 603-878-3285. *Innkeepers:* Judy and
Bill Wolfe. Open all year except three weeks in April.

Birchwood Inn began as a tavern in 1775, although the present brick
inn was probably built in the early nineteenth century, with its handsome large white barns added in 1848. Thoreau was once an overnight
guest here and noted the stay in his diary in 1852. Judy and Bill have
restored the inn's antique-filled rooms and salvaged the original
Rufus Porter murals decorating the main dining room, where breakfast and dinner are offered to the public from a blackboard menu that
changes daily. These usually include seafood and red meat entrées
along with a chef's surprise. The tavern, warmed by an old wood-
burning stove, is a popular gathering spot. An antique Steinway
square grand piano and an old Edison phonograph provide entertainment, as does the plentiful supply of table games, including the very
un-colonial Trivial Pursuit. Each guest room, furnished with antiques, is decorated around a particular theme such as a school room,
a train station, and an editorial room. Guests may bring their own al-
coholic drinks since this is a dry town.

Accommodations: 7 rooms with shared baths. *Pets:* Not
permitted. *Driving Instructions:* From Peterborough take Route 101
east to Route 45. Turn right and drive 1½ miles to the center of
Temple. The inn is on the left, facing the town common.

Rhode Island

Block Island, Rhode Island

THE ATLANTIC INN

359 High Street, Block Island, Rhode Island. Mailing address: P.O. Box 188, Block Island, RI 02807. 401-466-2005. *Innkeeper:* Vincent J. Ryan. Open mid-May to mid-October.

The Atlantic Inn is a reminder of earlier days when summer resorts meant old wooden dragons of hotels with manicured grounds dotted with shuffleboard courts and croquet greens. Although not on that "grand" a scale, the Atlantic Inn is a nice size with a manageable twenty-eight rooms, a restaurant, and a parlor and is more a country inn than a resort hotel. It sits on one of Block Island's hills overlooking rolling meadows and the picturesque old harbor and village below. Built in 1880, the inn went into gradual decline as summer resorts went out of fashion, but in 1981 it was totally restored and renovated. Its halls and rooms were papered with floral prints highlighted by fresh trim paint and white curtains. To complete the Victorian atmosphere, antiques original to the inn were restored, and more were added. The third-floor rooms have old-fashioned sloping eaves and dormered windows; the spacious veranda is ideal for watching the sunsets. The restaurant's interesting menu stresses nouvelle cuisine. Vegetables from the inn's gardens are served, along with the island's fresh seafood as well as lamb, steaks, and veal dishes. Be sure to save room for the chef's rich desserts. There is a bar and wine list.

Accommodations: 26 rooms, 11 with private bath, and 1 family suite. *Pets:* Not permitted. *Driving Instructions:* Ferries leave from Point Judith and Providence, Rhode Island, and from New London, Connecticut. Flights are from Westerly, Rhode Island, or by charter.

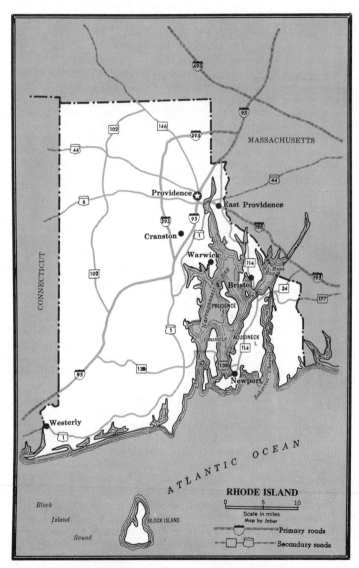

RHODE ISLAND

Scale in miles

0   5   10

Map by Jaber

━━━ Primary roads
━☐━ Secondary roads

MASSACHUSETTS

CONNECTICUT

Providence ⭐
East Providence

Cranston ●

Warwick ●

Bristol ●

PRUDENCE

Narragansett Bay

Mt. Hope Bay

CONANICUT

AQUIDNECK I.

Newport ●

Sakonnet River

Westerly ●

ATLANTIC OCEAN

Block

Island

Sound

BLOCK ISLAND

BLUE DORY INN

Dodge Street, Block Island, RI 02807. 401-466-2254. *Innkeepers:* Bob and Sandy Sherman. Open all year.

The Blue Dory Inn is a country Victorian charmer with Laura Ashley wallpapers, antique lace curtains that rustle in the sea breezes, period oak, walnut, and brass furnishings, and ocean views. On a knoll just 75 feet from Crescent Beach, a 3-mile stretch of sand and surf, the inn is a complex of weathered gray shingled buildings with shutters painted soft blue. Behind are three romantic hideaways: The Teahouse and Cottage, both efficiencies, and the aptly named Doll House, with a skylight over its Victorian bed. All rooms are furnished with Victorian pieces, and two upper rooms with skylights set into the sloping eaves offer ocean views from bed. Favorite spots with guests are the country kitchen and the parlor, which has camelback furnishings and a wood-burning stove. When we were there, a lively game of Trivial Pursuit was in progress at an old oaken table. In the morning the aroma of baking breads fills the kitchen, where Continental breakfasts are served. The Shermans recommend leaving your car on the mainland; the ferries dock just down the road and restaurants are within walking distance. Bike rentals are available next door.

Accommodations: 14 rooms with private bath. *Children under 10:* Not permitted. *Driving Instructions:* The inn is just up the hill from the ferry dock at the old harbor.

HOTEL MANISSES

Spring Street, Block Island, RI 02807. 401-466-2836 or 466-2421. *Innkeepers:* Joan and Justin Abrams. Open April 1 through January 1.

The Manisses, the showplace of Block Island when it opened in 1872, has entered its second century with a flourish—restored, renovated, and refurnished in Victorian splendor. The Abrams spared no effort getting the Manisses ready to receive guests once again. Its guest rooms are decorated with authentic Victorian hotel furnishings against the period wallpapers. With a bow to the comforts of the 1980s, the rooms have private baths; some even have Jacuzzis. The parlors glow with light from splendid stained-glass windows. Old-fashioned flower gardens can be seen from the windows here. High tea with sweets and savories is served in the afternoons at the hotel, where the Victorian atmosphere is enhanced by the authentic costumes worn by the staff. Included in the room rates are a buffet breakfast and wine and nibbles at cocktail hour.

Accommodations: 18 rooms with private bath. *Pets:* Not permitted. *Driving Instructions:* Block Island may be reached by ferry from Point Judith, Rhode Island, or New London, Connecticut.

Newport, Rhode Island

ADMIRAL BENBOW INN

93 Pelham Street, Newport, RI 02840. 401-846-4256. *Innkeeper:* Arlene McKenna. Open all year.

The Admiral Benbow, in the Historic Hill section of Newport, was built in 1855 by Augustus Littlefield, a mariner, and has been an inn ever since. Its freshly painted exterior is noteworthy for its tall, wide Romanesque windows. In restoring the Admiral Benbow, authentic Victorian colors and wallpapers were chosen. Following guidelines for historic preservation, the inn's exterior lines were not changed, but a number of private baths were tucked into guest rooms. All guest rooms have brass beds, except room 9, which has a canopied four-poster. All are furnished with a mixture of period reproduction pieces and antiques. Room 12, on the third floor, has its own deck and commands a fine view of the harbor.

In the morning a Continental breakfast is served that includes hot muffins and pastries, English jams, and beverages. The breakfast area is open all day, with hot coffee and tea available for guests. The inn offers off-street parking and is within walking distance of Bellevue Avenue and the bustling wharf area.

Accommodations: 15 rooms with private bath. *Pets and children under 11:* Not permitted. *Driving Instructions:* The inn is one block from Bellevue Avenue and two blocks from the wharf.

CAPTAIN SAMUEL RHODES GUEST HOUSE

3 Willow Street, Historic Point, Newport, RI 02840. 401-846-5486. *Innkeeper:* Pattie Murphy. Open all year.

Captain Samuel Rhodes, skipper of the schooner *Africa* before the Revolutionary War, made his fortune in the rum and slave trades. In 1740 he had a Colonial home built, complete with a secret tunnel to its "sacred grounds." Today the house has been beautifully restored and preserved. As an inn, the Rhodes House was awarded the coveted two pineapples of distinction for its hospitality by the city of Newport. Pattie Murphy lives at the inn and welcomes guests to her home with a get-acquainted cocktail. The house has fireplaces in most of the rooms—including two of the three guest rooms—wide-board pine flooring, and period antiques that reflect the age of the house. Coordinated bedspreads, dust ruffles, and curtains are used in each guest room, and bouquets of flowers are set out on the tables. A Continental breakfast is served to guests in the old "keeping" room, with its beehive oven. In summer the patio, a riot of color from the surrounding gardens, is a quiet place to sit and unwind. The Newport waterfront is just a few blocks away.

Accommodations: 3 rooms, 1 with private bath. *Pets and children:* Not permitted. *Driving Instructions:* Take the Newport Bridge to Newport, bear right to the first traffic light (Van Zandt Avenue), turn left onto Washington Street, proceed to Willow Street, and turn left.

INN AT CASTLE HILL

Ocean Drive, Newport, RI 02840. 401-849-3800. *Innkeeper:* Paul McEnroe. Open all year for bed and breakfast. The dining room is closed from December until just before Easter. Inquire first.

In 1874, Alexander Agassiz, son of the naturalist Louis Agassiz, built a fine summer home that would serve as a base for his studies in marine biology. The Woods Hole Marine Biological Laboratory eventually assumed the function of the Agassiz laboratory, and the property was later purchased by the O'Connell family, who still own it today. During World War II a local real estate agent persuaded Mr. O'Connell to rent rooms to young naval officers who could not find lodgings in crowded Newport. From that time the building's operation as an inn developed gradually. A public restaurant was added in 1950, and a separate shingled building added six rooms a few years

later. In the mid-1970s the inn was leased to Paul McEnroe, who redecorated all the rooms extensively.

The guest rooms, as well as the public rooms, have a refined country atmosphere. The flavor varies from print wallpapers and white wicker to the warmth of polished wood paneling. Besides the main inn, there are nineteen beach cottages, each with its own kitchen, which are rented by the week in the summer season. The shingled Harbour House, with more guest rooms, has been done in floral prints. Its porch is at the top of the cliff. A stairway leads down to a secluded bathing cove the family likes to call "Grace Kelly Beach." The stairs were built when the actress was a guest at the inn, to provide more privacy for her here than at the hotel's large sandy beach.

The dining rooms of the inn offer a wide sampling of Continental fare augmented by a selection of local seafood. Service is formal — appropriate to the Newport setting. There is live entertainment during the summer months, and the Sunday brunch draws a crowd, so be prepared to join in the activities.

Accommodations: 10 rooms in the inn, 7 with private bath. Rooms also in Harbour House and 19 cottages. *Pets:* Not permitted. *Driving Instructions:* From downtown Newport, follow all signs to Ocean Drive.

QUEEN ANNE INN

16 Clarke Street, Newport, RI 02840. 401-846-5676. *Innkeeper:* Peg McCabe. Open April to mid-November; thereafter, by special arrangement.

The Queen Anne Inn is a pretty Victorian town house in the heart of Newport's most historic district. The location is ideal for walking tours of the city; the inn is surrounded by tiny old Colonial houses and is just a short walk from the restored wharf area, with its many boutiques, antique shops, and waterfront restaurants. Built in 1890, the Queen Anne has a cheerful elegance, from its rose-and-pink Victorian exterior, through its oaken door with delicate flowers etched in its glass panes, to the bouquets of fresh flowers everywhere. When we were there, flowers adorned the staircase landings and were even placed on the washstands in the immaculate hall bathrooms. Innkeeper Peg McCabe has obviously had fun restoring and decorating her inn. The hardwood floors glisten with polish, and fresh floral wallpapers brighten the rooms and halls. The guest rooms are furnished with antiques and some newer pieces. Several rooms have large bay windows; one has heavy Victorian furnishings including a large armoire. Another has a quilt-topped four-poster.

Mornings find guests plotting the day's adventures in the parlor, where Peg puts out baskets of breads and sweet biscuits accompanied by pots of jam and butter, as well as coffee and tea, on the antique sideboard. Across the hall is a nook lit by a gem of a stained-glass window all lacy with pinks, blues, and greens. The Queen Anne has another bonus—off-street parking, quite a boon in this town of narrow side streets.

Accommodations: 12 rooms with 6 shared baths. *Pets:* Not permitted. *Driving Instructions:* Take the ramp from the Newport Bridge. Turn right on Farewell Street to Thames Street. Drive to Washington Square and Touro Street. Turn left on Touro, and take the first right onto Clarke Street.

WAYSIDE

Bellevue Avenue, Newport, RI 02840. 401-847-0302. *Innkeepers:* Dorothy and Al Post. Open all year.

If a visitor to Newport wants to experience the atmosphere of this elegant seaside resort, what better way than to stay in one of the large summer "cottages" on the famous mansion row along the cliff walk, high above the bay? Wayside is one such "cottage," a beige brick Georgian built in 1896. It is a favorite with members of syndicates that own America's Cup yachts. Al and Dorothy Post bought the mansion from Salve Regina College, which had used it as a dormitory, and created a guest house within the mansion, using lots of plants, comfortable furniture, and a variety of antiques and near antiques gathered at auctions and estate sales. All of this is set against dark paneled oak that rises to 15-foot-high ceilings. Elaborate fireplaces of marble and granite reinforce the sumptuous feeling of another era. A winding staircase leads upward from the entry hall to the guest rooms, each of which has its own sitting area. A favorite room has a marble hearth, a canopied bed of cherry wood, and wicker furniture in its sitting area. In warm weather it is enjoyable to sit on the veranda or the back porch, and there is a swimming pool for guests. A Continental breakfast is the only meal served. Wayside is just steps away from such famous Newport mansions as the Breakers, some of which are open to the public.

Accommodations: 8 rooms with private bath. *Pets:* Not permitted. *Driving Instructions:* Wayside is on Bellevue Avenue, between Parker Dixon and Narranset.

THE WILLOWS OF NEWPORT

8 Willow Street, Newport, RI 02840. 401-846-5486. *Innkeeper:* Pattie Murphy. Open all year.

The Willows, an elegant Newport bed-and-breakfast inn, was built in the early eighteenth century just three blocks from the waterfront. Pattie Murphy restored it in 1983, and it is now listed in the National Register of Historic Places. Its gardens are enclosed with cobblestones, and Pattie provides a private garage for guests' cars. The antique-filled rooms at the inn create an out-of-the-ordinary, fanciful vacation mood. The Victorian parlor, decorated in soft pinks, is where evening cocktails are served and where there is a wet bar for guests' use. The guest rooms have romantic solid brass canopied beds.

Pattie specializes in attention to detail, and guests returning at night find the beds turned down and the lights dimmed. In keeping with this pampering, breakfast arrives at bedside in the morning on trays set with bone china and sterling silver. The Willows is convenient to much that historic Newport has to offer.

Accommodations: 4 rooms with private bath. *Pets and children:* Not permitted. *Driving Instructions:* Take the Newport Bridge to Newport. Turn right at the first traffic light onto Van Zandt Avenue, then left onto Washington Street and left again onto Willow Street. The inn is on the right.

SHELTER HARBOR INN

U.S. 1, Shelter Harbor, Westerly, RI 02891. 401-322-8883. *Innkeepers:* Jim and Debbye Dey. Open all year.

Shelter Harbor Inn is set well back from the road, fronted by a large, grassy field. The inn was built as a farmhouse in the early nineteenth century and was converted to an inn in 1911. In 1978, innkeeper Jim Dey completed the conversion of the farm's barn into the inn annex with ten double rooms with baths, a large living room, and a redwood deck overlooking a secluded wooded area. The eight guest rooms in the old farmhouse are decorated with print wallpapers and old-fashioned country furnishings appropriate to the setting. Guests may use the inn's library.

The fields around the inn are filled with wild roses and blueberry and Juneberry bushes. Guests may use the inn's paddle-tennis facilities, and its private sandy beach is a short drive away.

Meals are served in the dining room, with its exposed beams, and in the garden room, cocktails in the sun parlor. The restaurant is open to the public for breakfast, lunch, and dinner, which features New England fare, including such specialties as finnan haddie, Rhode Island's ubiquitous johnnycake, and stuffed flounder.

Accommodations: 18 rooms with private bath. *Pets:* Not permitted. *Driving Instructions:* The inn is 5 miles east of Westerly, on U.S. 1.

Vermont

ARLINGTON INN

Arlington, VT 05250, 802-375-6532. *Innkeeper:* Ron Brunk. Open all year.

If you haven't been to the Arlington Inn in a few years, you are in for a real treat. This stately 1848 mansion has been renovated from stem to stern. Its long rows of columns and black shutters were given fresh coats of paint, and the interior woodwork was stripped and refinished to show off the no-expense-spared craftsmanship of the trim, stairways, wainscoting, and doors. The foyer sets the Victorian mood with potted plants, Oriental rugs, period antiques of walnut and mahoganies, and dark woodwork everywhere, even on the ceiling. The thirteen guest rooms are individually decorated in an authentic manner with heavy, dark carved wooden bedroom pieces set off by wallpapers of deep colors with miniature floral prints.

The dining rooms and the Deming Tavern downstairs — very popular spots with tourists, guests, and townsfolk — also feature Victorian pieces. The walls, decorated with Norman Rockwell prints, and the tables, attractively set with fresh linens and candles, blend to create a casually gracious feeling. Dinners feature a number of hot and cold appetizers, such as oysters Rockefeller, fettucine a' la Panna, or smoked salmon. Soups include cucumber and red onion or

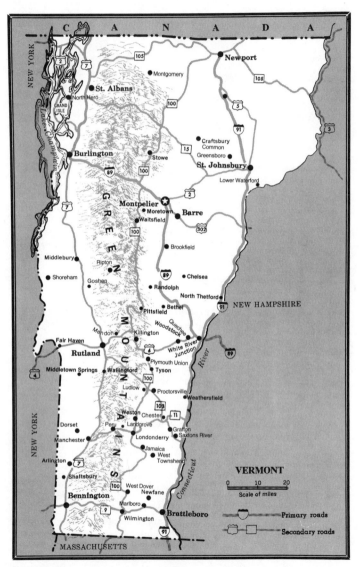

VERMONT

Scale of miles
0   10   20

Primary roads

Secondary roads

gazpacho, and among the salads are mushrooms and spinach or the Middle Eastern tabulee. Entrées are primarily steaks and chops from the grill, several fresh seafoods, and usually a vegetarian dish or two.

Guests enjoy exploring the inn, its well-maintained grounds, and even the ancient graveyard across the street. The front porch contains two of the largest rocking chairs we have ever seen. Guests who love the supernatural will be happy to learn that the Arlington has its own resident ghost, a fellow named Sylvester Deming. We've been assured that he is not troublesome and happens to be quite fond of children. Sylvester was the father of Martin Deming, "scion of a rich local family," who built the Arlington in 1848 for his family. Dad was so upset by the mansion's cost ($4,800) and ostentation that he tried unsuccessfully to destroy it. Sylvester died just after its completion, but his somewhat disgruntled spirit remains. He appears now and then and does nothing more than float about.

Accommodations: 13 rooms with private bath. *Pets:* Permitted only in the cottage units on the property. *Driving Instructions:* The inn is on Route 7 in Arlington.

WEST MOUNTAIN INN

Arlington, Vermont 05250. 802-375-6516. *Innkeepers:* Wes and Mary Ann Carlson. Open all year.

The West Mountain Inn, on a hill with spectacular views of the Battenkill River and the Green Mountains, is surrounded by 150 acres of woodland, meadow, and a spring-fed pond. It was originally a smaller farmhouse built in the late nineteenth century. During the 1920s, an affluent Texas couple enlarged the building for their summer home. They peaked the roof to form seven gables, built the spacious barn for their horses, and planted more than fifty species of evergreens, which along with maples, tower above the inn today. One of the barns is now a stoneware potter's studio.

On the main floor are the living area, plant room, lounge, and dining room. Meals are served by candlelight before an open hearth and feature New England country cuisine.

The bedrooms upstairs are individually decorated with authentic antiques, Colonial-style furniture, and homemade quilts. A bowl of fresh fruit is placed in each room. The African violet in each room is a gift from the innkeepers and may be taken home.

There are miles of wooded trails for hiking and quiet country roads for cycling. The Battenkill provides fly-fishing, swimming, and canoeing. In winter the estate offers wilderness cross-country skiing, as well as tobogganing and snowshoeing.

Accommodations: 12 rooms, 7 with private bath. *Pets:* Not permitted. *Driving Instructions:* The inn is ½ mile west of Arlington on Route 313.

WALLOOMSAC INN

67 Monument Avenue, Old Bennington, VT 05201. 802-442-4865.

Innkeeper: Martha Berry. Open Memorial Day through October.

We almost drove right by the Walloomsac Inn the first time we saw it. The building's exterior has been worn and weathered by time, and we were not even sure it was open. However, we knocked on the door and were warmly welcomed by innkeeper Martha Berry, who proceeded to show us through the inn that has been in her family for more than half a century. Inside, clean white curtains, polished pine floors, and antique furnishings belie the buildings exterior. Much of the inn looks as it must have when it was built before the Revolutionary War, although its furnishings date from the Victorian era. Elaborately carved highback Victorian beds are the rule, for example, and the historical mood is reinforced through the use of marble-topped dressers, Victorian mirrors, old photographs, and family memorabilia throughout the guest and public rooms. Fresh flowers add spots of color everywhere. At one time, the claim was made that meals had been served continuously at the inn since the War of Independence. However, gas rationing during World War II forced the closing of the kitchen, and although it resumed service after the war, it closed again in 1972, and no meals are now served here. Old Bennington is distinct and different from Bennington, the college town just down the hill. The preservationist movement is strong in this tiny hamlet with its picturesque village green, and dozens of beautifully restored, centuries-old homes are nearby.

Accommodations: 15 rooms with private or connecting bath. *Driving Instructions:* Take Route 9 west through Bennington to Old Bennington, where it becomes Monument Avenue.

Bethel, Vermont

GREENHURST INN

Bethel, VT 05032. 802-234-9474. *Innkeepers:* Lyle, Barbara, and
Claire Wolf. Open all year.

Greenhurst is a turreted, many-gabled mansion built in 1891 as a
private summer home for a wealthy Philadelphia family. Much of its
original elegance remains, including chandeliers hanging from high
ceilings and eight fireplaces, four of which are in guest rooms. It was
recently added to the National Register of Historic Places.

The inn, on 5 landscaped acres on the White River, is surrounded
by old lilacs and hydrangeas. After a day of antiquing or seasonal
recreation (the inn is quite near six major ski areas and Silver Lake), it
is a pleasure to curl up by the fire with a good book from the Wolfs'
library of more than three thousand volumes or join in songs after
dinner around the piano. Continental breakfast is included in the
room rates, and the Wolfs offer occasional evening meals for houseguests.

Accommodations: 12 rooms, 4 with private bath. *Driving Instructions:* Take Route 12 for ½ mile south from Bethel.

Brookfield, Vermont

GREEN TRAILS COUNTRY INN

By the Floating Bridge, Brookfield, VT 05036. 802-276-3412. *Innkeepers:* Betty and Jack Russell. Open all year.

Green Trails Country Inn stands near a lake and a floating bridge in the scenic Vermont village of Brookfield, established in 1820. The inn comprises two historic buildings — one built at the end of the eighteenth century and the other an 1840 farmhouse. The guest rooms are decorated with a variety of antiques from many periods and contain handmade quilts, fresh seasonal flowers, antique beds, and perhaps a Victorian settee or old-fashioned oil lamp.

The innkeepers serve family-style meals: a full Vermont breakfast complete with maple syrup from the trees across the lake, as well as dinners starting with homemade soups and including freshly baked breads, a single entrée, and desserts. For cross-country skiers, the inn offers 25 miles of marked trails through rolling terrain of pastures and woods. Instruction and ski rentals are available at the inn's ski-touring center.

Accommodations: 15 rooms. *Pets:* Not permitted. *Driving Instructions:* Bearing right at the fork on Route 66, follow Route 14 north for 6 miles to East Brookfield, then follow the sign to Floating Bridge and Green Trails (2 miles up to the Brookfield State Highway from Route 14).

Chelsea, Vermont

SHIRE INN

8 Main Street, Chelsea, VT 05038. 802-685-3031. *Innkeeper:* Jacqueline Arundell. Open all year.

Shire Inn is a striking brick Federal home built in 1832 and surrounded by 17 acres of peaceful Vermont land in a village of 900 people. The first branch of the White River flows through the property, which has its own private fishing bridge. The forest and back fields are ideal for cross-country skiing and hiking. One is immediately taken with the inn's "sunburst" doorway set back behind a tidy picket fence.

Inside, the original woodwork and old brass hardware are still in place after a century and a half. Wide spruce floorboards are set off by Oriental carpets. Throughout, the rooms are furnished with period antiques, many a legacy from earlier owners. A writing desk still stands in the hall, where it has been since 1866, and a spiral staircase leads to the guest rooms above. Four bedrooms have working fireplaces; two have four-poster beds; and one room has a canopied bed built in 1826. The inn serves breakfasts and candlelight dinners that stress regional produce (reservations required).

Accommodations: 6 rooms, 2 with private bath. *Pets and children under 10:* Not permitted. *Driving Instructions:* Take Route 110 to the center of Chelsea.

Chester, Vermont

THE HUGGING BEAR INN (and Shoppe)

Main Street, Chester, VT 05143. 802-875-2412. *Innkeepers:* Paul and Georgette Thomas. Open all year.

Hugging Bear Inn is special in many ways, the most obvious and endearing being bears — everywhere — bears peering out of tower attic windows and tucked into nooks and crannies of the inn and its much photographed Carriage House. Naturally all guests have teddy bears to hug for the night, and if they have been converted, there is a shop filled with bears of every shape and fuzziness in the attached barn.

The bare facts are that this inn is dedicated to the warmth and huggability of bears, but the Thomas's real goal is to promote hugs for humans. Georgette Thomas teaches classes in reevaluation counseling, a program to help people recover their full humanity. Both Georgette and Paul are excellent huggers, and naturally this inn is a friendly place decorated with comfortable family pieces, from antique to modern. The house was built in 1850, and its Victorian trappings such as the tower and Carriage House were added at the turn of the century. The inn is in the center of Chester overlooking the village green and an old cemetery. Out back are open fields and a little brook.

Accommodations: 6 rooms with private bath. *Pets:* Not permitted. *Driving Instructions:* Take exit 6 from I-91, then drive 10 miles west on Route 103, which becomes Route 11 in Chester.

THE OLDE TOWNE FARM INN

Route 10, Chester, Vermont. Mailing address: RD 4, Chester, VT 05143. 802-875-2346. *Innkeepers:* Fred and Jan Baldwin and family. Open all year except Thanksgiving and Christmas.

This 21-room white farmhouse on 11 acres of grounds is noted for its spiral staircase, a testimony to early craftsmanship. There are wide-board floors throughout, and the rooms are partially furnished with antiques.

The farm was built more than a century ago as the Chester Towne Farm. The indigent of the town were given food and lodging in return for a hard day's work there. A new brick patio overlooks the inn's spring-fed pond, used for swimming, fishing, and winter skating.

The inn is heated by a wood furnace whose fragrant smoke greets travelers during the winter. Meals at this inn vary from traditional Yankee-style to gourmet, featuring Jan's Roast Royale, Ham al Vermont, breast of chicken with cranberry glaze, quiches, and colonial desserts. In summer, Fred's garden provides spinach and lettuce and tomatoes for the salads.

The inn is part of the "Cycle Inn Vermont" program, and Fred and Jan will help plot out a tailored route.

Accommodations: 10 rooms, 2 with private bath. *Pets:* Not permitted. *Driving Instructions:* Take Route 103 north through Chester to Route 10. Turn east on Route 10 and drive ½ mile.

STONE HEARTH INN

Route 11, Chester, VT 05143. 802-875-2525. *Innkeepers:* Sharon and Andre Papineau. Open all year except Thanksgiving and Christmas.

The Stone Hearth Inn is a New England colonial farmhouse set behind stately pines. Built in 1810, it is one of Chester's oldest brick homes. The front porch overlooks the fields across the road and houses a collection of creaky rocking chairs and an old-fashioned porch swing. The farmhouse is attached to a big red barn. Upstairs a wing contains one particular bedroom with nooks and crannies and a dormer flanked by rough exposed logs, bark and all. The room is papered with a deep blue calico print, providing a backdrop for the exposed woods and brass bed. All of the guest rooms retain the period look with antique furnishings, exposed beams, rolling wide-plank pumpkin-pine floors, and low ceilings. Many of the beds are sturdy pine four-posters or brass and iron. The sloping eaves, print wallpapers, and scenic views add to the romance.

The centerpiece of the living room is the fieldstone fireplace. In back of the house are the dining room and sun porch with views of the stone walls and back field. Full country breakfasts are served to guests only. The inn is just minutes from eight of Vermont's major ski areas and many other recreational offerings, such as hiking, horseback riding, and fishing and rafting in mountain streams. It is part of the "Cycle Inn Vermont" tour for intermediate to experienced cyclists.

Accommodations: 8 rooms, 3 with private bath. *Pets:* Not permitted. *Driving Instructions:* The inn is a mile west of the green in Chester, on Route 11.

CRAFTSBURY INN

Craftsbury, VT 05826. 802-586-2848. *Innkeepers:* John and Susan McCarthy. Open all year.

The Craftsbury Inn is a handsome columned inn that was built as a private home about 1850 by Amasa Scott for his family. Scott spared no expense building a sturdy house that would stand the test of time well. He proudly installed one of the first central heating systems in the region.

One of the joys of visiting this inn derives from its abundance of original woodwork. Its tones have mellowed with the patina of the years, having been spared the coats of paint that so often were applied in other buildings. There are numerous built-in cabinets, handsome door and window trims, and random-width spruce floors.

Upstairs the guest rooms have an old-fashioned look, with Colonial wallpapers, flowers, hand-made quilts, and antique touches such as old wicker. Rooms in the front of the inn are sunny, with views of the surrounding mountains and the roofs of the houses of the tiny Vermont village.

The main dining room's picture windows overlook the gardens, which are illuminated at night. Every table is set with white linen and a bouquet of fresh flowers from the gardens. Specialties include fish quenelles, salmon with green sauce, and homemade ice creams. In winter Nordic skiers are given passes to the nearby ski center.

Accommodations: 10 rooms, 3 with private bath. *Pets:* Not permitted. *Driving Instructions:* Take Route 14 north of Hardwick for 7 miles to the turnoff for Craftsbury. Take the Craftsbury Road 2 miles to the town. The inn is on the main street, across from the general store.

Craftsbury Common, Vermont

THE INN ON THE COMMON

Main Street, Craftsbury Common, VT 05827. 802-586-9619. *Innkeepers:* Penny and Michael Schmitt. Open all year.

The Inn on the Common consists of three restored Federal buildings currently filled with a mixture of antiques and contemporary furniture. The Schmitts take great pride in their antiques, many of which are heirlooms, and in the extensive art work on the walls. Several guest rooms have working fireplaces. All are individually decorated with quilts, print wallpapers, and antiques. Two of the most popular bedrooms are in the annex and have Jotul wood-burning stoves, exposed beams, and bold colors contrasting with a Victorian loveseat and a brick hearth. A guest lounge with a fireplace contains a library of films on tape.

Guests eat together at three large tables under the watchful eyes of ancestral portraits. Meals feature vegetables and herbs grown in the inn's gardens and at the Schmitts' farm nearby accompanied by appropriate wines.

Behind the main house is a lighted formal rose garden and an herb garden, as well as an English-style croquet court, a bocce court, a clay tennis court, and a solar-heated swimming pool disguised as a pond. The Schmitts are affiliated with the nearby Craftsbury Sports Center,

where cross-country skiing is available on 50 miles of trails. Big Hosmer Pond offers boating and lake swimming in summer and skating in winter.

Accommodations: 18 rooms — 14 with private bath, 4 sharing 2 baths. *Driving Instructions:* Take Route 14 from the Montpelier-Barre area north to the village of Craftsbury Common. The inn is on the hill before the common.

Dorset, Vermont

BARROWS HOUSE

Dorset, VT 05251. 802-867-4455. *Innkeepers:* Charles and Marilyn Schubert. Open all year except November.

Barrows House is actually a collection of buildings in the center of Dorset. The inn's property includes a number of early buildings carefully renovated and redecorated by the Schuberts and offering a variety of accommodations. Ten of the guest rooms are in Barrows House, with the remainder in the other buildings. Larger families can stay in Truffle House, where they can share up to five rooms and a living room with a fireplace. The Stable has rooms with exposed beams and is one of the nicest sections of the inn. Most rooms have wall-to-wall carpeting, and many have coordinated drapes, quilts, and wallpaper.

The menu changes daily and features regional specialties and fresh vegetables.

Recreational facilities at Barrows House are excellent. Many cross-country skiers start right at the door (rentals are available at the inn's ski shop), and the inn has its own heated swimming pool, tennis courts, bicycle rentals, sauna, and gazebo for relaxing.

Accommodations: 29 rooms, 27 with private bath. *Pets:* Not permitted. *Driving Instructions:* From Route 7 in Vermont, take Route 30 northeast to Dorset.

DORSET INN

Church and Main streets, Dorset, VT 05251. 802-867-5500.
Innkeepers: Cissy Hicks and Gretchen Schmidt. Open all year.

The Dorset Inn is a beautiful old country inn, one of the oldest in the state. It stands, flanked by ancient sugar maples, at the edge of the town green. Worn slabs of Vermont marble form the inn's front porch where traditional granny rockers are set out. The inn was built in two sections, the first in 1796 and the later in 1850. It has recently undergone a major restoration by the new owners, Hanneke and Alex Koks, of the nearby Village Auberge. Now the low-ceiling reception parlor is decorated with country pine antiques set on polished pumpkin-pine floorboards. In the older section of the inn, the renovation process revealed lovely early stencilling, which has been preserved on one wall and duplicated on the others. Beyond this room is a parlor with a grouping of wing chairs and sofa surround the fireplace. On the pine-paneled mantel, a collection of old Willow pattern china is displayed. The inn's dining room, open guests and the public, is papered with a fresh blue-and-white pattern. Under the direction of chef-innkeeper Cissy Hicks, the dinner menu at the Dorset is refreshingly different, with recent offerings including breast of chicken with pear and cider cream, veal medallions with lime-ginger sauce, and fresh trout with lemon-curry butter. The inn's guest rooms have country antique furnishings and romantic print wallpapers.

Accommodations: 31 rooms with bath. *Pets:* Not permitted.
Driving Instructions: Take Route 30 to the center of Dorset and the inn.

THE LITTLE LODGE AT DORSET

Route 30, Dorset, VT 05251. 802-867-4040. *Innkeepers:* Allan and Nancy Norris. Open all year except for short spring and fall vacations.

This bed-and-breakfast country inn stands on a hillside overlooking its own trout pond. The building's white clapboarding stands out sharply against the greens of the pines on the wooded mountainside behind it. Twelve-over-twelve windows are topped by second-story "belly" windows, so named because one has to lie on one's belly to look out of them.

The Norrises opened their inn in 1981, and their enjoyment of this venture is clearly evident from the relaxed informality here. The inn is furnished with country antiques, while the guest rooms, with wide-board pine floors, are decorated with patchwork quilts and lots of calico.

A barnboard den has a bring-your-own-bottle wet bar, a fireplace, and wonderful mountain views through the picture windows. A light breakfast is served in the formal dining room or out on the porch. There is much to do right here, with ice skating and cross-country skiing on the grounds. Downhill skiing, tennis, and golf are nearby, and the Norrises will be happy to steer guests to a variety of restaurants in the area.

Accommodations: 5 rooms, 3 with private bath. *Pets:* Rarely permitted. *Driving Instructions:* Take Route 30 to Dorset. The inn is the sixth house north of the village green.

VILLAGE AUBERGE

Route 30, Dorset, Vermont. Mailing address: RD 1, Box 53, Dorset, VT 05251. 802-867-5715. *Innkeepers:* Alex and Hanneke Koks. Open May through October and December through March.

Village Auberge is an old clapboard Vermont farmhouse with a full-fledged European restaurant complete with formal table settings and a menu interesting and extravagant enough for the fussiest gourmet. Chef-owner Alex Koks is from Holland, where he trained at a hotel school in The Hague and operated several restaurants before coming to Vermont. The dining room is decorated with distinction, as is the rest of the house, thanks to Hanneke Koks's training as an interior decorator and fashion designer. The dining room with its large bay window can seat about fifty guests. Just off the dining room is an

intimate cocktail lounge papered with antique newspapers found in a forgotten corner of the attic.

The six guest rooms are individually done with miniature-print wallpapers and comfortable antique and contemporary furnishings. Each has its own private bath. Downstairs, the sitting room has a fireplace and lots of reading material, including magazines and books from Holland. The inn's lawns are shaded by maples, and there is an old-fashioned porch to relax on and view the Vermont scenery. Out back, by the kitchen door, is a very European herb garden. Hanneke operates a small antique shop in one of the outbuildings here.

Village Auberge is ideally located in the heart of southern Vermont. It is minutes away from the Dorset Playhouse, tennis courts, golf, and swimming. In winter three large ski areas, Bromley, Stratton, and Magic Mountain, are a short drive away, and cross-country skiing is available very near to the inn.

Accommodations: 6 rooms with private bath. *Pets:* Not permitted. *Driving Instructions:* The inn is 6 miles north of Manchester on Route 30.

East Dover, Vermont

COOPER HILL LODGE

Cooper Hill Road, East Dover, Vermont. Mailing address: P.O. Box 146, East Dover, VT 05341. 802-348-6333. *Innkeepers:* Ray and Shirley Parris. Open all year.

Cooper Hill Lodge began as a mountaintop farmhouse in the early nineteenth century. Wings, porches, and various other additions over the years have transformed the building into a sprawling country inn. The rambling white clapboard lodge stands on 18 acres at an elevation of 2,300 feet, with views of Vermont and New Hampshire mountains in the distance. No traffic noises break the peace and quiet here on the mountain, and the woods are crisscrossed by old logging trails, which are ideal for hiking or cross-country skiing. The inn is bright and cheerful, with early-American antiques in all the rooms. The innkeepers, Ray and Shirley Parris, keep things tidy but casual and informal. Meals are served family style and are available to house guests and, with advance notice, the public. The Parrises enjoy arranging and catering weddings, and indeed, the setting has inspired several couples each year to get married at the lodge.

Accommodations: 13 rooms with private bath. *Driving Instructions:* From Wilmington take Route 100 north toward West Dover and follow signs to Cooper Hill Lodge 5 miles off Route 100 in East Dover.

Fair Haven, Vermont

VERMONT MARBLE INN

12 West Park Place, Fair Haven, VT 05743. 802-265-8144. *Innkeeper:* Jerry Henkel. Open all year.

In 1867, Ira C. Allen built a mansard-roofed home faced with yellow marble hewn in Proctor, Vermont. The inn's exterior is made even more distinctive by the sets of paired columns that wrap around two sides of the inn. The Vermont Marble Inn, which faces the village green, is surrounded by 5 acres of grounds including stately trees, gardens, stone walls, and the river.

Both the public and guest rooms have been restored using warm colors and an eclectic blend of antique and occasional modern pieces. There are seven working carved marble fireplaces, including three in guest rooms. The wicker breakfast room is light, with plants in every corner. The dining room is open daily to guests and the public for all three meals, with a combination of American and Continental dishes.

The inn's guest rooms have brass and iron or high-backed wooden beds, antique quilts and crocheted coverlets, and rocking or easy chairs. Also on the grounds is a brick and slate carriage house, which serves in warmer months as a gallery of antiques and crafts.

Accommodations: 10 rooms, some with private baths. *Driving Instructions:* Take Route 4 to Route 22A and drive south 1 mile to the village green.

Goshen, Vermont

BLUEBERRY HILL

Goshen, VT 05733. 802-247-6735. *Innkeeper:* Tony Clark. Open all year except November and April.

Many people first find Blueberry Hill during the ski season; for it is as a cross-country ski center that the inn has gained most of its fame. Thirty miles of groomed trails, a complete retail and rental ski shop, and an expert staff keep the inn's guest rooms full all winter. Each of these rooms is fitted out with numerous antiques and with homemade quilts. By evening the inn fills with the tantalizing aroma of a dinner that might center around a dish such as blueberry Cassis roast duck or boursin veal birds. Breakfast is often served in the inn's greenhouse.

During the skiing season, the innkeeper organizes waxing clinics, ski seminars, night tours, and inn-to-inn ski tours. In the warmer months, the inn continues to welcome guests who appreciate the quiet of its mid-Vermont location. The inn is host to Vermont croquet and volleyball championships.

Accommodations: 8 rooms with private bath. *Pets:* Not permitted. *Driving Instructions:* Take Route 73 east of Brandon, and follow signs to the inn, north of Route 73.

Grafton, Vermont

THE OLD TAVERN AT GRAFTON

Grafton, VT 05146. 802-843-2231. *Innkeeper:* Lois Copping. Open all year except Christmas Eve, Christmas Day, and April.

The Old Tavern at Grafton is by far the most impressive piece of restoration as yet performed by the craftsmen at the disposal of the Windham Foundation. The Old Tavern, an imposing, shuttered, brick-and-clapboard white building, is distinguished by its seven two-story columns. The main inn, noted for its fine paneling, pumpkin-pine floors, and collection of antiques, is joined by a breezeway to the original barn, which now serves as the lounge for the inn's guests. Its exposed beams and ample use of board paneling give the barn a warm feeling.

The Old Tavern is our candidate for the most perfectly re-created inn in the northeast. Here no detail has been overlooked. This feeling of perfection, of every panel perfectly painted, of every piece of furniture perfectly placed, gives the inn a formality that would not appeal to those seeking the casual atmosphere of some Vermont inns. This is no feet-on-a-stool-in-front-of-the-fire inn, nor does it intend to be. This is an inn that makes few mistakes.

Fourteen guest rooms are in the Old Tavern building, and the remainder are in an assemblage of two old houses and a barn directly across the street. Known as the Homestead and the Windham Cottage, this complex also has function rooms that host meetings of business groups from all over New England. Each guest room has a collection of antiques including canopied or four-poster beds, interesting rugs, and comfortable furniture.

The inn has a natural swimming pond, tennis courts, and indoor-games rooms. There are well-marked hiking trails and, nearby, horseback riding and golf. Several miles of cross-country ski trails are maintained by the inn, and they can provide snowshoes, sleds, and toboggans for winter guests. Lunch and dinner are served at the inn for guests and the public, and breakfast is served for guests only. The menu has surprises like cold blueberry soup or cheese-and-bacon pie to augment some of its more standard items.

Woodrow Wilson, Theodore Roosevelt, General Ulysses Grant, Henry David Thoreau, Oliver Wendell Holmes, and Rudyard Kipling have all stayed at the Old Tavern. This is an extraordinarily well-thought-out inn for those guests who enjoy the ambience of this very special place. The secret is long since out, so plan to make reservations early. Families with children and pets are placed in one of several guest houses maintained by the Old Tavern.

Accommodations: 35 rooms and 5 guest houses, all with private bath. *Pets and children:* Permitted in guest houses only. *Driving Instructions:* Take Route I-91 to exit 5, then Route 121 to Grafton.

WOODCHUCK HILL FARM

Middletown Road, Grafton, VT 05146. 802-843-2398. *Innkeepers:* Anne and Frank Gabriel. Open May through October.

Woodchuck Hill Farm is the oldest house in Grafton, built about 1780. Originally built for the town's first minister, the inn has been completely restored. During the 1930s, a porch and other additions were built. On a hilltop with outstanding views, the inn is a comfortable place where the guests are joined in a family spirit. The living room has a big fireplace with a fire going on cooler days. In summer the large porch is a favorite gathering place before dinner.

In addition to the guest rooms in the main house, the Gabriels have created two new guest facilities: A studio apartment overlooking the fields and woods has its own entrance, kitchen, and large sliding-glass door opening onto a deck. The barn apartment, with a loft

bedroom, a large living room, and a modern kitchen with a wood stove, overlooks the apple orchard and farm pond where guests enjoy swimming, canoeing, and sunbathing in summer.

Each evening the Gabriels prepare a single-entrée meal served family-style with all the guests at a single large table. A recent dinner included Tomato Vintage, a spiced tomato bouillon; home-baked bread and muffins; pickled beets and caponata, a salad of home-grown greens; a mixed grill of filet mignon, loin lamb chop, kidney, sausage, and tomato served with mushrooms; and fresh vegetables and roast potatoes.

Although liquor is not served at the inn, setups are furnished with cheese and crackers in the lounge or porch area. The Gabriels also have an antique shop in a nearby outbuilding.

Accommodations: 6 rooms in the main house, 3 with private bath, and 2 apartments with kitchens. *Pets:* Not permitted. *Children:* Under eight not permitted. *Driving Instructions:* The inn is 2 miles west of Grafton on Middletown Road.

HIGHLAND LODGE

Craftsbury Road, Greensboro, VT 05841. 802-533-2647. *Innkeepers:* David and Wilhelmina Smith. Open Memorial Day weekend to mid-October and December to April.

The Highland Lodge is a wide, two-story lakefront inn with a full-length porch. Most of the inn dates from 1926, although one part was a farmhouse for a sheep farm before that. Nonhousekeeping cottages were added to the 180-acre property on Caspian Lake.

The lodge's public rooms include a large dining room with wood-burning stove, a pine-paneled breakfast room with hand-braided rugs, and several sitting rooms including a library with grand piano and grandfather clock. One of the nicest rooms in the main lodge takes up the entire end of the house. It has two new brass beds, carpeting, traditional mahogany furniture, and striped floral wallpaper.

At dinner the menu includes veal, seafood, chicken, pork, and locally raised lamb.

At the lakefront there is a private sandy beach where a beach house affords guests a place to change their clothes and enjoy the fireplace when engaging in cookout grills and other lake activities. The inn has a complete cross-country ski center with 30 miles of trails.

Accommodations: 11 rooms in the lodge, all with private bath; 12 cottages, each with 2 bedrooms, living room–kitchen, and fireplace. *Pets:* Not permitted. *Driving Instructions:* Take Route 15 to Route 16 (east of Hardwick), where you turn north. Take Route 16 to East Hardwick and follow the signs to Caspian Lake.

Jamaica, Vermont

THREE MOUNTAIN INN

Route 30, Jamaica, VT 05343. 802-874-4140. *Innkeepers:* Elaine
and Charles Murray. Open all year except April.

Three Mountain Inn is a small inn built in the late eighteenth century.
The white clapboard house with its original twelve-over-twelve windows and big center chimney has been carefully restored by the
Murrays, and there is nothing they like better than showing off their
handiwork. The living room's wide-planked floors and walls and its
original Dutch-oven fireplace set the colonial tone. Some of these
planks are the widest we have seen. A long, low sofa before the hearth
is the favorite spot for before- and after-dinner drinks. Beyond this
low-ceilinged room are the dining room and library, both used as
dining rooms. They are candlelit at dinner and, on chilly evenings,
have fires in their hearths. The library is well stocked with reading
materials to help while away the wintry Vermont evenings. The inn's

main entrance is through the low back door that opens directly into a little pub-lounge.

The guest rooms in the inn's wing are decorated with antiques and print wallpapers on one wall contrasting with stripes and floral prints on another. These rooms are unique, fashioned from the inn's former stable, whose old beams can still be seen. Upstairs in the main house is the "honeymoon suite." The third floor contains a family bunk room.

The dining rooms, open to guests and public alike, offer a menu that changes frequently. Elaine Murray's specialties are her vegetable quiche, a variety of hearty soups, and her desserts. Entrées usually include a fresh seafood dish and perhaps a beef Stroganoff or a chicken Jacques with a garlicky sour cream sauce. The evening we were there, fresh scallops, blue fish, and rainbow trout were on the menu. A selection of wines is available. For breakfast, you can choose a light Continental style with fresh-from-the-oven muffins, dough-nuts, or rolls; or you can take the heartier country route with locally smoked bacon or ham, pancakes with Vermont maple syrup, and eggs.

Accommodations: 10 rooms, 8 with private bath. *Pets:* Not per-mitted. *Driving Instructions:* Take I-91 to Brattleboro, second exit; then take Route 30 to Jamaica's Main Street.

Killington, Vermont

THE VERMONT INN

Route 4, Killington, VT 05751. 802-773-9847. *Innkeepers:* Judy and Alan Carmasin. Open all year except May and three weeks in November.

The Vermont Inn began life in the early nineteenth century as a farmhouse. It is set on an open rise of land overlooking the high peaks of the Green Mountains. Off to one side a woodland stream rushes past. Judy and Alan Carmasin have extensively renovated the farmhouse-inn, recently adding wall-to-wall carpeting in many of the rooms and polishing the hardwood floors in others. Today the inn's rooms have a contemporary look that sets off its antiques and green plants, which grow just about everywhere.

Just off the living room–lobby is the inn's cocktail lounge; beyond that, in what was formerly the barn, is the popular wood-paneled dining room. Here guests and the public dine by candlelight, warmed by a fire in the large fieldstone fireplace — the focal point of the room. The menu of New England and Continental cuisine features veal and fresh seafood that is trucked in from the New England coast. In addition to the full-service bar there is a well-thought-out wine list.

A swimming pool, a sauna, and an all-weather tennis court are available at the inn for guests' recreation, and the Killington and Pico ski areas are just across the highway.

Accommodations: 14 rooms, 8 with private bath. *Pets and cigars:* Not permitted. *Driving Instructions:* The inn is set back off Route 4, 6 miles east of Rutland and 4 miles west of Killington.

NORDIC INN

Route 11, Landgrove, VT 05148. 802-824-6444. *Innkeepers:* The Acton family. Open all year except April.

The Nordic Inn is a converted New England residence built in 1940 and now housing a small inn with a taste of Scandinavia. There are three fireplaces in public rooms, as well as one bedroom with its own fireplace. The innkeepers added a new ski shop, using rough-sawn lumber milled from trees cut on their own property. The cross-country ski area now has 12 miles of trails. Equipment rentals and instruction are available. Although cross-country skiing is the focus of many guests in the winter, the proximity of several fine downhill areas brings other skiers as well.

The inn is equally popular in the warmer months among those who seek the rural beauty of this area. In all seasons, guests are drawn to the inn to sample dinners prepared with an unmistakable Swedish touch, with a number of French specialties as well.

Each guest room is decorated differently. They were named Sweden, Norway, Finland, Denmark, and Vermont. If you want the room with the fireplace, ask to stay in Sweden. The lower level of the inn contains a fully licensed après-ski tavern.

Accommodations: 5 rooms, 3 with private bath. *Pets:* Not permitted. *Driving Instructions:* The inn is between Londonderry and Peru on Route 11.

Londonderry, Vermont

THE VILLAGE INN

RFD Landgrove, Londonderry, VT 05148. 802-824-6673. *Innkeepers:* Jay and Kathy Snyder. Open December 20 through March and late June through October 20.

The first part of the Village Inn was constructed in 1810 and has had various additions over the years. The most recent was made in 1976. The result is a series of low, interconnected buildings, mostly of clapboard, that has come to serve as a small resort rather than a country inn. On the property are private tennis courts, a heated outdoor pool, and a three-hole pitch-and-putt golf course. Inn guests who enjoy cross-country skiing can use trails that originate there, while downhill skiers have only short drives to Bromley, Stratton, Magic Mountain, Snow Valley, or Okemo. There is a Rafter Room Cocktail Lounge, a whirlpool spa, and a new game room. Guests can enjoy hayrides and sleigh rides for which the inn has horses.

The guest rooms are large, with curtains, comforters, and an old-fashioned look. Of the twenty rooms available, fourteen have private baths. Dinners at the inn are simple affairs featuring such main courses as roast beef with Bordelaise sauce or a seafood dish. Fresh breads and rolls are baked daily in the kitchen. The dining room is open to the public for breakfast and dinner.

Accommodations: 20 rooms, 14 with private bath. *Pets:* Not permitted. *Driving Instructions:* From Manchester, take Route 11 past the Bromley ski area and turn left into Peru. At the fork in Peru bear left and continue 4½ miles through the national forest to the crossroads in Landgrove. Turn left toward Weston; the inn is on the right.

Lower Waterford, Vermont

RABBIT HILL INN

Lower Waterford, VT 05848. 802-748-5168. *Innkeepers:* Eric and
Beryl Charlton. Open all year, except April and November.

The four large, hand-hewn Doric columns that support the front
porch of the Rabbit Hill give it a somewhat imposing look that is
quickly forgotten within the relaxed atmosphere of the inn. The property consists of a main inn built in 1827 and enlarged about fifteen
years later to its present size. It has always served as an inn, except for
a short period when it was used as a private home. In its early days it
served the active logging community in the area.

Guests who stay in this inviting inn can choose their accommodations according to their preference for more contemporary or old-
fashioned surroundings. The guest rooms in the main house are
upstairs off a sitting area. The "Briar Patch," built as a tavern in
1795, currently houses a cross-country ski center below and some old-
fashioned guest rooms above. In the mid-1850s an annex was constructed containing a ballroom that has since been subdivided into a
number of rooms.

Everywhere one looks — in nooks and crannies, on antique end
tables, and scattered on shelves and windowsills — are rabbits:
ceramic, wooden, every sort of rabbit. A Defiant wood stove warms
the sitting room–lobby and one of the dining rooms, while another
dining room has a working fireplace hung with brass and copper
buckets. Breakfasts and Continental menus at dinner are available to
guests and the public.

Accommodations: 20 rooms with private bath. *Driving Instructions:* The inn is on Route 18 between St. Johnsbury, Vermont, and
Littleton, New Hampshire.

Ludlow, Vermont

BLACK RIVER INN

100 Main Street, Ludlow, VT 05149. 802-228-5585. *Innkeepers:*
Rosemary Krimbel and John Garton. Open all year except April.
Black River Inn is a large red-brick Vermont farmhouse with a fanlight over the front entry and white trim highlighting the windows. A
side porch overlooks the Black River and not-too-distant Okemo
mountain. The house was built in 1835, and a family annex was attached in 1859. Modern conveniences came early to the house with the
introduction of electricity in 1893; the original fixtures are still in use.
Ludlow's very first indoor bath was the talk of the town and can be
seen here today, its solid copper tub trimmed in oak. Rosemary and
John scoured the countryside looking for suitable antique fixtures for
the newly installed bathrooms. Rooms are furnished with Victorian
antiques and a few overstuffed upholstered pieces for comfort. The
floors are left bare to show off the unusual pattern of alternating
maple and black cherry woods set in concentric squares. If guests
wish, breakfasts are served in bed on trays set with antique china and
silver. The guest rooms have a variety of Victorian beds in ash, oak,
and brass with painted iron. The family annex is a two-bedroom suite
with private bath for guests traveling with children, and for this
reason there are no antiques used in these rooms.
Accommodations: 6 rooms, 2 with private bath, and a family annex
with 2 rooms and private bath. *Pets:* Not permitted. *Driving Instructions:* Take I-91 to exit 6 (Route 103). Take Route 103 west to Ludlow.

THE COMBES FAMILY INN

RFD 1, Ludlow, Vermont. Mailing address: Box 275 TC, Ludlow, VT 05149. 802-228-8799. *Innkeepers:* Ruth and Nancy Combes. Open all year except April 15 to May 15.

As the name indicates, this is a true family inn on a quiet country back road in the heart of Vermont's mountains and lakes region. There are 50 acres of rolling meadows and woods to explore and to ski cross-country in winter. Cupcake and Brownie, reported to be the friendliest goats around, share the farm with lots of equally friendly cats, dogs, innkeepers, and guests. The inn itself is a century-old farmhouse that the Combeses have recently renovated. The dining room has exposed beams and a big bay window overlooking pastures and Okemo Mountain. The lounge area is paneled in Vermont barnboards and is furnished with turn-of-the-century oak. Cocktails (bring your own bottle), card games, and conversation are the specialties here.

There are five guest rooms in the old farmhouse, one with a private bath. Five other guest rooms in an attached motel unit come with private baths. The Vermont-style meals here consist of cream soups, turkey, lamb, or pork roasts, fresh vegetables, and home-baked breads and desserts.

Accommodations: 10 rooms, 6 with private bath. *Pets:* Not permitted. *Driving Instructions:* From Ludlow, proceed north on Route 103 to Route 100 North. Follow state signs for the inn.

THE GOVERNOR'S INN

86 Main Street, Ludlow, VT 05149. 802-228-8830. *Innkeepers:*
Charlie and Deedy Marble. Open all year except a short time in
spring.

One enthusiast for the town of Ludlow was Governor William
Stickney. His farm was in Tyson, 10 miles away, and at the turn of the
century he decided to build a townhouse for himself on Ludlow's
main street. Today his house has been restored and converted into the
Governor's Inn.

The inn's intricately carved oak woodwork exemplifies the attention paid to every detail. Furnishings in each guest room include Vermont country antiques and pieces from the Marble family collection.

The highlights of the inn's interior are its handsome woodwork
and the marbleized-slate fireplace mantels that display an art that is
virtually lost and is certainly worth seeing. The inn's six-course dinners often start with one of Deedy's unusual soups, such as blueberry
Chablis soup, and end with the dessert of the day, which might be
apricot Victorian or chocolate walnut pie. The Marble's teenage
daughter, Alison, bakes all the inn's breads including a tasty strawberry tea bread; and Deedy will pack picnic baskets for guests.

Accommodations: 8 rooms, 6 with private bath. *Pets:* Not permitted. *Children:* Under twelve not permitted. *Driving Instructions:*
Take Route I-91 to exit 6 (Route 103) to Ludlow and the inn.

THE OKEMO INN

R.F.D. #1, Box 133, Ludlow, VT 05149. 802-228-8834. *Innkeepers:* Ron and Toni Parry. Open all year.

The Okemo Inn is an 1810 Vermont home that was a private residence in the nineteenth century. It became the Locust Hill Inn in the early 1900s and has had its present name since 1962. The inn's interior is distinguished by hand-hewn beams, wide-board pine flooring, and a diversified collection of Vermont antiques. Two of the eight fireplaces still function, offering warmth and atmosphere in the cooler seasons. Meals at the Okemo Inn, available in summer, fall, and winter, are served family style with a single entrée prepared each evening. Meals often start with homemade soup and fresh salad and end with a freshly baked dessert. Dishes that are favorites include roast beef, chicken saltimbocca, and pork schnitzel. The inn has a fully licensed lounge. A parlor affords a place for quiet reading and games and has a fireplace. The only television set is in what the Parrys call their "Public Room."

Among the inn's more modern amenities are its large coed sauna room and an outdoor pool for summer guests. The area has many recreational attractions in all seasons. Most winter guests are drawn to the Okemo Inn because the Okemo Mountain Ski Area, with its twenty-two trails and nine major lifts, is virtually in the inn's backyard. Cross-country skiing trails start from the inn's door, and major Nordic skiing centers are nearby.

Accommodations: 12 rooms, 10 with private bath. *Pets:* Not permitted. *Driving Instructions:* Take Route I-91 north to exit 6 (Route 103). Take Route 103 for 23 miles northwest to Ludlow. The inn is 1½ miles north of the village.

Manchester, Vermont

BIRCH HILL INN

West Road, Manchester, VT 05254. 802-362-2761. *Innkeepers:* Jim and Pat Lee. Open late December to early April and late May to late October.

Built in 1790, with an addition dating from just after the turn of the century, Birch Hill has been part of innkeeper Pat Lee's family since 1917. The family large, homey New England house was a family summer home until Pat and Jim bought it and transformed it to a country inn in 1981. Its spacious, sunny rooms contain woodburning stoves and fireplaces as well as the Lee's many antiques and houseplants. The living room, with its extensive library, opens onto a marble terrace that offers panoramic views of the Green Mountains. The living room is a popular spot in the evening.

Guest rooms are decorated with antiques and have exposed-beam ceilings. Meals are served family style near the big wood stove.

The grounds, with vegetable and flower gardens and a trout pond, are surrounded by beautifully crafted stone walls and fences; 15 kilometers of cross-country skiing trails begin at the inn and wind through open fields and peaceful woods.

Accommodations: 5 rooms, 3 with private bath, and a summer cottage. *Pets:* Not permitted. *Children:* Under six not permitted. *Driving Instructions:* West Road joins U.S. 7 to the south and Vermont 30 to the north.

THE 1811 HOUSE

On the Green, Manchester, Vermont. Mailing address: Box 39, Manchester Village, VT 05254. 802-362-1811. *Innkeepers:* Mary and Jack Hirst. Open all year.

The 1811 House is a New England frame home built in the 1770s. It has operated as an inn since 1811, except for the years from 1905 to 1935, when it was the home of Mary Lincoln Isham, granddaughter of Abraham Lincoln. Mary and Jack Hirst, after buying the inn in 1982, completely restored it and furnished it in keeping with its Federal-period origin. Inside, the rooms were totally repainted, papered, and decorated with a collection of English and early-American antiques, paintings, some canopied beds, and Oriental rugs. The house has eight working fireplaces, including three in guest rooms and one in the dining room, where a full English-style breakfast is served. The lawn and gardens behind the inn afford views of the Equinox Golf Course and the Green Mountains.

Accommodations: 10 rooms with private bath. *Children:* Under sixteen not permitted. *Driving Instructions:* The inn is on Route 7A in Manchester Village, a mile south of Manchester Center.

RELUCTANT PANTHER INN

West Road, Manchester Village, VT 05254. 802-362-2568. *Innkeepers:* Ed and Loretta Friihauf. Open Memorial Day to early November and early December to early April.

The Reluctant Panther Inn was fashioned out of a clapboard home built in 1850. It is well landscaped and is painted in the unusual hues of mauve and purple. The decor inside, equally daring, shows a decorator's flair. The public rooms blend modern and antique furnishings. One dining room is a greenhouse with healthy plants everywhere, another has a Colonial motif, and the third has a display of wood carvings from old furniture. The cocktail lounge is a good place to relax on chilly evenings when innkeeper Ed Friihauf lights a fire in its hearth. The dining rooms are open to the public. Hors d'oeuvres include broiled trout and bacon-wrapped asparagus with Vermont cheddar cheese sauce. Nine entrées include roast loin of smoked pork, duckling à l'orange, and trout stuffed with shrimp and crabmeat.

The bedroom decor is imaginative. Some rooms have carpeting that continues up the wall. Six feature working fireplaces, and all have color television, room phones, and oversize bath towels.

Accommodations: 10 rooms with private bath. *Pets and children:* Not permitted. *Driving Instructions:* The inn is in the center of Manchester Village, about 20 miles north of Bennington and just off Route 7A.

Manchester Center, Vermont

MANCHESTER HIGHLANDS INN

Highland Avenue, Manchester Center, Vermont. Mailing address: P.O. Box 1754, Manchester Center, VT 05255. 802-362-4565. *Innkeepers:* Harry and Donna Williams, Marge and Connie Bellestri. Open all year.

This attractive Victorian inn with its gingerbread-trim and fanciful tower was built in 1898 and is on the crest of a hill overlooking a valley and the mountains beyond. The slightly older Carriage House, connected to the inn by a tunnel, served as a mill during the construction of the main house and now contains four guest rooms above a game room that offers table tennis, pool, and a putting green. Homey, comfortable upholstered furniture mingles with family antiques and mementoes collected by the two generations of Bellestris at the inn. Guests may relax and visit in several common rooms, including the library, where beverages and freshly baked goodies are set out. The bar, the Remedy Room, has comfortable chairs and an old piano by the stone hearth. The candlelit dining room is open to the public for dinner. Marge and daughter Donna prepare single-entrée meals, often featuring family Italian recipes—lasagna, baked Italian sausage and peppers—or simple country fare such as pork chops baked in cider or chicken pot pie with corn bread topping. A full breakfast that often includes waffles or pancakes is served to overnight guests.

Accommodations: 13 rooms, 11 with private bath. *Pets:* Not permitted. *Driving Instructions:* From Route 7A, turn east onto Route 11 and 30. Drive about ¾ mile and turn left onto Highland Avenue.

Marlboro, Vermont

LONGWOOD INN

Route 9, Marlboro, Vermont. Mailing address: Box 86, Marlboro, VT 05344. 802-257-1545 and 802-257-7272. *Innkeepers:* Thomas and Janet Durkin. Open all year.

The Longwood Inn was already getting along in years as a dairy farmhouse when the Revolutionary War broke out. The clapboard inn was built in 1729 and, in addition to serving the milk-drinking public, spent a few years as a dormitory for nearby Marlboro College. The restored building now welcomes travelers. Two of the nine guest rooms feature wood-burning fireplaces that are still in use. Throughout the inn hearths are kept going twenty-four hours a day in the winter months. There are two sitting rooms for guests. The grounds contain an old red barn that houses a summer theater, and a carriage house that has been converted into four studio apartments. The farm pond is a perfect spot for fishing or swimming in summer or for skating on when the ice isn't covered with a foot of snow. The land is crisscrossed with horse trails for hiking and jogging, and Alpine skiing is just minutes away at three major sites. In 1961 an addition was built to house the inn's restaurant, which specializes in Italian food.

Accommodations: 9 rooms, 7 with private bath, and 4 studio apartments. *Pets and children:* Not permitted. *Driving Instructions:* Take I-91 north to exit 2 at Brattleboro. Take Route 9 to Marlboro, approximately 10 miles. The inn will be on the right.

Mendon, Vermont

RED CLOVER INN

Woodward Road, Mendon, VT 05701. 802-775-2290. *Innkeepers:*
Dennis and Bonnie Rae Tallagnon. Open Thanksgiving to mid-
April and mid-June to mid-October.

The Red Clover Inn, named for the Vermont state flower, is a small
farm whose main lodge was built about 1840. In 1923 the property
was bought by General J. E. Woodward of Washington, D.C., who
dreamed of creating a miniature working farm. It is in a hidden mountain valley just minutes from Killington and Pico.

The inn today consists of the lodge, a separate carriage house now
called the Plum Tree House, and the farm barn. In the main lodge a
dining room has views of the distant hills. Here, and in a second
room, Dennis's Continental meals are served.

Bonnie Rae painstakingly restored each of the inn's guest rooms,
some of which are in the main inn and some in the Plum Tree House.
The old-fashioned rooms in the inn have print wallpapers and are furnished with a mixture of antiques including brass beds and old desks.
Some of the rooms in the inn share hall bathrooms with old-fashioned
tubs. Rooms in the Plum Tree House are more spacious —
several are suites — and done in a more modern decor. Recent additions include a tennis court and a billiard room.

Accommodations: 15 rooms, 11 with private bath. *Pets and children under 5:* Permitted in the Plum Tree House only. *Driving Instructions:* From Rutland, take Route 4 east for 5.2 miles; turn right
on Woodward Road.

Middlebury, Vermont

THE MIDDLEBURY INN

17 Pleasant Street, Middlebury, Vermont. Mailing address: Box 631, Middlebury, VT 05753. 802-388-4961; from out of state: 800-842-4666. *Innkeepers:* Frank and Jane Emanuel. Open all year.

The Middlebury Inn, overlooking the village green, consists of a large brick building constructed in 1827, the 1825 Porter House mansion, and a motel unit behind the main inn. The Middlebury is a fine example of a dignified college-campus inn. The Emanuels undertook a major face-lifting for the old inn and Porter House, with the help of a grant from Vermont's Division of Historic Preservation. The outside of the buildings and the public rooms have all been freshened up. The rooms were redecorated and wallpapered, and shag carpeting is used in the hallways. Most of these guest rooms have been carefully redone, including such details as wallpapering the sprinkler pipes.

The old ballroom houses the Country Peddler Shop. The Tavern and the inn's dining room are open to guests and the public for breakfast, lunch, and dinner.

Accommodations: 65 rooms with private bath. *Driving Instructions:* The inn is on Route 7 in the town of Middlebury.

Middletown Springs, Vermont

MIDDLETOWN SPRINGS INN

On-the-Green, Middletown Springs, VT 05757. 802-235-2198. *Innkeepers:* Jean and Mel Hendrickson. Open all year.

The Middletown Springs Inn is an 1879 Victorian mansion with Italianate overtones. Downstairs are a welcoming country kitchen and two high-ceilinged dining rooms where breakfast is served every morning; in the Music Room on this floor, a grand piano awaits a guest's talents, and in the library a wood stove adds its warmth. A doll-and-miniature collection, assembled by three generations of collectors, is on display at the inn. The guest rooms upstairs include the Honeymoon Suite, with its private bath. The Hendricksons provide velour robes for the rooms with shared baths. At night, covers are turned down and mints are placed on guests' pillows. Guests may sleep late and still have the breakfast.

The inn is a favorite with bicyclers and skiers. Auctions, antique shops, and swimming holes are nearby.

Accommodations: 7 rooms, 1 with private bath. *Pets:* Not permitted. *Driving Instructions:* From Rutland, take Route 4 west and then Route 133 south to the inn.

Montgomery, Vermont

BLACK LANTERN INN

Route 118, Montgomery Village, VT 05470. 802-326-4507. *Innkeepers:* Rita and Allan Kalsmith. Open all year.

The Black Lantern Inn was built as a stagecoach stop at the turn of the nineteenth century. The old brick building is fewer than 10 miles from the Canadian border and minutes from the big Jay Peak Ski Area to the east. The guest rooms are each individually decorated with antiques. One room has a balcony overlooking the mountains. A large suite has a fireplace and a Jacuzzi. There is a television room and a sitting room warmed by an open wood-burning stove. A dining room and a taproom are open to guests and the public and are popular with skiers from Jay. The bar has exposed beams and a casual atmosphere. The candlelit dining room offers a Continental menu.

In winter the area offers a variety of skiing choices in addition to Jay Peak. Cross-country skiing is just outside the door of the inn, and for downhill skiers there are four nearby Canadian mountains. Spring and summer bring numerous recreational activities, including fishing in many nearby streams and swimming in the old swimming hole.

Accommodations: 11 rooms, 9 with bath. *Pets:* Not permitted. *Driving Instructions:* Take Route 100 north to Route 118 in Eden. Follow Route 118 through Montgomery Center to Montgomery.

Moretown, Vermont

CAMEL'S HUMP VIEW FARM

Route 100B, Moretown, VT 05660. 802-496-3614. *Innkeepers:* Jerry and Wilma Maynard. Open all year.

This northern-Vermont farmhouse was built about 1831. The even older kitchen has hand-hewn wooden-pegged beams and wide floor boards. Throughout the house are antiques and innkeeper Wilma Maynard's handmade rugs and quilts. Antique copper and old brick add to the warmth of the interior. A fountain and pool surrounded by losts of greenery have been built into the living room. Meals are served to guests family style, with one dinner entrée offered each evening. Most of the fruits and vegetables are grown in the Maynards' garden. The farmhouse is near downhill and cross-country skiing at Sugarbush, Sugarbush North, Stowe, and Mount Mansfield, as well as the Appalachian Trail, known as the Long Trail where it runs through Vermont. Nearby Camel's Hump, part of the Green Mountains, has a 4,083-foot-peak, one of the highest in the area, and is the source of the inn's name.

Accommodations: 7 rooms, 1 with private bath. *Pets:* Not permitted. *Driving Instructions:* The inn is a mile south of Moretown on Route 100B.

Newfane, Vermont

THE FOUR COLUMNS INN

230 West Street, Newfane, VT 05345. 802-365-7713. *Innkeepers:* Sandy and Jacques Allembert. Open all year except several weeks in April and November.

The Four Columns Inn is a handsome white structure that looks out over the picturesque little town of Newfane and its green. On the tree-shaded grounds guests enjoy trout ponds and a pool. The restaurant, which is closed Tuesdays, has many seasonal specialties including fresh trout or breast of duck with rhubarb or raspberries.

Canopy, four-poster, and brass beds — all queen-size — are the rule. Gardening is one of Jacques Allembert's hobbies, as evidenced by herb gardens, which not only add beauty but provide condiments for the kitchen, and by perennial beds which bloom all spring and summer. There are several hiking and cross-country ski trails on the inn's 150 acres.

Accommodations: 12 rooms with private bath. *Driving Instructions:* The inn is 100 yards off Route 30 in the center of Newfane.

OLD NEWFANE INN

Route 30 and the Common, Newfane, VT 05345. 802-365-4427.
Innkeepers: Eric and Gundy Weindl. Open May to October and
December through March.

Built in 1787, the Old Newfane is filled with early American antiques
and retains the wide-board floors, beamed ceilings, and red-brick fireplaces characteristic of this period. It was built on Newfane Hill and
moved to the present location on the Common in 1825. The extensive
menu of French dishes prepared by chef-owner Eric Weindl lists more
than a dozen appetizers and even more entrées. The restaurant has
won accolades from many national publications such as *Gourmet,* the
New York Times, and *Bon Appetit.* The guest rooms are decorated in
traditional New England style, with tiny-print wallpapers and colonial antiques.

Accommodations: 10 rooms, 8 with private bath. *Pets and children:* Not permitted. *Driving Instructions:* Take Route 30 to Newfane. The inn is in the center of town.

North Hero, Vermont

NORTH HERO HOUSE

Route 2, Champlain Islands, North Hero, VT 05474. 802-372-8237. *Innkeepers:* Roger and Caroline Sorg. Open mid-May to mid-October.

The North Hero House is actually a group of buildings dating from the last century. The Champlain Island inn, built in 1890, has been completely renovated to contain guest rooms with private baths, dining rooms, a craft shop, and the Green Mountain Lounge. There are waterfront accommodations in the granite-walled Wadsworth House and Store. A suite was fashioned out of the old cobbler's shop, which now has a bedroom, a bath, a sitting room with the original fireplace, and a screened porch. Rooms are decorated with sturdy modern country-style furniture and attractive wallpapers or paneling. The waterfront area provides a carefully preserved steamship dock, as well as swimming, boating, waterskiing, and canoeing. A different menu with three entries is offered each evening in the dining room, including a Friday-evening dockside lobster picnic. Dinner guests are welcome to select a wine from the wine cellar personally.

Accommodations: 24 rooms, 22 with private bath. *Pets:* Not permitted. *Driving Instructions:* The Champlain Islands are reached by ferry from Plattsburgh, New York, or by bridge 35 miles northwest of Burlington on Route 2. On the islands, take Route 2 to North Hero.

North Thetford, Vermont

STONE HOUSE INN

Route 5, North Thetford, Vermont. *Mailing address:* P.O. Box 47, North Thetford, VT 05054. 802-333-9124. *Innkeepers:* Art and Dianne Sharkey. Open all year except 2 weeks in April.

The Stone House Inn is just feet from the Connecticut River, and guests can arrive by canoe, landing at the public boat-launch just behind the inn. Railroad buffs will be happy to note that the B & M (Boston and Maine) line also runs just behind the inn.

The Sharkeys were once schoolteachers. They decided to become innkeepers and were delighted to find that all their family furniture fitted perfectly in the inn. The living room has a tiled-hearth fireplace; over its mantel is an oak-framed mirror bearing a carved lion's head. The bright guest rooms upstairs continue the country atmosphere of the inn. The inn is part of the "canoe inn to inn" program. Canoers in the program are served breakfast and dinner, and all other guests are served only breakfast, in the dining room overlooking the 2-acre pond out back.

Accommodations: 6 rooms with shared bath. *Pets:* Not permitted. *Driving Instructions:* Take I-91 north of White River to exit 14. Take a right on Route 113 to Route 5. Turn left on Route 5, and drive 2 miles. The inn is next to a red barn by a sharp curve.

Peru, Vermont

JOHNNY SEESAW'S

Route 11, Peru, VT 05152. 802-824-5533. *Innkeepers:* Gary and Nancy Okun. Open December through April and July through October.

This Vermont log country inn offers lodging and fine food with a special "houseguest" atmosphere. Originally built as a dance hall in 1926, Johnny Seesaw's has undergone renovation and expansion while still maintaining a very special rustic ambience. Accommodations range from a room in the inn with private bath to one of several large cottages complete with king-size bed, fireplace, and television. Bunk rooms are also available.

During the summer the inn's Olympic-size, marble-edged pool is inviting, and a clay tennis court is nearby. Bromley Mountain's Alpine Slide is only 500 yards away, and Stratton and Magic Mountain ski areas are a short drive.

Nightly, the inn's chef prepares country fare, served by candlelight. All soups, breads, and desserts are homemade; special dishes will be prepared for vegetarians or those on a restricted diet. Children are served early, allowing the adults to enjoy a more leisurely meal. After their dinner, youngsters may enjoy the game room.

Accommodations: 30 rooms, 24 with private bath. *Driving Instructions:* Peru is midway between Manchester and Londonderry on Route 11. The inn is ¼ mile east of Bromley Mountain.

Joanne M Feding

Pittsfield, Vermont

PITTSFIELD INN

Box 526, Pittsfield, VT 05762. 802-746-8943. *Innkeepers:* Tom and Sue Yennerell. Open all year except mid-October to mid-November.

Pittsfield is a pretty Vermont village centered around a village green complete with a bandstand and liberty pole. The Green Mountains and nearby ski areas form a backdrop for picturesque white clapboarded Colonial houses. At the north end of the green stands the Pittsfield Inn, a three-story Colonial built in 1903 after a fire destroyed the original 1835 inn. First- and second-story balconies overlook the green and in warm weather are complete with the obligatory rows of rocking chairs. The inn's dining room is open to guests and the public for dinner. A grouping of a couch and chairs around a wood stove is the focal point of the tavern. Each of the guest rooms is decorated with antiques and traditional furnishings. One has a fourposter bed, a walnut chest of drawers, and a portrait of an ancestor of one of the innkeepers. Another has basket-patterned wallpaper with matching drapes.

Accommodations: 8 rooms, 4 with private baths. *Pets:* Not permitted. *Driving Instructions:* Pittsfield is 20 miles northeast of Rutland, Vermont via U.S. 4 and Route 100.

Plymouth Union, Vermont

SALT ASH INN

Plymouth Union, VT 05056. 802-672-3748. *Innkeepers:* Ginny and Don Kroitzsh. Open in the summer, fall, and winter.

The Salt Ash Inn has had a history as, at various times, a stagecoach stop, post office, inn, and general store. Most of the antiques in the building were originally used there. The lounge is paneled with barnboard, and its walls are decorated with skis, crutches, and other wintry memorabilia. A large circular fireplace is the room's focal point, a pleasant spot to relax by the fire and look out at the hillside through the big picture window. A small pub is adjacent to this room. The old post-office boxes remain here, and if you look carefully you can still see the Coolidge name on one mailbox. Nearby Plymouth is the birthplace of President Calvin Coolidge, and the Calvin Coolidge National Historic Restoration and family homestead are there.

The guest rooms are country casual, their pine beds covered with colorful homemade quilts. Some are larger family rooms with bright plaid blankets on the beds and rough-sawn wooden walls. This casual family inn appeals to active people who love the outdoors. The dining room serves family-style meals including home-baked breads and a salad bar. Breakfast and dinner are served to overnight guests.

Accommodations: 12 rooms, 4 with private bath. *Pets:* Not permitted. *Driving Instructions:* The inn is at the junction of Routes 100 and 100A.

Proctorsville, Vermont

CASTLE INN

Junction of routes 103 and 131, Proctorsville, Vermont. Mailing address: Box 157, Proctorsville, VT 05153. 802-226-7222. *Innkeepers:* Michael and Sheryl Fratino. Open mid-May to the end of October and mid-December to the end of March.

A great variety of inns dot the countryside in this state, but far and away the most unusual we have run across is the Castle Inn. As its name indicates, guests here are treated to a night at a small stone castle complete with mahogany and oak paneling, carved plaster ceilings, an oval dining room, library, and ten fireplaces scattered throughout the building, many with elaborate carved mantels.

The inn, once a governor's mansion, offers ten guest rooms with a distinct baronial feeling in keeping with the public rooms of the estate. Outside are clay tennis courts and a pool. A hot-tub and a sauna are also available. Breakfast is served to guests; and dinner, to guests and the general public, featuring duck, shrimp, and veal specialties.

Accommodations: 10 rooms, 8 with private bath. *Pets:* Not permitted. *Driving Instructions:* Take Route 103 north through Chester to Proctorsville; the inn is 2 miles south of Ludlow on Route 103.

THE GOLDEN STAGE INN

Route 103, Proctorsville, Vermont. Mailing address: Box 218, Proctorsville, VT 05153. 802-226-7744. *Innkeepers:* Tim and Shannon Datig. Open all year except November and April.

Built in 1796, the Golden Stage has been a stagecoach stop and private home for 180 years. Once a link in the underground railroad, the inn is a rambling clapboard building with wraparound porches and an attached barn, 5 acres of lawns, gardens, and a large pool.

There are ten guest rooms, two with private baths; the others share four baths. The rooms are spacious, with comfortable beds, quilted bedspreads, wide-pine floors, and Colonial wallpaper and ruffled curtains.

A plant-filled living room with a fireplace provides enough space for guests to relax. The dining room (open to the public with advance reservations) serves traditional New England dishes and Continental cuisine. The menu features homemade soups, crepes, quiches, breads, and fish trucked in fresh from the sea. During the summer and fall, the vegetables come straight from the innkeepers' garden. Breakfast and dinner are served.

This inn is one of the most attractive ones we've encountered. Sheep graze on the hillside, and a clever parrot named Roger entertains with his antics.

Accommodations: 10 rooms, 2 with private bath. *Pets:* Not permitted. *Driving Instructions:* Take Route 91 to exit 6, then go north on Route 103 for 18 miles to the inn.

OKEMO LANTERN LODGE

Route 131, Proctorsville, Vermont. Mailing address: Box 247, Proctorsville, VT 05153. 802-226-7770. *Innkeepers:* Charles and Joan Racicot. Open all year.

Okemo Lantern Lodge has welcomed guests since the late 1940s. Built early in the nineteenth century, the house has many Victorian touches. Within, its natural butternut woodwork and stained-glass windows give the lodge a warmth. In its kitchen, an old-fashioned Model Stewart wood stove often has a kettle of soup simmering on its top. Comfortable couches, chairs, and even a chaise longue in a bay window invite guests to linger and relax. The guest rooms are on the second floor. They contain antiques, wall-to-wall carpeting, and — in some cases — beds with canopies. The one suite has its own sitting area. Be sure to ask about the "Tumble in the Rumble."

Dinner and breakfast are served family style at Okemo Lantern Lodge. Joan Racicot bakes her own breads and often serves corn-cob–smoked bacon and homemade jams for breakfast.

Accommodations: 7 rooms, including a 2-room suite with private bath; other rooms share baths. *Pets:* Not permitted. *Driving Instructions:* Take Route 91 north to Route 103. Go 18 miles northwest on Route 103 to the intersection with Route 131. Turn right to the lodge, the ninth house on the left.

Quechee, Vermont

THE QUECHEE INN AT MARSHLAND FARM

Clubhouse Road, Quechee, Vermont. Mailing address: Box T 747, Quechee, VT 05059. 802-295-3133. *Innkeepers:* Michael and Barbara Yaroschuk. Open all year except three weeks in April and one in early December.

Colonel Joseph Marsh, the first lieutenant governor of Vermont, built his home, known as Marshland, in 1793. The farmhouse and associated barns were used as a private residence until the mid-1970s, when they were restored and converted.

The renovation of the inn was done with care so as to maintain the original feeling of the guest rooms while providing fully modern private bathrooms and color cable television for the rooms. Furnishings are largely Queen Anne in style, with most rooms featuring wideboard pine floors, braided rugs, and old-fashioned print curtains.

There are two dining rooms: one small room with French doors overlooking the lake and a larger room warmed by an antique stove. Dinners are served to the public Wednesday through Sunday.

Guests at the inn are given passes for the Quechee Club recreational facilities. For a nominal fee, inn guests have access to boating, racquet ball, squash, skiing, tennis, golf, indoor and outdoor swimming, and canoe and bicycle rentals.

Accommodations: 22 rooms with private bath. *Pets:* Not permitted. *Driving Instructions:* From Route I-91, take I-89 north to exit 1 — Route 4. Take 4 west about 1 mile; turn right on Clubhouse Road and proceed 1 mile.

THREE STALLION INN

Stock Farm Road, Randolph, VT 05060. 802-728-5575. *Inn-keeper:* Roxanne Sejerman.

The Three Stallion Inn is a part of the Green Mountain Stock Farm, a 1,500-acre estate once occupied by Robert Lippitt Knight, the originator of the Lippitt strain of the Morgan horse. The inn's second and third floors date from the early eighteenth century; the first floor was built beneath the upper stories sometime in the first part of the nineteenth.

The Three Stallion Inn, offering overnight accommodations, is the focal point of a popular cross-country skiing center. Although some of the surrounding acreage has been reserved for private house lots and a small number of condominiums, the rest is available for skiing on groomed and tracked trails including one lighted night trail. There is a wood-fired Finnish sauna for after-skiing, or anytime. Other resort activities include tennis, horseback riding, golfing at the Montague Golf Course, and hiking and bicycling throughout the Stock Farm. Horse shows are held on the property each summer, and there is an active dairy farm on the land.

The inn has three floors. On the first floor are the dining room, entrance parlor, and two sitting rooms, all with working fireplaces. An oaken staircase leads to the upper floors, which house several antique-furnished guest rooms. At the back of the inn is an appealing two-floor suite with bedroom over the first-floor living room. Views from the guest rooms include large meadows, a horse paddock, and the Third Branch of the White River. During the ski season, home-cooked family-style single-entrée dinners are served to guests.

Accommodations: 13 rooms, 3 with private bath. *Pets:* Not permitted. *Driving Instructions:* From I-89, take exit 4 and proceed west for 2 miles.

Ripton, Vermont

CHIPMAN INN

Route 125, Ripton, Vermont. Mailing address: Box 37, Ripton, VT 05766. 802-388-2390. *Innkeeper:* Joan Bullock. Open all year except April and November.

In this small, fully restored 1828 farmhouse the guest rooms are furnished with country antiques, and some have hand stenciling. The Tavern Room sports a Dutch-ovened fireplace and a bar-lounge. Other public rooms include a combination reading and sitting area and a dining room with a fireplace and piano. Guests enjoy hors d'oeuvres followed by a four-course New England–style dinner served at a trestle table. Alpine and Nordic skiing are nearby.

Accommodations: 10 rooms, 8 with private bath. *Pets:* Not permitted. *Driving Instructions:* Take Route 125 to the inn.

Saxtons River, Vermont

SAXTONS RIVER INN

Main Street, Saxtons River, VT 05154. 802-869-2110. *Innkeeper:* Averill Campbell Larsen. Open April through December.

The current Saxtons River Inn was built in 1903. The Campbell family, with help from friends and neighbors, revived and restored it. The inn is now run with energy and talent by Averill Campbell Larsen, who not only cooks all the meals but is equally at home with a hammer and saw or a swatch of wallpaper.

The inn has a spacious public dining room, a bar with a copper top, and several public sitting rooms in addition to individually decorated guest rooms. Throughout the inn Ms. Larsen has shown tireless care in taking wood to its natural state and augmenting that look with a novel selection of wallpapers.

Saxtons River Inn serves dinner to the public and offers breakfast to overnight guests. The dinner menu changes twice a week and often includes exotic gourmet specialties. Desserts may be selected from a display on the inn's former coal-burning cookstove. The restaurant is closed on Tuesdays.

Accommodations: 20 rooms, 11 with private bath. *Pets:* Not permitted. *Driving Instructions:* From I-91, take exit 5 to Route 121 (left). Take Route 121 to 4 miles west of Bellows Falls.

Shaftsbury, Vermont

MUNRO-HAWKINS HOUSE

Route 7A, Shaftsbury, VT 05262. 802-447-2286. *Innkeeper:* Ruth Ann Myers. Open all year.

The Munro-Hawkins is a classic Georgian-style home built in 1808 from designs by Lavius Fillmore. Joshua Munro, the builder, was a shoemaker-turned-farmer who made his fortune selling wheat to France after the Napoleonic Wars. Two generations later, his granddaughter, Mary Munro, married another local wheat farmer, Anson Hawkins, and the house has been known as the Munro-Hawkins House ever since. The House has fluted Ionic columns, triangular gables and fanlight, and Palladian windows with their original wavy glass lights. This symmetrical white clapboard frame building has high ceilings, hand-carved moldings in its more formal "receiving" room, and exposed, hand-hewn beams in the common rooms. All five bedrooms have working fireplaces, and a wood-burning stove adds its warmth to the common room. Full country breakfasts served in the dining room include fresh fruit, eggs, hot homemade breads, and bacon, sausage, or pancakes with Vermont maple syrup.

Accommodations: 5 rooms with shared bath. *Pets:* Cats not permitted; dogs by prior arrangement. *Driving Instructions:* The inn is 4 miles north of Bennington on Route 7A.

Shoreham, Vermont

THE SHOREHAM INN AND COUNTRY STORE

Shoreham, VT 05770. 802-897-5081. *Innkeepers:* Cleo and Fred Alter. Open all year.

The Shoreham is a small, informal, family-run inn that dates back to 1799. Unlike many inns in Vermont, the Shoreham has always been an inn serving this small community. The dining room and especially the guest rooms are furnished with comfortable "country auction" antiques. The dining room, with its exposed beams, is currently used only for guest breakfasts, often served before a fire in the fireplace. Cleo and Fred strive to emphasize the informal atmosphere here — guests share tables for breakfast and often strike up friendships. Adjacent to the inn is the 150-year-old Shoreham Country Store, also run by the Alters. Cleo has stocked the shelves with a selection of local Vermont crafts, as well as wines and cheese and maple-sugar products of the state. The store also offers simple lunches for travelers, who often choose to eat them on picnic tables on a small green across the street. Be sure to try the ice cream! The Alters now have groomed hiking and ski trails nearby.

Accommodations: 9 rooms with shared baths. *Pets:* Not permitted. *Driving Instructions:* The inn is on Route 74 West, 22 miles north of Fair Haven and 12 miles southwest of Middlebury, across Lake Champlain from New York State's Fort Ticonderoga.

Stowe, Vermont

EDSON HILL MANOR

RD 1, Edson Hill Road, Stowe, Vermont. Mailing Address: Box 2480, RR 1, Stowe, VT 05672. *Innkeepers:* The Heath family. Open all year.

The original Manor house was built as a private ski lodge for a wealthy landowner in 1939. No expense was spared, as evidenced by Delft tiles surrounding several of the inn's fireplaces, Oriental rugs, and hand-hewn beams in the main living room. Much of the inn's interior is paneled in pine, and about half the guest bedrooms have working fireplaces. Throughout there is a comfortable mixture of antiques and functional furniture. A wing was added to the Manor house in 1952, an annex in 1957, and two new carriage house buildings in 1984 — the latter with pine-paneled rooms, beam ceilings, brick fireplaces, and private baths. Below the inn are fully stocked trout ponds (with equipment provided), a terraced swimming pool, and a riding stable for fifteen horses, with instruction and trail rides available. There is a cross-country ski touring center, also with instruction, equipment rentals, and more than 40 kilometers of scenic trails which connect with Stowe's other trail systems, including those at nearby Mt. Mansfield. Situated on 400 acres of woods, the Manor offers a fully licensed lounge and candlelight dining.

Accommodations: 23 rooms, 16 with private bath. *Pets:* Not permitted. *Driving Instructions:* From Stowe, take Mountain Road (Route 108) north 3.3 miles to Edson Hill Road, turn right and proceed 1.2 miles to the Manor entrance.

FOXFIRE INN AND RESTAURANT

Route 100, Stowe, Vermont. Mailing address: R.R. 2, Stowe, VT 05672. 802-253-4887. *Innkeepers:* Art and Irene Segreto. Open all year.

The main section of the Foxfire Inn was built early in the nineteenth century as a farmhouse and later served as a stagecoach stop. It is one of the oldest frame houses in Stowe. Modified over the years, it has served as a guest house, a summer resort, and even a Chinese restaurant. Despite its diverse heritage the building still retains what is best described as the "Vermont look." The inn is set against a 70-acre wooded hillside.

The guest rooms with their wide-board floors, truncated ceilings, and nook-and-cranny layout have been carefully renovated, and several have exposed hand-hewn wood beams. Each room has its own bath: some big, some small, and one across the hall.

Probably the most distinctive feature of the Foxfire Inn is its fine Italian restaurant. It offers a classically structured menu—antipastos followed by prima (pasta) and secundi (entrée) courses followed by salad and cheese or sweets and fruit. A cross section of antipastos includes rolled eggplant, stuffed mushrooms, prosciutto and melon, and assorted antipasto. A selection of pasta dishes includes all the expected ones plus special treats like baked ziti with ricotta and eggplant, or baked ziti with broccoli, tomato, and ricotta. Entrée choices include veal prepared seven different ways, five kinds of chicken, steak, eggplant, and shrimp. Many dinner guests complete their meal by having their dessert and coffee in the living room by the open fire.

Accommodations: 5 rooms with private bath. *Driving Instructions:* The inn is on Route 100, 1½ miles north of Stowe village.

THE GABLES INN

Mountain Road, Stowe, VT 05672. 802-253-7730. *Innkeepers:* Lynn and Sol Baumrind. Open all year.

The Gables Inn consists of a 120-year-old house to which additions were made in the 1930s. A motel was added in 1977. This many-dormered inn is a place where you feel comfortable relaxing with your feet up on the coffee table enjoying the warmth of the fire and good conversation with new friends. The ground floor contains the main dining room, which seats forty, and the living room with its paneled fireplace, upholstered furniture, and coffee table–bench. In the skiing season, family-style candlelight dinners feature such dishes as spadini, veal, baked chicken, homemade manicotti, and a dish whimsically called toothache stew (a beef stew redolent of cloves).

Several of the guest rooms are tucked into the eaves and dormers upstairs. Each is papered with a different print. We especially like the one that has a canopy bed, a cranberry-colored Oriental rug, and floral-print papers. A new solarium overlooks the inn's swimming pool and hot tub.

The Gables has one of the most interesting breakfast menus we have seen in a country inn. In addition to the standard breakfast of eggs and bacon or pancakes, one can order kippers with onion, curried poached eggs with chutney, sautéed chicken livers and scrambled eggs, corned beef hash, or matzo brei. These meals are served in summer on the lawn or the inn's front porch, with its views of the valley and Mount Mansfield.

Accommodations: 16 rooms with private bath. *Pets:* Permitted in the motel only. *Driving Instructions:* The inn is 1.6 miles northwest of Stowe, on Route 108.

Sunderland, Vermont

THE INN AT SUNDERLAND

Route 7A, Sunderland, Vermont. Mailing address: Box 2440, RR 2, Arlington, VT 05250. 802-362-4213. *Innkeepers:* Tom and Peggy Wall. Open all year.

The Inn at Sunderland, midway between Manchester and Arlington on historic Route 7A, is a handsome 1840 farmhouse on 7 acres of land on the Battenkill River. There are a large barn, a pond, and a yard with views of the mountains. The barn is home to a string of ponies who adore visitors, especially those bearing gifts of carrots or apples, and the official greeter, Nannie, is probably Vermont's friendliest goat. Peggy and Tom Wall have restored the inn and decorated it with country antiques and floral-print wallpapers, all enhanced by chestnut, walnut, and cherry woodwork. Guest rooms are furnished with oak and walnut antiques. One room has a sleigh bed; another, an unusual bonnet chest. Breakfasts are get-acquainted events in the dining room. Complimentary hors d'oeuvres and hot cider are offered when it's chilly, and if guests wish something a little stronger, the Walls have a full-service bar with wines and beers. Golfers and tennis buffs can arrange guest privileges at the Manchester Country Club.

Accommodations: 5 rooms. *Pets:* Not permitted. *Children:* By advance reservation only. *Driving Instructions:* The inn is on Historic Route 7A midway between Arlington and Manchester.

Tyson, Vermont

ECHO LAKE INN

Route 100, Ludlow, Vermont. Mailing address: P.O. Box 142, Ludlow, VT 05149. *Innkeepers:* The Cocco family. Open all year. Echo Lake Inn, built in the last decade of the eighteenth century, has over the years been host to Presidents McKinley and Coolidge, Andrew Mellon, and other dignitaries. Recently, the white frame inn was purchased by the Cocco family who have maintained many of the inn's fine traditions. Their presence is felt most strongly in the kitchen where breakfast, lunch, and dinner are all supervised by Kathy Cocco. Specialties include breakfast crepes with salmon mousse and a variety of "gourmet" pasta dishes. A tradition in the Cocco family is an Italian cornmeal dish known as polenta, which often appears as a companion to full soups. Before dinner, guests may have drinks in the Basket Case Lounge where Kathy's antique basket collection is on display. The Stoned Tavern, dug out from the inn's foundation, offers a rathskeller for evening socializing. The recently redecorated guest rooms have print wallpapers and reproduction colonial furnishings. In addition, condominiums have been created from a former cheese factory on the property. The grounds include a lighted tennis court and a heated swimming pool; boating, fishing, and swimming are available across the street at Echo Lake.

Accommodations: 20 rooms, 4 with private bath. *Pets:* Not permitted. *Driving Instructions:* The inn is 5 miles north of Ludlow.

KNOLL FARM COUNTRY INN

Bragg Hill Road, RFD Box 179, Waitsfield, VT 05673. 802-496-3939. *Innkeepers:* Ann Day Heinzerling and Harvey and Ethel Horner. Open all year except April and November.

The Knoll Farm Inn, on 150 acres of hillside pasture and woods, is a converted farmhouse with four guest rooms, a large family kitchen with an old wood stove, dining room, study, and living room. This was a working farm in the last century and was converted to a combination farm and inn in 1937. It continues to produce its own meats, vegetables, fruits, eggs, and breads. Dinners feature these ingredients in hearty meals, and the inn serves what may be the biggest breakfast of any in Vermont.

The inn has its own pond with a dock and a rowboat in the summer and good skating in the winter. Ann is an accomplished naturalist and is happy to guide the inn's guests on nature walks. Riding horses and lessons are available. The inn has a collection of old buggies and sleighs, which are used for rides. Guests are welcome to help with chores.

Innkeepers and guests all eat together, meet and talk together, and gradually a special relationship of friendship evolves. If this appeals to you, reserve early. The inn can be booked for the summer months a year in advance.

Accommodations: 4 rooms. *Pets:* Not permitted. *Children:* Under six not permitted. *Driving Instructions:* The farm is half a mile up the hill (Bragg Hill Road) from the junction of Routes 100 and 17.

LAREAU FARM COUNTRY INN

Route 100, Waitsfield, Vermont. Mailing address: P.O. Box 563, Waitsfield, VT 05673. 802-496-4949. *Innkeepers:* Dan and Susan Easley. Open all year except April.

The Lareau Farm Country Inn nestles among the rolling hills of central Vermont. The 150-year-old white-clapboard farmhouse and its red barns occupy a meadow on 45 acres of farmland and woods bordered by the Camel's Hump State Forest and the Mad River. The innkeepers restored the inn, papering the guest rooms with old-fashioned print wallpapers, and polishing bare pine-board floors. The rooms are simply decorated with country antiques, many original to the farmhouse. Guests wake to the aroma of breads baking in the wood-burning cookstove in the kitchen. There is a family room where breakfasts are served and a parlor where the cable television set resides, along with "bring your own bottle" setups and hors d'oeuvres for hungry skiers returned from a day on the slopes. Some of Vermont's best downhill and Nordic ski areas are nearby.

Accommodations: 10 rooms, 4 with private baths. *Pets:* Not permitted. *Children:* Under six not permitted. *Driving Instructions:* The inn is on Route 100, ¼ mile south of its junction with Route 17.

MOUNTAIN VIEW INN

Route 17, Waitsfield, Vermont. Mailing address: RFD Box 69, Waitsfield, VT 05673. 802-496-2426. *Innkeepers:* Fred and Suzy Spencer. Open all year.

Built early in the nineteenth century as a farmhouse, the building became one of Mad River's first ski lodges in the 1940s. The Mountain View today is an attractive New England inn, with many heirloom antiques and green plants. A favorite spot is the couch by the wood-burning Vigilant stove in the living room, where guests may share space with an old cat or a handmade quilted pillow. A piano awaits talented visitors. Innkeepers Fred and Suzy Spencer serve skiers mugs of hot mulled cider by the fire. The inn accommodates up to fourteen guests, who dine together family-style around the large pumpkin-pine harvest table. Fred and Suzy grow their own vegetables, serve eggs laid by their pet chickens, and top off the meals with homemade breads and desserts. Dinners are served only to guests.

The guest rooms are decorated with braided rugs and handmade quilts. One room has a bird's-eye–maple canopied bed, while another is done up with colorful quilts and stenciled walls.

Accommodations: 7 rooms with private bath. *Pets:* Not permitted. *Driving Instructions:* From the junction of Route 100 and Route 17 near Waitsfield, take Route 17 west for 2 miles.

TUCKER HILL LODGE

Route 17, Waitsfield, VT 05673. 802-496-3983. *Innkeepers:* Zeke and Emily Church. Open all year.

Although Tucker Hill Lodge was built in 1948, its traditional lines often create the first impression among guests that it is more than a century old. On 14 acres of a wooded hillside away from the road, Tucker Hill is popular in all seasons. Innkeepers Zeke and Emily Church are from North Carolina and pride themselves on their "Southern hospitality that has been transplanted to Vermont."

The focal point of the living room is a large fieldstone fireplace, before which winter guests frequently gather after a day of skiing at the nearby Sugarbush and Mad River Glen ski areas. Baskets of plants hang beneath a row of skylights in the atrium addition to the dining room. Here guests and the public are treated to French and regional cuisine that changes daily and includes such specialties as Norwegian salmon sautéed with Carolina peaches and beurre blanc.

The guest rooms have fresh flowers on the bureaus and old-fashioned quilts on the beds. Over the years many antiques have been added to the public rooms and guest rooms. In the winter, in addition to downhill skiing, many guests enjoy the more than 40 miles of cross-country trails offered by the Tucker Hill Ski Touring Center. In warmer months there is tennis on the lodge's clay courts, swimming in its pool, nearby golf, and plenty of hiking, biking, and horseback riding.

Accommodations: 20 rooms, 12 with private bath. *Pets:* Not permitted. *Driving Instructions:* The inn is 1½ miles from the junction of Routes 100 and 17 in Waitsfield.

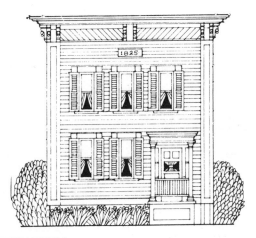

WAITSFIELD INN

Route 100, Waitsfield, Vermont. Mailing address: P.O. Box 362, Waitsfield, VT 05673. 802-496-3979. *Innkeepers:* Ted and JoAnne Campbell. Open all year except six weeks in late fall.

The oldest section of the Waitsfield Inn dates from 1825 when church elder Rufus Barrett began construction on his home. Over the years additional bedrooms, a barn, a woodshed, and other rooms have been added in typical New England fashion. When Ted and JoAnne decided to change careers and leave the Santa Cruz Mountains in California for a life of innkeeping in Vermont, they explored the state until they found the former Bagatelle Inn in Waitsfield just waiting for the time and affection their family could give. Its transformation into a Vermont charmer required thousands of hours of family energy. The inn presently offers guest rooms in the main house and in the barn and woodshed. Two of the rooms in the latter have exposed beams and skylights. Fireplaces and a sitting room were added, while JoAnne made the cozy comforters that grace the antique beds.

The Campbells place great emphasis on the preparation of food. Their chef's evening specialties include roast duck with raspberry glaze and poached sole with lobster sauce. Breakfast is served daily to overnight guests, and brunch is a Sunday tradition.

Accommodations: 16 rooms with private bath. *Pets and children under 10:* Not permitted. *Driving Instructions:* Take Route 100 to Waitsfield and the inn.

Wallingford, Vermont

THE WALLINGFORD INN

9 North Main Street, Wallingford, Vermont. Mailing address: P.O.
Box 404, Wallingford, VT 05773. 802-446-2849. *Innkeepers:* The
Groggets. Open all year except for short vacation periods.

A mansarded Victorian building built in 1876, the inn retains most of
its original details, including fine oaken woodwork, arched marble
fireplaces, elegant chandeliers, and polished wood floors. One reason
that the Wallingford still has so many of its original features is that
until 1969 the mansion was owned by the family that built it. That
family's holdings included a small company that was to grow to become the True Temper Corporation. The son of the original owner of
the building invented the pneumatic mailing tube, once a mainstay of
virtually every department store in America.

The Wallingford Inn's high-ceilinged dining rooms offer candlelight meals with a number of seafood specialties, including shrimp
scampi and broiled trout amandine. In addition to meat, poultry, and
Italian specialties, the inn's creamy Caesar salad is a favorite of many
diners'. The guest rooms are spacious and furnished with antiques,
including many from the Victorian period.

Accommodations: 6 rooms with private bath. *Pets:* Not permitted. *Driving Instructions:* The inn is about 7 miles south of Rutland
on Route 7.

Weathersfield, Vermont

THE INN AT WEATHERSFIELD

Route 106, Box 165, Weathersfield, VT 05151. 802-263-9217. *Innkeepers:* Mary Louise and Ron Thorburn. Open all year.

The initial six rooms of what became the Inn at Weathersfield were built from 1795 to 1798 by Thomas Prentis, a Revolutionary War veteran. A carriage house was attached three decades later, and finally an antebellum-style columned gallery was added to the front of the building. Over the years the building has been a homestead, a stagecoach stop, a stop on the Underground Railroad, and, until its restoration in the 1960s, a summer estate.

The inn is set well back from the road on a 12-acre site. Its dining room has exposed beams, a stone fireplace, and antique furnishings. Menu highlights include sole with lemon, dill and caper butter, lamb cutlets in puff pastry, and chicken Weathersfield. Guest rooms have brass and canopy beds and antique furnishings and quilts. Several rooms have working fireplaces. Even a rainy day can be a blessing at the inn, whose library has more than forty-five hundred books. High tea is served each afternoon.

Accommodations: 12 rooms with private bath. *Pets and children:* Not permitted. *Driving Instructions:* Take Route 106 from Springfield 1 mile past the airport to the inn.

West Dover, Vermont

INN AT SAWMILL FARM

Route 100, Mt. Snow Valley, West Dover, VT 05356. 802-464-8131. *Innkeeper:* Rodney C. Williams. Open all year.

This 1779 property has undergone a renovation that has completely transformed the interior of the buildings into facilities with modern conveniences, while still retaining the old Vermont feeling. The buildings use the original structure with exposed beams and time-softened barnboard in an effective way. Many of the guest rooms and suites have fireplaces for added comfort. The inn is filled with brass, copper, and other antiques. A pond on the property provides swimming and trout fishing in summer and skating in winter.

The restaurant, with its exposed timbers and old mill tools on display, features an array of dishes. Appetizers include Irish smoked salmon, coquille of lobster; escargots, and the famed Vermont appetizer asparagus tips wrapped in ham and baked with Vermont cheddar cheese. Dinner entrées include scallopini à l'Anglaise, roast duck au poivre vert, frogs' legs Provençal, and breast of chicken.

Accommodations: 22 rooms including 10 fireplace suites in cottages, all with private bath. *Pets and children:* Not permitted. *Driving Instructions:* Take Route 100 north of Wilmington 5 miles to the inn.

1830 INN ON THE GREEN

Box 104, Weston, VT 05161. 802-824-6789. *Innkeeper:* Arlene Jordan. Open May—October and mid-November—mid-March.

The 1830 Inn is a large white clapboard farmhouse overlooking the town green in the picturesque Vermont village of Weston, home of the Weston Country Store and Weston Playhouse. In the nineteenth century, the inn was used as a blacksmith shop and later served as the town hall and then a poorhouse. Arlene Jordan opened her restored home as an inn in 1983 after completely repainting and papering the rooms and installing five modern bathrooms. A curving staircase, salvaged from the home of the "Witch of Wall Street," Hetty Green, rises to the third floor. A spacious living room, furnished with antiques collected around the world, is a favorite spot with houseguests, who enjoy sipping wine and swapping the day's adventures by the fireside. Each guest room is decorated with coordinated Laura Ashley linens and comforters and includes upholstered chairs and well-stocked bookcases. Arlene serves a country breakfast of homemade breads, preserves, and coffee cakes as well as hors d'oeuvres and wine in the evening. In warm weather guests can relax on the terrace overlooking a small pond.

Accommodations: 6 rooms, 2 with private bath. *Pets:* Not permitted. *Driving Instructions:* From Londonderry take Route 100 north 4 miles to Weston.

West Townshend, Vermont

WINDHAM HILL INN

West Townshend, VT 05359. 802-874-4080. *Innkeepers:* Ken and
Linda Busteed. Open all year except November and April.

The road from Windham Road to the inn borders a deeply cleft
valley. Windham Hill Inn, fashioned out of a 135-year-old farmhouse
on the edge of a steep hill, is a happy place where innkeepers Ken and
Linda Busteed are joined in their family effort by their three sons. The
feeling here is that of being a houseguest rather than a transient. The
Busteeds often call their inn the "best-kept secret in Vermont."

Meals are served by candlelight. Inn specialties include beef
bearnaise, coquilles St. Jacques à la Provençal, and breast of chicken
tarragon. Windham Hill is fully licensed, and a wine list is available.

Each guest room is decorated in a different way, and all have
pleasing views of the woods, valley, or mountains. One of the most
popular is the Wicker Room with its collection of Victorian wicker
pieces. Linda, an interior decorator, has transformed the barn into
five guest rooms with exposed beams. In winter there are cross-country skiing and skating on the frog pond.

Accommodations: 15 rooms with private bath. *Pets:* Not permitted. *Driving Instructions:* West Townshend is 21 miles northwest
of Brattleboro. In West Townshend, turn up Windham Road, and go
1¼ miles to the inn sign on the right.

Wilmington, Vermont

THE HERMITAGE INN

Coldbrook Road, Wilmington, VT 05363. 802-464-3511. *Innkeeper:* Jim McGovern. Open all year.

The Hermitage has been developed from a farmhouse that dates back to the early eighteenth century. At one time it was the residence of Bertha Eastman, editor of the famed Social Register, the "Blue Book" of society. The building and its grounds have since been renovated by its present owner, Jim McGovern.

The reputation of the Hermitage Inn rests primarily on cuisine. The restaurant, which received much praise from the press, is one of those most frequently recommended by innkeepers in the area. The inn has four separate intimate dining rooms. Among the specialties are an assortment of homemade soups, Wiener schnitzel, frogs' legs Provençal, fillet of sole Veronique, shrimps scampi, and chicken amandine. Daily specials are special indeed: game birds such as partridge, pheasant, and quail, all raised on the property. Saturdays and Sundays brunch is offered. The inn has a 1000-label wine celler.

Each guest room at the Hermitage Inn is individually decorated and furnished with antiques. Ten have working fireplaces. The carriage house contains a sauna.

The grounds were once the site of one of the largest maple-sugar operations in the state, and Jim McGovern has revived the business in the old sugar house. The maple-sugaring started out as a hobby for Jim, but it is now a full-scale operation.

Accommodations: 15 rooms with private bath. *Driving Instructions:* Take Route 9 to Wilmington. At the traffic light, turn right onto Route 100 N. Go about 3 miles to Coldbrook Road on your left. The inn is another 3 miles down Coldbrook Road.

NUTMEG INN

West Main Street (Route 9N), Wilmington, Vermont. Mailing address: P.O. Box 818, Wilmington, VT 05363. 802-464-3351. *Innkeepers:* Del and Charlotte Lawrence. Open all year.

The Nutmeg Inn is a little Green Mountain farmhouse with a brook nearby. The red and white inn consists of a late-eighteenth-century main house with connecting carriage house and barn from a later date. In summer the Nutmeg Inn is ringed with beds of flowering annuals and perennials. In 1957 the farmhouse was restored, its beams were exposed, and in combination with the carriage house, it was opened as an inn. The connected barn is the family home. The carriage house is now the parlor, with its piano, television set, and fireplace. Books are available for guests, as are games and a bar (bring your own bottle). Rooms have fresh print wallpapers, and beds are topped with comforters.

Meals are available to guests only. In the morning there is an à la carte menu as well as a combination eggs, bacon, and muffin breakfast available. In the evening a family-style dinner with a single entrée is served by candlelight.

Accommodations: 9 rooms, 4 with private bath. *Pets:* Not permitted. *Children:* Under 9 not permitted. *Driving Instructions:* The inn is on Route 9, ½ mile west of the traffic light in Wilmington.

THE WHITE HOUSE OF WILMINGTON

Routes 9 and 100, Wilmington, Vermont. Mailing address: Box 757, Wilmington, VT 05363. 802-464-2135. *Innkeeper:* Robert Grinold. Open all year.

The White House of Wilmington was built in 1914 as the summer estate of a lumber baron, who mysteriously ordered a staircase hidden in the mansion's innards. A popular pastime with new guests is attempting to discover the whereabouts of the staircase.

The inn is surrounded by landscaped grounds, fountains, and formal gardens. A 60-foot outdoor pool is in this attractive setting. In winter there is a complete cross-country ski-touring center with about 14 miles of well-marked and groomed trails. After skiing, guests may enjoy the indoor pool, sauna, and whirlpool bath.

The central section of the inn's ground floor features elaborate French doors topped by fan-shaped windows flanked on two sides by symmetrical two-story porches. Three of the twelve guest rooms have fireplaces that work, as do the main dining rooms and lobby–living room. One favorite retreat for guests is the Patio Lounge, where drinks are served accompanied by mountain and valley views.

The inn's dining rooms are popular with skiers for lunches of hot chili and stews. The dinner menu offers Continental cuisine by candlelight. This inn combines hospitality with the elegance of a turn-of-the-century mansion.

Accommodations: 12 rooms, 8 with private bath. *Pets and children under 11:* Not permitted. *Driving Instructions:* Take Route 9 West from Brattleboro 16 miles to Wilmington. From there take Route 9 East for ½ mile.

Woodstock, Vermont

THREE CHURCH STREET

3 Church Street, Woodstock, VT 05091. 802-457-1925. *Innkeeper:* Eleanor Cole Paine. Open all year except April.

Three Church Street was built near the end of the first quarter of the nineteenth century. There is some evidence that the Marquis de Lafayette may have lodged at the inn on his visit to Woodstock in 1825. William Howard Taft dined here in 1912. (A special chair had to be built by a local craftsman to seat the portly president.) Each of the inn's guest rooms is differently decorated, most with at least one piece of antique furniture. The several guest sitting rooms have either a fireplace or a wood stove. There is a drawing room with a piano and a set of six chairs that were at one time given to Queen Victoria, as well as a library and a small, informal sitting room and a larger living room. In the attic is a small room that was probably used to hide runaway slaves.

The breakfast menu here offers juice, hot cereal, sausages, chicken livers, corned-beef hash, eggs of any style, and pancakes with Vermont maple syrup. On the grounds are seven tennis courts and a swimming pool.

Accommodations: 11 rooms, 5 with private bath. *Driving Instructions:* Take Route 4 to the center of Woodstock; the inn is next to the Town Hall.

THE VILLAGE INN OF WOODSTOCK

41 Pleasant Street, Woodstock, VT 05091. 802-457-1255. *Innkeepers:* Anita and Kevin Clark. Open all year except two weeks in April and two in November.

The Village Inn, until recently known as the New England Inn, was built in 1899 as a private home and office for a wealthy doctor and his family. The Victorian house, now the inn, its carriage house, and the caretaker's cottage are all that remain of what was once a 40-acre estate. Decorations in the restored house recapture the long-lost qualities of the turn of the century. The oaken wainscoting and moldings, beveled glass, and ornate tin ceilings were in the original house. Antiques were gathered from all over New England, and an intimate cocktail lounge was added downstairs. Here one finds stained-glass windows and an antique oaken bar with brass and nickel-plated fittings. The inn's dining room is open to the public for breakfasts and dinners by the fireside. Specialties include prime ribs of beef and rack of lamb.

The guest rooms, done in the Victorian manner, include two that now occupy Dr. Merrill's former billiard room on the third floor. Some guest rooms retain their original marble-topped washstands.

The inn is just a quarter mile from the historic town green and Woodstock's many craft and antique shops. Skiing is the primary winter attraction here, with Suicide Six in Woodstock and the Killington ski area just twenty-five minutes away. In warmer months there are auctions, festivals, and a number of water sports, including swimming, fishing, and canoeing in the nearby lake and Ottauquechee River.

Accommodations: 9 rooms, 2 with private bath. *Driving Instructions:* The inn is a quarter mile east of the village on Route 4.

Index of Inns

WITH ROOM-RATE AND CREDIT-CARD INFORMATION

Index of Inns

WITH ROOM-RATE AND CREDIT-CARD INFORMATION

Inns are listed in the chart that follows. In general, rates given are for two persons unless otherwise stated. Single travelers should inquire about special rates. The following abbreviations are used throughout the chart:

dbl. =   double. These rates are for two persons in a room.

dbl. oc. =   double occupancy. These rates depend on two persons being registered for the room. Rentals of the room by a single guest will usually involve a different rate basis.

EP =   European Plan: no meals.

MAP =   Modified American Plan: rates include dinner and breakfast. Readers should confirm if stated rates are per person or per couple.

AP =   American Plan: rates include all meals. Readers should confirm if stated rates are per person or per couple.

BB =   Bed and Breakfast: rates include full or Continental breakfast.

Credit-Card Abbreviations

AE =   American Express   MC =   MasterCard
CB =   Carte Blanche   V =   Visa
DC =   Diners Club

Important: All rates are the most recent available but are subject to change. Check with the inn before making reservations.

Addison Choate Inn, 132; rates: $57 to $95 dbl. BB

Admiral Benbow Inn, 219; rates: $40 to $85 dbl. BB; AE, MC, V

Altenhofen House, 40; rates: $70 to $100 dbl. BB; MC, V

Arcady Down East, 41; rates: $45 to $65 dbl. BB

Arlington Inn, 227; rates: $45 to $85 dbl. BB; MC, V

Asheton House, 125; rates: $25 to $70 dbl. BB

Atlantic Inn, 215; rates: $55 to $110 dbl. EP; ME, MC, V

Aubergine, 46; rates: $65 to $75 dbl. BB; AE

Barrows House, 241; rates: $126 to $160 dbl. MAP

Bayview Inn, 27; rates: $65 to $150 dbl. BB; AE, MC, V

Beal House Inn, 191; rates: $35 to $70 dbl. BB; AE, CB, DC, MC, V

Beechwood Inn, 83; rates: $65 to $95 dbl. BB; AE, MC, V

Bee and Thistle Inn, 19; rates: $50 to $75 dbl. EP; AE, MC, V

Bernerhof Inn, 179; rates: $25 to $30 per person BB; AE, MC, V

Bethel Inn and Country Club, 37; rates: $43 to $80 per person MAP; AE, CB, DC, MC, V

Birch Hill Inn, 262; rates: $100 dbl. MAP

Birchwood Inn, 214; rates: $34 to $140 dbl. BB

Bishopsgate Inn, 7; rates: $60 to $85 dbl. BB

Black Lantern Inn, 270; rates: $38 to $40 per person MAP; AE, MC, V

Black River Inn, 258; rates: $40 dbl. BB; AE, MC, V

Blue Dory Inn, 217; rates: $75 to $110 dbl. BB; AE, MC, V

Blue Hill Inn, 42; rates: $48 dbl. EP; AE, MC, V

Blueberry Hill, 247; rates: $60 to $72 per person MAP; MC, V
Boulders Inn, 17; rates: $120 dbl. MAP; MC, V
Bradford Gardens Inn, 126; rates: $69 to $74 dbl. BB; AE, MC, V
Bradford Inn, 169; rates: $38 to $45 dbl. EP; MC, V
Bramble Inn, 86; rates: $50 dbl. BB; MC, V
Brannon-Bunker Inn, 76; rates: $40 to $45 dbl. BB; MC, V
Breezemere Farm Inn, 44; rates: $46 to $56 per person MAP; MC, V
Butternut Farm, 10; rates: $48 to $58 dbl. BB
Camel's Hump View Farm, 271; rates: $21 per person BB, $42 per person MAP
Captain Dexter House, 106; rates: $55 to $75 dbl. BB; MC, V
Captain Ezra Nye House, 143; rates: $35 to $50 dbl. BB
Captain Freeman Inn, 87; rates: $40 to $50 dbl. BB; MC, V
Captain Jefferds Inn, 61; rates: $65 to $75 dbl. BB
Captain Lord Mansion, 62; rates: $89 to $119 dbl. BB
Captain Lorenz Perkins House, 72; rates: $30 to $60 dbl. BB
Captain Samuel Rhodes Guest House, 221; rates on request
Captain's House (Chatham, MA), 90; rates: $35 to $40 dbl. BB
Captain's House Inn (Newcastle, ME), 69; rates: $60 to $80 dbl. BB; AE, MC, V
Carriage House, 115; rates: $55 to $90 dbl. BB
Castle Inn, 279; rates: $55 to $65 per person MAP; AE, MC, V
Central House Inn & Restaurant, 28; rates: $45 to $60 dbl. BB; AE, DC, MC, V
Charlotte Inn, 107; rates: $75 to $250 (less off-season); MC, V
Chebeague Inn by-the-Sea, 50; rates: $50 to $80 dbl. EP; MC, V
Chetwynd House, 63; rates: $52 to $65 BB
Chipman Inn, 284; rates: $55 per person dbl. oc. MAP; MC, V
Cleftstone Manor, 29; rates: $32 to $90 dbl. BB; AE, MC, V
Coach House, 141; rates: $52 dbl. EP; AE, MC, V
Colby Hill Inn, 181; rates: $58 to $65 dbl. BB; AE, MC, V
Colonel Ebenezer Crafts Inn, 153; rates: $69 dbl. BB; AE, DC, MC, V
Colonial House Inn, 165; rates: $50 dbl. MAP, summer and holidays $50 dbl. BB;
     AE, MC, V
Combes Family Inn, 259; rates: $80 dbl. MAP; AE, MC, V
Cooper Hill Lodge, 245; rates: $38 per person MAP
Copper Beech Inn, 12; rates: $65 to $90 dbl. BB; AE, DC, MC, V
Cornell House, 102; rates: $30 to $55 dbl. BB; MC, V
Corner House Inn, 171; rates: $32 to $40 dbl. BB; AE, MC, V
Country Inn, 100; rates: $55 to $65 dbl. BB; AE, MC, V
Country Inn at Princeton, 124; rates: $95 to $115 dbl. BB; AE, MC, V
Country Inn on Jefferson Hill, 189; rates: $20 to $26 dbl. EP
Crab Apple Acres, 77; rates: $18 per person EP
Craftsbury Inn, 238; rates: $84 to $110 dbl. MAP; MC, V
Craignair Inn, 51; rates: $80 dbl. MAP; MC, V
Cranmore Inn, 200; rates: $30 per person BB, AE, DC, MC, V
Cranmore Mountain Lodge, 201; rates: $45 to $61 dbl. BB; AE, MC, V
Curtis House, 24; rates: $20 to $38 dbl. EP; MC, V
Daggett Houses, 109; rates: $45 to $125 dbl. BB; MC, V
Dana Place Inn, 186; rates: $30 to $42 per person dbl. BB; AE, MC, V
Darby Field Inn, 173; rates: $50 to $65 per person dbl. oc. MAP; AE, MC, V
Dr. Shiverick House, 110; rates: $115 dbl. BB; MC, V
Dorset Inn, 242; rates: $90 to $100 dbl. MAP; MC, V
Downeaster Inn, 52; rates: $33 to $50 dbl. BB

Dunscroft Inn, 101; rates: $55 to $70 dbl. BB
Echo Lake Inn, 292; rates: $22 to $53 per person AE, MC, V
Eden Pines Inn, 133; rates: $55 to $74 dbl. BB
Edencroft Manor, 192; rates: $35 to $50 dbl. EP; AE, MC, V
Edgartown Inn, 111; rates: $70 to $95 dbl. EP
Edson Hill Manor, 288; rates: $58 to $85 per person dbl. oc. MAP
1802 House, 64; rates: $54 to $69 dbl. BB; MC, V
1807 House, 127; rates: $40 to $55 dbl. BB; MC, V
1811 House, 263; rates: $60 to $120 dbl. BB; AE, MC, V
1830 Inn on the Green, 301; rates: $50 to $60 dbl. BB
1895 House Country Inn, 193; rates: $35 to $65 dbl. BB; AE, MC, V
Elms, 20; rates: $75 to $105 dbl. BB; AE, DC, MC, V
English Meadows Inn, 65; rates: $40 to $65 dbl. BB
Essex Street Inn, 120; rates: $45 per person EP, suites higher; AE, DC, MC, V
Farmhouse, 94; rates: $45 to $60 dbl. BB; MC, V
Follansbee Inn, 205; rates: $30 to $50 dbl. EP; MC, V
Four Chimneys Inn, 116; rates: $85 to $150 dbl. BB; AE, MC, V
Four Columns Inn, 272; rates: $55 to $90 dbl. BB; MC, V
Foxfire Inn, 289; rates: $48 to $56 dbl. BB; AE, MC, V
Franconia Inn, 176; rates: $45 to $65 per person dbl. oc. MAP (EP avai.) MC, V
Gables Inn, 290; rates: summer $35 to $44 dbl. EP, winter $80 to $92 dbl. MAP
Garden Gables Inn, 103; rates: $38 to $70 dbl. EP; MC, V
Golden Stage Inn, 280; rates: $50 per person MAP, BB available; MC, V
Goodspeed's Guest House, 48; rates: $35 to $65 dbl. BB, suite higher
Governor Bradford Inn, 112; rates: $50 to $115 dbl. BB; suites higher; AE, MC, V
Governor's Inn, 260; rates: $60 per person dbl. oc. MAP; AE, MC, V
Grane's Fairhaven Inn, 35; rates: $35 to $55 dbl. EP
Green Trails Country Inn, 233; rates: $49 to $65 dbl. BB, MAP available
Greenhurst Inn, 232; rates: $40 to $60 dbl. BB; AE, MC, V
Grey Havens Inn, 58; rates on request
Griswold Inn, 8; rates: $55 dbl. BB; AE, CB, DC, MC, V
Harbor Hill, 81; rates on request BB; MC, V
Harraseeket Inn, 57; rates: $65 to $75 dbl. BB; AE, MC, V
Haven Guest House, 113; rates: $35 to $70 dbl. BB; AE, MC, V
Haverhill Inn, 180; rates: $50 dbl. BB
Hawthorne Inn, 93; rates: $85 dbl. BB
Hearthside Inn, 30; rates: $42 to $62 dbl. BB: MC, V
Herbert Hotel, 67; rates: $39 per person dbl. oc. MAP (EP avail.); MC, V
Hermitage Inn, 303; rates: $70 to $80 per person MAP; AE, CB, DC, MC, V
Hide-away Lodge, 197; rates: $34 dbl. EP
Highland Lodge, 251; rates: $75 to $100 dbl. MAP; MC, V
Holbrook Inn, 31; rates: $50 to $65 dbl. BB; AE, MC, V
Holden Inn, 159; rates on request
Holiday Inn, 183; rates: $43 to $47 per person MAP, BB available; AE, MC, V
Home Hill Inn, 206; rates: $75 to $90 dbl. BB; MC, V
Homeport Inn, 74; rates: $45 to $60 dbl. BB; AE, CB, DC, MC, V
Homestead, 211; rates on request
Homestead Inn, 11; rates on request; AE, DC, MC, V
Horse and Hound Inn, 176; rates: $45 to $55 dbl. BB; MC, V
Hotel Manisses, 218; rates: $60 to $150 dbl. BB ; AE, MC, V
Hugging Bear Inn, 235; rates: $45 to $60 dbl. BB; MC, V

Inn at Castle Hill, 221; rates: $75 to $200 dbl. BB; MC, V
Inn at Christian Shore, 207; rates: $40 to $50 dbl. BB; MC, V
Inn at Crotched Mountain, 175; rates: $40 to $60 dbl. EP
Inn at Duck Creeke, 160; rates: $35 to $60 dbl. BB; AE, MC, V
Inn at Sunderland, 291; rates: $55 to $65 dbl. BB; AE, MC, V
Inn at Mystic, 15; rates: $55 to $125 dbl. EP; AE, MC, V
Inn at Sawmill Farm, 300; rates: $140 to $200 dbl. MAP
Inn at Stockbridge, 151; rates: $50 to $135 dbl. BB; MC, V
Inn at Strawberry Banke, 208; rates: $45 dbl. BB; MC, V
Inn at Weathersfield, 299; rates: $55 per person dbl. oc. MAP; AE, MC, V
Inn on Cove Hill, 134; rates: $29 to $59 dbl. BB
Inn on the Common, 239; rates: $50 to $80 per person MAP; MC, V
Islesboro Inn, 60; rates: $44 to $84 per person MAP
Ivanhoe Country House, 145; rates: $38 to $72 dbl. BB
Jared Coffin House, 117; rates: $80 to $125 dbl. EP; AE, DC, MC, V
Johnny Seesaw's, 276; rates: summer $40 to $60 dbl. EP; winter $44 to $65 per
    person MAP; MC, V
Kawankee Inn, 78; rates: $33 dbl. BB
Knoll Farm Country Inn, 293; rates: $38 per person MAP
Kona Mansion Inn, 196; rates $40 to $97 dbl. EP; MC, V
Land's End Inn, 128; rates: $44 to $75 dbl. BB
Lareau Farm Country Inn, 294; rates: $26 to $30 per person dbl. oc. BB; MC, V
Le Domaine Restaurant and Inn, 59; rates: $55 dbl. EP; AE, CB, MC, V
Lincoln House Country Inn, 55; rates: $45 to $50 dbl. EP; MC, V
Lion's Head, 161; rates: $38 to $50 dbl. BB
Little Lodge at Dorset, 243; rates: $44 to $59 dbl. BB; AE
Longfellow's Wayside Inn, 156; rates: $45 dbl. EP; AE, CB, DC, MC, V
Longwood Inn, 266; rates: $58 to $75 per person MAP; MC, V
Lyme Inn, 194; rates: $55 to $70 dbl. BB; AE, MC, V
Madison Beach Hotel, 14; rates: $60 to $95 dbl. BB; AE, DC, MC, V
Manchester Highlands Inn, 265; rates: $30 to $40 per person MAP (BB avail.); AE,
    MC, V
Manor House Inn, 32; rates: $69 to $135 dbl. BB; MC, V
Marlborough Bed and Breakfast Inn, 164; rates: $40 to $60 dbl. BB
Martin's Guest House, 118; rates: $65 to $95 dbl. BB
Merrell Tavern Inn, 150; rates: $40 to $95 dbl. BB; AE, MC, V
Middlebury Inn, 268; rates: $60 to $86 dbl. EP; AE, MC, V
Middletown Springs Inn, 269; rates: $65 dbl. BB; MC, V
Mira Monte Inn, 33; rates: $45 to $75 dbl. BB; AE, MC, V
Monadnock Inn, 188; rates: $35 to $45 dbl. BB; MC, V
Morrill Place, 121; rates: $45 dbl. BB
Morse Lodge and Inn, 190; rates: $30 to $38 dbl. EP; MC, V
Mostly Hall, 98; rates: $35 to $65 dbl. BB
Mountain View Inn, 295; rates: $45 per person MAP
Munro-Hawkins House, 286; rates: $40 dbl. BB
Nauset House Inn, 95; rates: $35 to $65 dbl. EP; MC, V
Nestlenook Inn, 187; rates: $36 to $60 dbl. BB; MC, V
New England Inn, 184; rates: $55 to $125 dbl. BB, MAP available; AE, MC, V
New London Inn, 198; rates: $44 to $49 dbl. EP; MC, V
Newcastle Inn, 70; rates: $29 to $49 dbl. BB
Nordic Inn, 255; rates: $33 to $53 dbl. BB, MAP available; AE, MC, V
Norseman Inn, 38; rates on request

North Hero House, 274; rates: $35 to $80 dbl. EP

Northfield Country House, 122; rates: $30 to $60 dbl. BB; MC, V

Nutmeg Inn, 304; rates: summer and fall $48 to $77 dbl. BB, winter $39 to $59 per person MAP

Okemo Inn, 261; rates: $45 per person MAP; AE, CB, DC, MC, V

Okemo Lantern Lodge, 281; rates: $55 per person MAP; MC, V

Old Babcock Tavern, 25; rates: $55 dbl. BB

Old Farm Inn, 135; rates: $48 to $60 dbl. BB

Old Manse Inn, 88; rates: $40 to $60 dbl. BB; AE, MC, V

Old Newfane Inn, 273; rates: $65 to $85 dbl. EP

Old Riverton Inn, 22; rates: $44 to $70 dbl. BB; AE, CB, DC, MC, TRADEX, V

Old Sea Pines Inn, 89; rates: $32 to $55 dbl. BB; CB, DC, MC, V

Old Tavern at Grafton, 248; rates: $45 to $85 dbl. EP

Old Towne Farm Inn, 236; rates: $40 to $45 per person MAP; AE, MC, V

Old Village Inn, 73; rates: $55 to $75 dbl. EP; AE, MC, V

Olde Rowley Inn, 71; rates: $40 dbl. BB; MC, V

Palmer House, 174; rates: $60 dbl. BB, $85 per person MAP

Pasquaney Inn, 170; rates on request; MC, V

Philbrook Farm Inn, 209; rates: $62 to $72 dbl. MAP

Pilgrim's Inn, 53; rates: $55 to $65 per person MAP

Pittsfield Inn, 277; rates: $38 to $45 per person MAP; MC, V

Pleasant Lake Inn, 199; rates: $32 to $42 dbl. EP; MC, V

Point Way Inn, 114; rates: $50 to $150 dbl. BB; AE, MC, V

Publick House, 154; rates: $65 dbl. EP; AE, CB, DC, MC, V

Quechee Inn at Marshland Farm, 282; rates: $60 to $135 dbl. BB; AE, MC, V

Queen Anne Inn (Chatham, MA), 91; rates: $87 to $115 dbl. BB; MC, V

Queen Anne Inn (Newport, RI), 223; rates: $35 to $60 dbl. BB

Rabbit Hill Inn, 257; rates: $35 to $60 dbl. EP; MC, V

Red Brook Inn, 16; rates: $70 to $85 dbl. BB; AE, MC, V

Red Clover Inn, 267; rates: $40 to $54 per person MAP; AE, CB, DC, MC, V

Red Lion Inn, 152; rates on request; AE, DC, MC, V

Reluctant Panther Inn, 264; rates: $50 to $90 per room EP; AE, MC, V

Riverwind, 5; rates: $60 to $65 dbl. BB; MC, V

Rocky Shores Inn and Cottages, 136; rates: $52 to $67 dbl. BB

Rose and Crown Guest House, 129; rates on request BB

Salem Inn, 142; rates: $55 to $70 dbl. BB; AE, CB, DC, MC, V

Salt Ash Inn, 278; rates: $39 to $46 dbl. BB, winter MAP; MC, V

Saxtons River Inn, 285; rates: $30 to $60 dbl. BB

Seacrest Manor, 137; rates: $54 to $72 dbl. BB, less in winter

Seafarer, 138; rates: $44 to $56 dbl. BB

Seaward Inn, 139; rates: $50 to $65 per person MAP

1780 Egremont Inn, 147; rates on request; MC, V

Shelter Harbor Inn, 226; rates: $48 to $72 dbl. BB; AE, CB, DC, MC, V

Ships Inn, 119; rates: $50 to $80 dbl. BB; AE, MC, V

Ship's Knees Inn, 96; rates on request

Shire Inn, 234; rates: $55 to $75 dbl. BB

Shoreham Inn and Country Store, 287; rates: $50 dbl. BB

Silvermine Tavern, 18; rates: $62 to $67 dbl. BB; AE, CB, DC, MC, V

Snowvillage Inn, 210; rates: $62 to $69 per person MAP, BB available; AE, MC, V

Somerset House, 130; rates: $38 to $65 dbl. EP; MC, V

Squire Tarbox Inn, 79; rates: $96 MAP

Stafford's-in-the-Field, 172; rates: $50 to $85 per person MAP; MC, V

Stagecoach Hill Inn, 146; rates: $35 to $55 dbl. EP; AE, CB, DC, MC, V
Stone Hearth Inn, 237; rates: $24 to $32 per person BB
Stone House Inn, 275; rates: $35 dbl. BB; MC, V
Stonebridge Inn, 182; rates: $35 to $40 dbl. BB; MC, V
Stonehenge, 21; rates: $70 to $170 dbl. BB; AE, CB, DC, MC, V
Stonehurst Manor, 202; rates: $65 to $115 dbl. EP; AE, MC, V
Stratford House Inn, 34; rates: $50 to $80 dbl. BB; MC, V
Sugar Hill Inn, 178; rates: $40 to $65 per person MAP; $29 to $35 per person EP;
    AE, MC, V
Summer House, 144; rates: $40 dbl. BB; MC, V
Tamworth Inn, 213; rates: $50 to $60 dbl. EP; MC, V
Tarry-a-While Resort, 43; rates: $55 to $60 per person MAP
Three Church Street, 306; rates: $40 to $52 dbl. BB; MC, V
Three Mountain Inn, 252; rates: $45 to $70 per person MAP
Three Stallion Inn, 283; rates: $36 dbl. EP, $38 to $45 per person MAP in season
Tollgate Hill, 13; rates: $70 to $80 dbl. BB; AE, MC, V
Town House Inn and Lodge, 92; rates: $95 to $105 dbl. BB; AE, CB, DC, MC, V
Tucker Hill Lodge, 296; rates: $48 to $59 per person dbl. oc. MAP; AE, MC, V
Under Mountain Inn, 23; rates: $85 to $95 dbl. BB
Vermont Inn, 254; rates: summer $32 to $42 dbl. BB, winter $38 to $48 per person
    MAP; AE, MC, V
Vermont Marble Inn, 246; rates: $50 to $60 dbl. BB; AE, MC, V
Victorian, 163; rates: $79 to $98 dbl. BB; AE, MC, V
Village Auberge, 243; rates: $55 to $75 dbl. EP; MC, V
Village Inn (Lenox, MA) 104; rates: $70 to $105 dbl. EP, lower off season; MC, V
Village Inn (Londonderry, VT) 256; rates: $45 to $55 dbl. BB; MC, V
Village Inn (Yarmouth Port, MA), 166; rates: $44 to $60 dbl. BB
Village Inn of Woodstock, 307; rates: $35 to $45 dbl. EP; MC, V
Waitsfield Inn, 297; rates: $45 to $65 per person dbl. oc. MAP; AE, DC, MC, V
Walker House, 105; rates: $40 to $110 dbl. BB
Wallingford Inn, 298; rates: $55 dbl. BB; MC, V
Walloomsac Inn, 231; rates: $25 dbl. EP
Waterford Inne, 56; rates: $40 to $60 per room EP
Wayside, 224; rates: $45 to $65 per room BB
Weathervane Inn, 149; rates: $30 per person BB weekdays, $55 per person MAP
    weekends; MC, V
Wedgewood Inn and Gallery, 167; rates: $75 to $115 dbl. BB; MC, V
West Mountain Inn, 230; rates: $40 to $65 dbl. EP; AE, MC, V
Westwinds on Gull Hill, 131; rates: $30 to $100 dbl. BB; MC, V
Whalewalk Inn, 97; rates: $75 to $95 dbl. BB
White House of Wilmington, 305; rates: $55 to $90 per person MAP; AE, MC, V
Whitehall Inn, 49; rates: $57 to $90 dbl. BB, MAP available
Wildflowers Guest House, 204; rates: $40 to $44 dbl. BB
Wildwood Inn, 158; rates: $27 to $49 dbl. BB
Williamsville Inn, 162; rates: $69 to $115 dbl. EP; MC, V
Willows of Newport, 225; rates on request
Windflower Inn, 99; rates: $100 to $130 dbl. MAP
Windham Hill Inn, 302; rates: $55 per person MAP; MC, V
Winter's Inn, 68; rates: $65 per person MAP; AE, MC, V
Winterwood at Petersham, 123; rates: $60 to $85 dbl. BB; MC, V
Woodchuck Hill Farm, 249; rates: $45 to $85 dbl. BB
York Harbor Inn, 82; rates: $35 to $60 dbl. BB; AE, MC, V

THE COMPLEAT TRAVELER'S READER REPORT

To: *The Compleat Traveler*
    c/o Burt Franklin & Co., Inc.
    235 East 44th Street
    New York, New York 10017 U.S.A.

Dear Compleat Traveler:

I have used your book in _____ (country or region).
I would like to offer the following ☐ new recommendation, ☐ comment,
☐ suggestion, ☐ criticism, ☐ or complaint about:

Name of Country Inn or Hotel:

_____

Address: _____

_____

Comments:

Day of my visit: _____   Length of stay: _____

From (name): _____

Address _____

_____ Telephone: _____